The Pecan Orchard

The Pecan Orchard

Journey of a Sharecropper's Daughter

PEGGY VONSHERIE ALLEN

THE UNIVERSITY OF ALABAMA PRESS
Tuscaloosa

The University of Alabama Press
Tuscaloosa, Alabama 35487-0380

The recipes in this book are intended to be followed as written by the author.
Results will vary.

Manufactured in the United States of America

Typeface: ACaslon

∞

The paper on which this book is printed meets the minimum requirements of
American National Standard for Information Sciences-Permanence of Paper for
Printed Library Materials, ANSI Z39.48-1984.

Library of Congress Cataloging-in-Publication Data

Allen, Peggy Vonsherie, 1959–
The pecan orchard : journey of a sharecropper's daughter / Peggy Vonsherie Allen.
    p.   cm.
    ISBN 978-0-8173-1672-3 (cloth : alk. paper) 1. Allen, Peggy Vonsherie,
1959-—Childhood and youth—Anecdotes. 2. African Americans—Alabama—
Butler County—Social life and customs—20th century—Anecdotes.
3. Sharecroppers—Alabama—Butler County—Social life and customs—20th
century—Anecdotes. 4. Butler County (Ala.)—Social life and customs—20th
century—Anecdotes. 5. Allen, Peggy Vonsherie, 1959-—Family—Anecdotes.
6. Country life—Alabama—Butler County—Anecdotes. 7. Allen family—
Anecdotes. I. Title.
    F332.B9 A45
    305.896'073076137—dc22
                                                              2009007061

I dedicate this book to the loving memory of my father, Charlie Allen; my mother, Willie Joe Allen; my sister Mae Nell; my brothers Floyd and Calvin; and to my great-grandmother Moa. Without their memories, I would not have had the strength nor the courage to write our family story.

They are no longer with us, and the entire family misses them dearly.

Contents

CONTENTS / ix

Acknowledgments

I thank those who have assisted me with this project—my father, Charlie Allen; my mother, Willie Joe Allen; and my twelve sisters and brothers, Thomas, Mae Nell, Betty, Ediffie, Gracie, Sadie, Floyd, Charlie Jr., Calvin, Brenda, Janice, and Diane—for giving me these memories. I also thank my great-grandma Moa, who was the glue that held our family together.

In addition to my family, I thank my agent, Sally Hill McMillan, of Sally Hill McMillan and Associates. She believed in my story and was willing to take a chance on me. I will always appreciate her assistance and hard work. And a special thanks to Holly Hollan.

The Pecan Orchard

Introduction

I suppose at least half of the black folks who grew up in southern Alabama in the 1940s, '50s, and '60s could say that they were born the child of a poor black sharecropper. I am one of those folks with a story to tell. This book is an account of some of the people, places, and events that impacted my mother, father, and twelve sisters and brothers, as well as my own youth in southern Alabama. All the stories are true.

I was born the daughter of a poor black sharecropper on November 29, 1959, in Greenville, Alabama, and, as the saying goes, the rest is history.

Greenville is a typical small southern town located in Butler County, Alabama. Butler County lies in the south-central portion of the state. It is truly deep in the heart of Dixie. Greenville also lies in a part of the country known as the Black Belt. It is a crescent-shaped region stretching through several of the most southern states. The term was first used to designate a part of the country that was distinguished by the color of the soil, which is thick, dark, and extremely rich. By the 1830s the area had become prime land for cotton plantations. And with cotton plantations in place, slaves soon followed. The term Black Belt took on a different meaning after the Civil War. It became known as an area with a high population of African Americans struggling with poverty, inadequate education, poor health care, substandard housing, and high unemployment rates. There is only one Black Belt, but there are two meanings for the term.

In addition to being a part of the Black Belt, Greenville is also on the fringes of Wiregrass Country, so named for its native tall grass. It's an area with deeply rooted southern cultural traditions, sugarcane mills, hog killing, and shotgun houses.

While Greenville is the county seat, other smaller towns and communities within the county include Chapman, McKenzie, and Georgiana. Butler County played an active role in the formation of the state and the country. Its land is among the most fertile on earth and the people are among the most resilient. Civil war, slavery, and reconciliation are part of its history.

A county older than the state, Butler County was created by the first session of the Alabama legislature on December 13, 1819. The county was named for Captain William Butler, who fought in the Creek Indian War of 1813–14. Captain Butler was killed during that war and was buried in the Pioneer Cemetery, which is near the First United Methodist Church of Greenville, the oldest church in Butler County. Many historic battles of the Creek War were fought on Butler County soil, including the infamous Butler Massacre. In this battle, Creek Indians led by Savannah Jack killed a well-armed party of settlers carrying dispatches to Fort Dale, the first Butler county seat.

Cotton was king in most of the southern states for more than a century, and so it was in Butler County, as well. Because of the rich fertile soil, it is not surprising that our chief industries were agriculture related, including cotton, timber, and textiles. All these industries required a tremendous amount of labor to bring a product to market. Initially it was slave labor, which eventually gave way to sharecropping.

The institution of slavery and the eventual emancipation of slaves figured prominently in the formation of the county. To that end, the Civil War had a tremendous effect on the community. Many of the county's young men joined Confederate regiments and went off to fight for their beliefs in Civil War battles all over the South. Some didn't have to go far to join up because Greenville had Civil War regiments of its own, including the Greenville Guards. Camp Pollard, a military camp, was just south of town. Greenville was an active participant in the war, and many of its young soldiers are interred in cemeteries all over the county, like Mount Zion Church Cemetery, Mount Carmel Baptist Church Cemetery, Magnolia Cemetery, and Pioneer Cemetery, the final resting place of our county's namesake, Captain William Butler.

Soon after the Civil War, blacks were employed first in the timber industry and then in the cotton industry as farm laborers and sharecroppers. The back-breaking labor contributed by blacks whether as slaves or as freedmen was instrumental in Greenville's survival. But trade would have been difficult without the railroad. The old L&N station was a bustling depot that shipped our cotton, timber, and textile goods to faraway places north, south, and beyond. The railroad transportation system, which followed old federal roads and stagecoach routes, played an important role in making Greenville a major regional trade center. For many years Greenville was the sole shipping point for a six-county area of south-central Alabama.

There were prominent citizens who also helped build the Butler County and Greenville community. There was John T. Milner, a civil engineer, who in the mid-1800s helped to engineer the Alabama and the Pensacola Railroads, which provided Greenville with its depot.

There was the McGowin family, headed by the patriarch James Greeley McGowin, who in 1905 purchased the W. T. Smith Lumber Company in Chapman. His family owned and operated the sawmill for more than six decades, providing jobs for many of the families in the surrounding community. James Greeley and his son Earl were both inducted into the University of Alabama's Alabama Business Hall of Fame. Earl McGowin also served for twenty years in the Alabama State Legislature as a representative from Butler County.

There was the Stabler family, a family of doctors headed by L. V. Stabler, who in 1916 entered into practice with his brother, Andrew Lee Stabler; together they opened the Stabler Infirmary in Greenville. L. V. Stabler had two sons, Ernest and Aubrey Stabler, who joined the practice in 1932 and 1940, respectively. Early versions of the infirmary, like most public places throughout the south prior to the civil rights era, had a segregated section for colored patients only.

Hank Williams, one of the county's most famous citizens, was born on September 17, 1923, in Georgiana, south of Greenville. There was a time when Hank's father worked for the W. T. Smith Lumber Company like most families in the community, including mine. In 1934 Hank's family moved to Greenville, where his mother opened and operated a boardinghouse next to the Butler County courthouse. While Hank was living there, Rufus Payne introduced him to the blues and other African American musical influences.

Rufus Payne, also known as "Tee-Tot," was a well-known Greenville citizen. His nickname was a play on the words "tea" and "teetotaler" because he always carried a homemade mixture of alcohol and tea wherever he went. Payne, a talented African American blues artist and a street musician, was born in 1884 on the Payne plantation in Lowndes County, one county north of Butler.

James Herbert was one of Greenville's most prominent and influential African American citizens. A property owner and entrepreneur, he was a pillar of the black community. James Herbert was born on July 18, 1888, to parents who were former slaves. In 1914, he received a diploma in plastering from Tuskegee Institute. At the time he received his diploma, Booker T. Washington was still principal of the young institute. In 1929 he established the James Herbert Funeral Home.

Mr. Herbert was the first African American in the city to own a telephone and the first to own a store. It was in space outside his store affectionately known to the community as "Saul's Corner" in the heart of the black community where Rufus "Tee-Tot" Payne mentored Hank Williams.

By the 1930s there were other prominent white families, large and small, of wealth and position in the area. Many were business and mercantile owners, large farm and landowners, and sawmill owners. There were even more families of lesser means. Those poor families lived each day from hand to mouth. They were families like mine, descendents of slaves and sharecroppers. During those years, even at the height of the Depression, there was work for families like mine, splitting logs, picking cotton, planting vegetables, gathering pecans, and working as nannies and domestics. There was not enough work for them to live comfortably, just enough to survive, if they were lucky. I consider my family one of the lucky ones. We survived, not without scars, but we survived.

The city of Greenville, Alabama, a place of historical significance in its own right, lies only thirty miles as the crow flies, from Montgomery, the first capital of the Confederate States of America and, ironically, the birthplace of the 1960s civil rights movement. Greenville's founding fathers can be found in the history books of the state and the nation. The city was forged on the backs of rich men and poor, freedmen and slaves, sharecroppers and tenant farmers.

Families like mine, whose names can't be found in the history books, the Alabama Business Hall of Fame, the Alabama state archives, or the Country Music Hall of Fame, lived, worked, and died building our city, our county, and our nation. Though their names are unknown, their contributions live on. You are invited to take a look at their lives, to see their struggles, their triumphs, and their ultimate survival. In order to hear their stories, you must read mine.

I was born the daughter of a poor black sharecropper on November 29, 1959, in Greenville, Alabama, and this is my story.

I
The Beginning

In the Beginning

My immediate family history began on June 4, 1939, the wedding day of Willie Joe Hall and Charlie Allen, my mama and daddy.

Mama and Daddy struggled very hard to provide for our extraordinarily large family. Over a span of more than twenty hard years they reared thirteen children with me being number twelve. We were reared on hard work in cotton fields and pecan orchards, moonshine to supplement the family income, education from the back of the bus, and the discipline of an iron hand from Daddy. The fact that all of us kids lived long enough to grow up was a miracle. Many times we did not think we would make it, but we always did.

Mama and Daddy married young. Daddy wasn't even twenty, and Mama was only in her midteens. Mama's daddy, Papa, was not in favor of their marriage. He constantly told Mama that Daddy came from poor folks and that he didn't want her to get mixed up with his kind. Of course everyone was poor in 1939 including Papa, who was a sharecropper, but I guess Papa thought that excuse was as good as any to try to keep Mama and Daddy apart. The more Papa warned Mama, the more they wanted to get married. Papa also cautioned Mama that Daddy already had a family. At his young age Daddy had already fathered a son out of wedlock, and Papa warned Mama time and again not to get involved with him. He said there would always be trouble if she married Charlie. But Charlie was the one she wanted to marry no matter what Papa had to say about him.

Daddy used to saunter by the house every day on his way to work.

Mama said he just did it to get a glimpse of her because his job was too far out of the way for him to be strolling by her house every day. It appears as though that's how courting was done back then.

After considerable thought, Papa eventually gave Mama his permission to get married—and his blessing. In early June 1939, Mama and Daddy got married. The wedding wasn't very big because no one could afford anything big in those days. It was a simple ceremony with just a few friends, family, and neighbors. Papa did kill two hogs for the festive occasion. One was for the wedding celebration, to feed the guests who had walked for miles to be there, and one was for Mama and Daddy. He wanted to get their new family off on the right foot because a family starting out with meat to eat was starting out right.

That was the beginning of the Allen family, my family.

Mama and Daddy started their life together moving from one white man's land to the next, sharecropping. There was always some old run-down shack in the middle of a field somewhere, owned by a white man who needed some colored folks to keep things going. There were also plenty of colored folks to go around. It seemed as if the white folks owned everything, including the black folks. Maybe they didn't actually own black folks, but they definitely controlled every aspect of black folk's lives.

After the wedding, it seemed as though in no time at all Mama was expecting her first child. In the dead of winter Mama began to have her first labor pains. The old house that she and Daddy lived in had holes in the walls and in the floors. It seemed to be just as cold inside as it was outside. Cold wind didn't hit the side of the house and go around, it went straight on through.

Mama was still a young teenager and the labor pains were scaring her as she did not know what to expect. Her mother had died when she was very young and she didn't have any knowledge of or experience with childbirth. All she knew was that it was extremely painful and she wanted it all to end. She had been having pains all day alone in that old cold house, and when Daddy came home from work that night, she told him about them.

It was time for the baby to come. And in those days a doctor was out of the question. There was, however, an old black woman who was the mid-

Willie Joe (*left*) and Charlie Allen shortly after they were married in 1939.

wife for the black community. Everyone called her black but actually she was only half black; her daddy was an old white man and her mama was a black woman who worked for him. Each black community or settlement had its own midwife. Ours was named Rachel Driggers; she was as old as time itself and was full of wrinkles. No one in the community could

Mama and Mae Nell when Mae Nell was about three
or four. She was the first of Mama's "baker's dozen" of
children.

remember her ever looking any younger, and she seemed to be at least a
hundred years old.

Daddy headed out right away to get Miz Rachel. It only took about
half an hour or so, but to Mama it seemed as if an eternity had passed.
Miz Rachel went to work immediately and after a long night of labor
Mama gave birth to a healthy baby girl, Mae Nell Allen. She had been
named Mae after Mama's younger sister who had died in a fire several
years earlier.

For the next twenty years, every eighteen months to two years, Mama
gave birth to another child, constantly increasing the number of hungry
mouths to feed. My sister Betty was born about two years after Mae Nell.

Miz Rachel helped bring Betty into the world also. After Betty was born, my oldest brother, Thomas, whom Daddy had before he and Mama married, came to live with Mama and Daddy. Until this time he had lived with his own mama, but she had fallen ill and was unable to care for him. His mama died from tuberculosis, and soon after her death Thomas moved in permanently with Mama and Daddy and took his place in the family.

Ediffie was born a couple of years after Betty, and once again Miz Rachel came to assist. After Ediffie, Gracie was born. And then came my brother Floyd, the second son. He was followed by another sister Sadie, and then Charlie Allen Jr., whom we called Sonny. After Sonny, came Calvin, the forth and final son. Brenda was next, and then Janice, nicknamed Jan. After Jan, on November 29, 1959, I was born. And though I evened out the dozen, I was not the last to arrive. In July 1961, baby Diane was born. Since Mama bore children for more than twenty years, she spent a large part of her life pregnant. I know it was difficult caring for all of us, but I never heard her complain about having such a large family. Instead, Mama often called us her baker's dozen because she had thirteen of us. Growing up in lower Alabama was difficult for any black family, but it was especially difficult for such a large family. Just getting enough to eat was hard. The entire family struggled together to survive.

Mama and Daddy had struggled with difficult childhoods of their own. Both their foundations were rocky but strong, and they had each other in addition to all of us. Our family history was interwoven with the will and determination to survive, and against all odds, they gave life their best efforts. We labored fervently to surmount everything that life threw at us.

Sunshine

The word "sunshine" has a special meaning for the Allen family, especially for Daddy. That was the nickname given to him by Zell Coouie and his family. Zell Coouie was an old white man who lived with his family down in the woods off Highway 31, in the Wild Fork community.

Daddy was born on August 9, 1919, in Greenville, Alabama. He had a tough and troubled childhood that ended much too quickly. He was born to a young, unmarried, and quite beautiful woman named Betsy. His father, Anthony Allen Sr., had many older sons and daughters by his wife. There was Attie, Maple, Anthony Jr., Glen, Ed, and Mason. And then there was Daddy, who was fathered out of wedlock. His being fathered out of wedlock signaled the beginning of his difficult life. Many years later Daddy would boast about being his mama's best-looking child and her only boy. He was correct. His mama, my grandmother Betsy, didn't live long enough to bear any more children. Nor did she live long enough to raise Daddy to adulthood.

Grandma Betsy was a beautiful woman. Everyone said so. It was said by many that her beauty rivaled that of Cleopatra. She had fair skin, long black hair, and an elegant body. All the men loved her, or at least they wanted to, and it would be fair to say that she liked most of them too. Likewise, the women in the community hated her, whether they had a reason to or not. They were most likely envious of her gorgeous appearance. Grandma Betsy's beauty was both a blessing and a curse. Daddy often spoke of the time he and his mother were brutally assaulted in a hay field when he was a small boy. The two of them were returning home after visiting with a neighbor. The walk home was only a couple of miles and by taking a shortcut through the hay field the walk would be even shorter. It was a route they had taken many times before without incident. It was early summer and the grass in the field was about waist-high for Daddy, knee-high for his mama, Betsy. It was early evening; darkness was still hours away.

As they reached the halfway point in the field, they could see a large man coming toward them. As he drew closer, they recognized the figure. It was a white man who lived in the area, though Betsy did not know his name. Since walking was a common mode of transportation at the time, it was not uncommon to meet other walkers black or white when traveling, so Betsy was not alarmed by meeting someone else in the hay field.

According to Daddy, when he and his mama were within a few feet of the white man he began making remarks to Betsy, comments that were inappropriate, out of line, explicit. Before Betsy could react, the man grabbed her, tearing her dress, and began forcing his unwanted attentions on her. When she resisted, he began to punch her about the head and face. As the man beat on Betsy, Daddy beat on him. Daddy was only a child and Betsy was very petite; they didn't stand a chance against a man that outweighed them by two hundred pounds or more. Each time Daddy got close to the man trying to protect his mama, the man would turn his attentions to him, hitting him and throwing his small body onto the ground. After a few minutes, both Daddy and Grandma Betsy lay exhausted and bleeding. When they could fight no longer even though they continued to try, the man took from Betsy what he wanted. She had no money, jewelry, or gold. Even the now torn and tattered dress she was wearing was a hand-me-down garment, given to her by a stranger. So he took from her all that she had. He took her self-respect. As a parting gesture he forcefully slammed her head to the ground once more, pinned her there for a moment, and then spit in her face, taking the last remaining ounce of her dignity.

There was no one to tell and no place to go seeking justice for such an incident. There was no law that would take Betsy's side in what had happened to her and Daddy. In those days white men often took what they wanted from black women. And sometimes, as in Grandma Betsy's case, they took everything. After a time, both Grandma Betsy and Daddy's physical wounds healed. But Daddy's mental injuries never did heal.

Grandma Betsy, who continued to be a free spirit, never married. But she died when she was fairly young. In the early 1920s on a cold Sunday morning an altercation occurred outside the church. Of course church was where every black soul went on Sunday morning in those days. Where else would they be but taking their burdens to the Lord? And Mount Ida Baptist Church, a small single-room building nestled among a grove of trees on a dirt road about one-quarter mile off Highway 31, was no different from all the rest. The little whitewashed church had a small steeple on top. The steeple was the only thing that distinguished it from any of the other old small buildings. Small and plain, it was typical for the time. All the folks in the surrounding community attended Mount Ida.

That Sunday, as Grandma Betsy was leaving the churchyard, she was confronted by a woman. Some said she was a jealous wife, but no one really knew for sure. The woman accused Grandma of spending time with her husband. Grandma Betsy denied her allegations, but to no avail. The entire congregation quickly gathered around to watch as the women started yelling and screaming at each other. They began pushing and shoving as the argument grew more heated. Back and forth they went until suddenly the woman pulled a knife on Grandma Betsy. After a brief struggle, and with many so-called Christian eyes looking on, Grandma was stabbed several times. No one intervened. Finally, when Grandma was near death, a few onlookers pulled the woman off of her.

In those days medical care for poor black folks was nonexistent. So Grandma's wounds were never properly treated. Some folks said that even a doctor would not have been able to save her. Grandma Betsy hung on for a few days. Painful days for her and agonizing for Daddy, who watched his beautiful mother slowly die from her horrible injuries.

The sad funeral in the dead of winter was held at the same church where she had been mortally wounded just a few days earlier. Grandma Betsy was buried on a cold, wet day marked by a persistent pouring rain that had pelted the community for several days. Her body had been laid in a simple pine coffin that was placed on a wagon for the short trip to the graveyard. The wagon was flat bottomed, with neither side rails nor a tailgate that could be closed. It was drawn by a single mule that struggled to

Grandma Betsy's pine coffin was placed on a wagon for the short trip to the graveyard. This drawing, inspired by Charlie Allen, was designed by Peggy Vonsherie Allen and illustrated by Michael Gardner.

pull the weight of the wagon, driver, and coffin in the pouring rain; the wagon wheels dug deeply into the mud.

En route to the cemetery the wagon had to climb a steep hill that led to a bridge with an almost vertical incline. The old bridge was made of large noisy wooden planks, like those used for railroad ties, and the rain made them very slippery. By the time the mule and wagon approached the hill, the mule's strength was waning. Several men tried to pull the mule along from the front and prod him from the rear. The driver, who had started the trip atop the wagon, jumped to the ground to lighten the load for the struggling mule.

The mule reached the steepest part of the incline and could go no farther. He was stuck. The wagon began to slide backward down the incline. And then, without warning, the coffin tumbled off the wagon, landed on its side, and Grandma Betsy's body fell out onto the cold, muddy ground. The procession of mourners stood stock-still. No one knew what to do. This was the stuff of late-night tales, except it was real. Grotesque and terrible, but real. The water and mud washed over the stiff body as the men struggled to put it back into the coffin. Daddy watched as the men placed the coffin back on the wagon. How much pain could one little boy be expected to endure? The cold, wet group of mourners finished the trip to the graveyard in silence. No one spoke a word, the picture of that overturned coffin and his mother's body lying in the mud was etched in Daddy's mind forever.

The men in the community thought that what happened to Grandma Betsy was a tragedy; the women thought she got just what she deserved for messing around with a married man. Actually there was no evidence that Grandma Betsy had done anything wrong at all. And surely no one deserved to meet such a tragic end. From that day forward, Daddy's life changed for the worse.

The years he spent with his mama were the best of Daddy's entire childhood. Times then were hard, but not terrible. After his mother died, he went to live with his grandma (Betsy's mama). When she took up with an evil old man who went by the name of Henry Gregory, he became Daddy's stepgranddaddy by default. Ol' Man Henry already had a family of children. He made it known that he neither needed nor wanted a stepgrandson. But Daddy's daddy, Anthony Allen, also had a family, and he did not want him either, so he was stuck with Ol' Man Henry.

Henry Gregory didn't care much for work and never held any job that amounted to much. It was said that his profession of choice was a two-headed man. He told fortunes and dabbled in roots for a living. He put spells and hexes on folks for money. Even when money was scarce, folks always seemed to find enough to put spells on or get spells off somebody else. And Ol' Man Henry was always there to take advantage of the situation.

Daddy, who was younger and smaller than all his stepuncles and stepaunts, was treated badly by the whole family. He wore hand-me-down clothes, ate seldom, and was the workhorse for the entire family. If there was a hard, dirty, tough job to do, Charlie did it. It was common practice for Ol' Man Henry to hire him out for days at a time to black folks and white folks alike. If anyone needed a hired hand, Ol' Man Henry had a boy.

By the time Daddy was ten or eleven he was being hired out for weeks at a time. One such time was when Zell Coouie needed a boy for a spell. Daddy's job was to help with anything and everything around the house and farm. He had to feed the cows, mules, chickens, and pigs. He also had to cut, split, and haul the firewood for the house. Zell Coouie had a wife, son, and two daughters, but he still needed a boy to take care of the hard labor around the house. And black folks could be hired for little or nothing. Daddy was small in stature and this work was extremely difficult. In return for this hard work he received food, lodging, and a few cents. Stepgrandpa Henry, on the other hand, received a couple of dollars a week for Daddy's work. The first few months with Mr. Coouie were tough. It was winter and the family used wood as fast as Daddy could cut it. He had to get up each morning before the chickens and make fires in all the stoves and fireplaces throughout the house. He had to have all the animals fed before the Coouies arose each morning. Nevertheless there were some things he liked about the job, that is, if one could like anything about being hired out like a slave. He ate better than he had since his mother Betsy had died. He even walked around with ten or twenty cents in his pocket at a time. He was also able to sleep in the house with the white folks. In fact, he slept in the room with the Coouie's son. Times were better than they had been in a long time. He periodically went back home to his family for short periods, and the harsh treatment would resume immediately. In time, he preferred working and living with the white folks.

Each time he returned from home to work for the Coouies, he was chipper. Whether working in the hot sun or the freezing cold, whatever the chore, he always had a good attitude and a smile. He was so gleeful, in fact, that the Coouies began to call him Sunshine, a name that stuck with him for the rest of his life. The entire family liked him, even the Coouie daughters, which was definitely forbidden. Of course, being black, he had been warned to stay away from the daughters, at least one of whom was young and attractive; he was told not to even look at her. The other daughter was large and ugly; Daddy said he thought she was mildly retarded. Every black man in the South during that time knew better than to even address a white woman, much less make advances toward her. Daddy was no exception. He knew better. A black man could be hung for even thinking such thoughts. A lot of them had been hung for less.

Daddy worked off and on for the Coouies for a number of years, occasionally moving back to stay with Ol' Man Henry. Soon the money Daddy was making with the Coouie family was not enough to support his big stepfamily. Since the burden of support was mainly his, he had to find more work. Daddy did everything he could to earn money for the family, and he got absolutely no help from them. Ol' Man Henry took every dime Daddy could make.

On one occasion, Daddy went to the woods and picked almost ten gallons of blackberries in one day. He hauled them to an old white man's house who had said he would pay him for them. But instead of paying Daddy cash, which was what he really needed, the man gave him a little sick calf that was close to death. He probably only gave it to Daddy so he would not have to bury the poor thing in a few days. Daddy took the sickly calf home, and within a couple of months, he had nursed it back to health. He figured this calf could grow up to be food for the family. But one evening when he returned from work at Zell Coouie's place, the calf was gone. Ol' Man Henry had sold him and kept all the money for himself. He hadn't even used any of the money to purchase food for the family. He just wasted it. Daddy didn't dare confront him about it; he just lowered his head and went on. He didn't think the calf was worth the beating he would get if he said something, so he didn't say a word.

Daddy had heard that they were hiring down at the sawmill in Chapman. The sawmill was actually W. T. Smith Lumber Company. It was owned and operated by the McGowins, a well-to-do white family in the community. The place was a community of trees, men, and saws down south of town. The mill itself was really just a large clearing in the middle of the woods, which consisted of some of the largest pine and hardwood trees in the South. The trees were so tall that they appeared to touch the clouds themselves. The mill was like a town. It was a self-sufficient, self-sustaining community that had everything including buildings for sleeping, eating, and sawing. It even had its own store and its own money. The money was a metal token. People who worked at the mill got paid mostly in tokens, which they could only spend at the mill store. No store outside the mill would accept the Chapman money. It was not real money at all. It was only legal tender at the company store.

Early one morning Daddy walked for miles to be at the mill in time for the opening bell. Although he arrived early, so did dozens of other men, black and white, who needed work as badly as he did. As the boss man walked through the crowd, he picked men to work for the day. He would point to a man here and a man there. Since logging work was hard labor, only the big and apparently strong men were chosen. After choosing ten or so men, the boss man said, "That's all I need today. The rest of y'all can come back tomorrow." This process went on day after day. Daddy walked for miles to the mill only to be overlooked in favor of the larger and stronger men. But Daddy kept coming back.

After a few days of the same routine, the boss man noticed that Daddy had been there every day, and every day he had been overlooked. He was just too small to work at a sawmill. He was only about fourteen. One day, the boss yelled to Daddy. "Boy, you're too damn small to work at a mill. What can you do?"

"I can do anything you want me to do," said Daddy.

"Well stand over here out of the way," he told Daddy. So Daddy stood there until the boss had chosen a dozen or so men for the day. After he sent the other men off to work, he returned to Daddy and said, "What is your name boy? Follow me."

"Charlie," Daddy replied as he followed the man into a large tent. All the buildings at the mill were made from tents. There was not one permanent building on the place.

This tent was large and had a wooden floor that looked as if it was made from newly split logs that could have come from some of the trees right there on the property. It had rows and rows of wooden tables and benches and a wood-burning stove at each end of the building and one in the middle. The top and sides of the building were made of some sort of thick waterproof cloth to keep the weather out. As they walked toward the far end of the building, Daddy could see a collection of pots, pans, cans, buckets, and dishes. As he got closer he noticed five-gallon cans of flour, meal, sugar, and syrup. And hanging from posts that were fixed to the floor were large carcasses of cured beef and pork. There was more food in that one building than Daddy had seen in all his life. He thought there must be enough food to feed an army, though at the time, Daddy didn't really know how many men constituted an army. He only knew that there was an awful lot of food there. In a distant corner of the building, working with the pots and pans, stood an older black man. He seemed to be cooking.

Daddy was passed off to the old man and the only instructions were, "Hey, uncle, put this boy to work." "Uncle" was a disparaging term used for old black men. He looked as if he had been tall in his time; however, work and time had turned his tall frame into a short, humpbacked old man. He was wearing an apron that reached well past his knees. In a quiet voice, he said, "Come on, boy, and let's get started." This was the beginning of Daddy's days as a cook for the Chapman sawmill. He had gotten a paying job at last. He was so proud of himself. He could finally help feed his family. In reality, he was their primary provider.

His new job was cook's helper. Food had to be prepared for all the men who worked at the mill. When Daddy arrived at the sawmill he didn't know anything about cooking, but he was a fast learner. He had to learn fast if he wanted to keep his new job. The two men prepared two meals a day, breakfast and supper. While some of the men went home at the end of each day, most of them ate and slept at the camp. Some went home to their families on weekends and some rarely left the mill. In any case, those who were there had to eat. And somebody had to do the cooking.

Daddy usually spent all week at the camp, going home to Ol' Man Henry and his family on weekends. He was in no rush to get home. The only thing there with his stepfamily was more work and poor treatment. Of course they were glad to see him. Well, they were glad to see the money he brought home and the food that he stole for them. They didn't really care whether they saw him or not. They only cared about what he had to give them. There were a lot of mouths to feed at home. And he was

W. T. Smith Lumber Company, Chapman, Alabama, circa 1900. Photo courtesy of Kay Taylor-Bryant Anderson.

the only one with a real job. As before, times were hard. It was even harder to steal food to take home. If he were caught stealing, he would lose the best job he had ever had, and he would probably be sent to jail as well, or worse. It was not uncommon in those days for a black man to be killed for stealing. But with so many hungry mouths to feed at home, he had to take a chance.

Daddy often spoke of how he got stealing food down to an art. He said he hated the stealing but he didn't have much of a choice in the matter. There was so much food at the mill, while his family was nearly starving at home. He saw no other alternative. He said he would take an empty syrup can and fill it with biscuits, bits of dried pork and beef, and canned salmon. Anything the men ate, he would take. He would put a lid on the can and when no one was looking, he would sneak out into the woods and bury the can in the ground. He would then cover the can with leaves and bushes, taking care not to be discovered. Since syrup cans were commonly used around the mill as lunch pails, no one would find it unusual to see him carrying one. He would work all week at filling the can. And then at the end of the week, he would carefully retrieve the can to take home to his family. He ate with the men all week, but sometimes that single can of food was all his entire family back home had to eat until he returned with another can. These were tough times. Daddy said that black folks didn't know much about the Great Depression, because things were always hard for black folks, Depression or not. In terms of survival it was "hard to get, hard to keep, and hard to eat," he always said.

Daddy worked as a cook at the sawmill for several years. The pay wasn't very good but at least he had a job, and the food he stole helped to supplement his pay. After a few years when he was a little older and a little bigger and stronger, he left his job as cook's helper and went to work in the mill. He split, stacked, and hauled wood, swept sawdust, and did any other job that needed doing. The work inside the mill paid a little more money than the cooking job. The work, however, was also a lot harder than cooking, and he no longer had the fringe benefit of stealing food to take home. Even though blacks and whites worked together at the mill, their duties were quite different. The work was dangerous; men could lose an arm or a leg or their lives. The most dangerous jobs went to the blacks and the very poor whites. When a black man died, which happened quite often, there was no fanfare; he was merely replaced. Daddy had often heard the boss man say that "niggers" were a dime a dozen, and they were surely treated that way. Poor whites ranked only about one notch above the blacks. Most of them had rough lives as well.

None of this really mattered to Daddy. It was not like he could just quit his job. Jobs were hard to come by, and anyone who found a job kept it. Daddy worked off and on at the sawmill for many years; he was working there when he met and married Mama. It was hard work but it was better than being a field hand and working on some white man's farm. A certain amount of influence and respect among your peers also went with a job at the sawmill. There wasn't much money, but Daddy managed to survive.

Mama

Mama's childhood may have been a little better than Daddy's, but not significantly so. Mama was born on May 5, 1923, to Willie and Josie Hall. She had two brothers, Woodrow and Wilson, and two sisters, Susan and Mae Liza. They had a nice normal family for black folks, at least for a while. Mae Liza was the youngest of the children, and when she was about two or three she was killed in an accident.

It had been a typical morning around the house. It was barely daylight but Papa and Grandma Josie had already left for the cotton field. Mama was the oldest child, and she had been left at the house to take care of her younger sisters and brothers. Even though they were young, they all had chores to do. It was Mama's responsibility to cook breakfast and watch over the house and the kids while her brothers Woodrow and Wilson brought in firewood for the kitchen stove and fireplace. Even though it was summertime, there was no electricity in the house and a fire was needed to cook and to heat water for the chores.

Wilson was mixing kerosene and kindling in a bucket to jump-start a fire. Papa had chastised him numerous times, warning him that it was dangerous and telling him not to do it. As usual Wilson had not heeded Papa's advice; with no one there to scold him, he prepared his dangerous mixture. Mae Liza, the youngest, had not yet been dressed for the day and was still wearing a long cotton nightshirt. The nightshirt, which was too long for her small body, dragged on the floor a few inches behind her as she walked. When Wilson tossed the bucket of kerosene and kindling into the fireplace, the kerosene led a deadly liquid trail from the fireplace right to where Mae was standing. Embers in the fireplace were still smoldering from the night before, and in a flash a trail of flames jumped from the fireplace onto Mae Liza. Her gown went up in flames like a torch. Mae screamed in pain. Mama yelled for Wilson to go to the kitchen for some water, but when he got there he found the water bucket empty.

Mama ran to the back door, yelling for Papa to come in from the field. The field was about fifty yards away and they could hear the yelling and screaming from the house. Before Papa reached the house he was shouting, "What's wrong, what's wrong?" Mama yelled back, "Its Mae Liza, she's on fire." By the time Papa and Grandma Josie got to the house Wilson had not drawn even one bucket of water from the well. Each time he got the bucket of water halfway up the side of the well he would lose his grip on the rope and the bucket would plunge back down into the well.

When Papa got to Mae the fire had burned her gown completely off. All the hair on her head had been singed off by the flames. Papa quickly grabbed a blanket and threw it around her to put out the flames that were still smoldering, but it was already too late. She had been so badly burned all over her body that when Papa picked her up in the blanket, her tiny body slid right out of it. Only her burned skin was left inside the blanket. The smell of Mae Liza's burning flesh was horrible. When Grandma Josie got to the house she began sobbing uncontrollably and calling out Mae Liza's name.

Papa handed Mae Liza over to Grandma Josie and ran outside to hitch up the mule and wagon. It normally took twenty minutes; this time Papa did it in less than five. He went as fast as he could go to town for the doctor, driving that old mule to exhaustion. It was a long ride, about eight miles. And it was all for naught; there was no hope for Mae Liza. The doctor took one look at Mae Liza and told her grieving parents that she could not recover from the massive burns. He said all they could do was try to make her comfortable. He gave them something for her pain and said it was all he could do.

The whole family stayed up all night keeping watch and praying for Mae, but nothing helped. Before dawn the next morning she was gone. Her little body just gave up. Grandma Josie never got over the death of

Mae Liza. I don't think Papa ever did either. Wilson may have had the hardest hard time dealing with Mae Liza's death because his actions had created the deadly fire that had taken her life.

Times were hard and soon the family had to get back to the business of trying to survive. Papa did a little bit of everything to make money for the family. Farming was what most black folks did. They tried to work a field of vegetables and cotton for the white folks and a field of the same for themselves. Most folks were like Papa, sharecroppers.

Papa also had another job—making moonshine. This art was passed down to him and his brothers and sisters by their mama. Her real name was Mary Henderson but everyone called my great-grandma Moa. She was the moonshine matriarch of the family. She passed her recipe down to everyone in the family; I still have it. Papa would make moonshine to sell to the local white folks. He also sold it to the few black folks who could afford to buy it. Making moonshine was the one job Papa was really good at, maybe because he had more practice at that than any other job.

Not long after Mae Liza's death, another tragedy arrived on Papa's doorstep. A terrible fever was going around the community. No one knew what was causing the sickness but folks from near and far were ill. Some of them got better, but some of them died. Soon everyone in Mama's house was sick: Woodrow, Wilson, Susan, Papa, Grandma Josie, and Mama herself. The sickness went on for days in Mama's house and weeks in others. No one ever put a name to the illness for sure. Some said it was scarlet fever, some, yellow fever or malaria or other names. All they knew was that there were high fevers, chills, and diarrhea associated with the sickness, and people were dying. In Mama's house everyone except Grandma Josie soon got better. Papa tried home cures and even took her to the doctor in town, but she continued to get worse, getting weaker and weaker each day. Then suddenly, she was gone. The fever with no name had taken her life, leaving Papa all alone with four kids to rear.

Mama was the oldest but she was only about ten, still too young to be the woman of the house. Papa had to go to work and while he was in the fields, Mama was at home taking care of the house and her three younger siblings. She worked hard and learned to do a little of everything. She had to cook and clean for the entire family. She also had to work in the fields at home and tend the hogs and chickens. Papa always raised several hogs at a time. The primary responsibility for keeping things in order at home was Mama's. Times were hard, but they were making it. In fact, they were managing to do much better than many colored folks in the community.

Mama was so small that every job was a chore, even washing dishes. In those days very few black people had running water. The well was about thirty feet from the house, out the back door. She had to draw water by the bucketful, pour it into a separate bucket, and carry in into the house. The water had to be heated on the wood-burning stove. In order to heat the water a fire had to be made in the stove, in summer as well as winter. The work would be hard for an adult; for a child it was grueling. But Mama never complained about her family responsibilities.

As times grew harder Papa took more chances making moonshine. The more he made, the more dangerous it became for him in two ways. The danger of selling to white folks increased the risk of being arrested and sent to jail. The danger of selling to black folks increased the risk of being robbed or even killed for the money or the liquor. His chances of getting into trouble were high. Eventually, Papa's luck ran out but not in the way he had thought it would.

Papa had a run-in with a mean old nasty Negro, a local bully. This old man used to rob and steal from other poor folks in the area. One day he decided he would rob Papa of his moonshine earnings. Late one evening after a moonshine run he stopped Papa on the road and raised a big stick, telling Papa to hand over all his moonshine money. Papa refused. As the man was about to beat up on Papa, Papa reached into his hip pocket and pulled out a revolver. That old Negro dropped the stick and ran as if he'd seen a rattlesnake. After word of the incident got around town, the would-be robber swore he would get back at Papa, and eventually he did. Back then it was against the law for a black man to carry a weapon, but most people knew that Papa had a revolver he sometimes carried for protection when he was making a moonshine run. After that old man threatened him, Papa began to carry it almost all the time.

One Sunday morning, in the middle of church service, right in the middle of a prayer, the doors of the church burst open. The loud noise startled everyone. I suppose some thought maybe God himself had come down to take them to glory. It wasn't God but the large, menacing figure of Sheriff Thompson, the meanest sheriff Butler County had ever known. The prayer stopped and the congregation fell silent. The sheriff walked in with two deputies at his side and headed straight for Papa, who was still kneeling in prayer. Without hesitation he reached over and patted Papa's right hip pocket; he pulled the pistol out and placed it in his own pocket. Papa was placed under arrest, put in handcuffs, and led out of the church. Everything took place right in front of Mama, the children, and the rest of the congregation. Everyone knew that the nasty old Negro who had sworn he would get back at Papa was the one who had told the sheriff about Papa's gun.

Papa spent a few days in jail before he was given a makeshift trial. There was no lawyer and no jury, just a judge. After a trial that lasted all of twenty minutes, he was sentenced to a year and a day in jail. He had been making and selling the moonshine in an effort to provide for his family. Now, he would be forced to abandon them. Mama, the oldest, who was eleven years old at the time, and the three younger children would be left to fend for themselves. There was no way they could survive on their own for a year, and no single family could afford to take in four young children for such a long time; they were too small to be of much help to anyone. So for a year, Mama and her sister and brothers bounced around from family member to family member, unloved, unwanted, and often mistreated.

Her brothers Woodrow and Wilson finally ended up at Grandpa Willie's house; he was Papa's daddy. Mama and Susan did not fare as well. The worst were the months that they spent with Papa's sister Sue. Sue, who had children of her own, was mean and did not want to be bothered with Mama and Susan. She worked them hard, making them perform chores every day, including chopping and stacking firewood, cooking, and cleaning. They had to do everything in the yard too. Aunt Sue would not allow a single leaf to be left on the ground in the fall. They had to sweep and pick up after everyone. They even had to take care of Aunt Sue's bad children. They were nothing more than unpaid hired hands. This poor treatment went on for months. Everyone noticed. People would come to the house and ask, "Sue, why are you so hard on those girls?" They were being treated like slaves by their own family. Papa did not know what his sister was putting his daughters through. But even if he had known, what could he do about their predicament? He was in a predicament of his own.

The girls were miserable, but they had no one to turn to, nowhere else to go, or so they thought. Eventually Moa, Papa's mama, got word that they were being mistreated and hired a man to take her by wagon to Aunt Sue's place. She got there and without even sitting down she told Mama and Susan to get their things because they were coming to stay with her. Aunt Sue was angry about losing her help but she didn't dare cross Moa. Few people had the nerve to do that and Aunt Sue was not one of them. Mama and Susan were happy to be rescued by their grandmother. Times were easier living with Moa. While Moa was a hard, strong-willed black woman, she was also fair. They had to work around Moa's house, too, but not quite as hard as they had to work at Sue's. And Moa taught them a lot. She taught them how to make jams and jellies, and how to pickle vegetables and fruits so they would keep for years. Moa also raised hogs like Papa. She taught them how to kill hogs, preserve them in salt, and smoke the meat. Her kitchen always seemed to have a large piece of smoked pork hanging from the ceiling behind the stove. Moa was good to them. She was the closest thing to a mother they had known since their mama, Josie, had died of the fever.

During the time Mama and Susan spent with Moa, she also passed down the famous family recipe—the moonshine recipe that had in a way landed Papa in jail. Moa had learned to make moonshine as a small child. The recipe had been passed down from her mama. Our family had been making moonshine for as long as anyone could remember; it was a family legacy, passed down from generation to generation, and the entire family became quite good at it.

A year and a day passed very slowly. But the time passed a little easier for Mama and Susan at Moa's house. Eventually Papa's time was done and he was let out of jail. He was able to return home to his family. They were all relieved and happy to see him. The girls had learned a lot while he was away, not least of all the family recipe.

Moa

My great-grandmother Moa was the matriarch of the family. I remember visiting her as a small child when she lived over in Crenshaw County, about twenty miles or so east of Greenville. While I cannot recall the first time I saw her, she always seemed to me to be the oldest woman I had ever seen. She was wrinkled from head to toe; her skin was dark and leathery. She was blind by the time I knew her, but she had a good mind and her memory was better than many people younger than her. She was sharp tongued and witty. By the time I first laid eyes on her, she had to have been well past her one hundredth year. We went to visit her often, and during the summer months there was plenty of activity in and around her house, including men working in the fields. Even in her old age she planted large fields of corn, peas, beans, pepper, tomatoes, sugarcane, and the like. She canned, or put up as they called it, most of the food. There was always more than enough for herself and enough to share with the rest of the family.

The sugarcane she grew was a special treat. I liked to peel it, and chew it whole, just for the sweet juices. The stalks of cane grew ten to fifteen feet tall. When you saw the cane fields from a distance, with a slight breeze blowing, the stalks swaying in the wind looked like water rippling in a creek or river. It was a beautiful sight. But Moa didn't raise sugarcane just for chewing or because it looked pretty swaying in the wind. She raised it to make syrup and sugar. I will never forget the taste of Mama's hot biscuits dipped in Moa's homemade syrup. She always grew more than enough cane for sale and processing into regular table sugar. Sugar was one of the main ingredients for her moonshine business. So it was crucial for her to always have enough sugar around the house.

Our trips to visit her in the fall of the year were just as memorable as the summer trips. That was hog-killing season, and Moa always had lots of hogs. On hog-killing days people came from all around the community to help. Mama, Daddy, and my sisters and brothers were among those who came. There was a lot of work to do on hog-killing days and Moa needed all the help she could get. Sometimes she would butcher as many as five hogs at a time. Not many black folks could afford to kill five hogs at once, but Moa could. It was always a festive occasion. I was too small to help out with the hog killing so I just mostly watched as the work was being done. A lot was happening and I wanted to take it all in. Moa was ordering people around like soldiers and everything was orderly. The smell of freshly killed pork filled the air. The best part about hog-killing day at Moa's was that I knew we would get to take some of the fresh meat home. There were numerous bonfires going all at once. There were buckets and barrels of water all about, cold and hot. After the hogs were killed they were taken to different tables to be dismembered. The precision would rival any operating room. The pork had to be cut up just right for curing. Learning how to properly cut up a pig was something of an art. Not just anyone could do it.

I also remember moonshine making time at Moa's. There were not quite as many people around for the making of moonshine as there were for hog-killing day. Only a few key, trusted people were on hand. There was still a lot of work going on however. And the smell, yes, even the smell was intoxicating. If you have ever smelled the scent of cooking moonshine, the smell will be with you forever. You will never forget it; I haven't. The smell is putrid. It is a mixture of foul brackish water combined with rotting vegetation and a hint of rotting animal flesh, topped off with a nauseating sweet smell, probably from all the sugar in the mixture. When I got within fifty yards of a moonshine still my eyes burned as if I had been hit in the face with a gasoline-soaked cloth. Just when I was about to vomit from the smell, I would remember. The horrible smell only lasts for a few days and after the sale of the finished liquor, life would be better for a while. Food, shoes, or maybe even a piece of hard candy for us children would be purchased from the proceeds of the sale. Those thoughts of what the moonshine promised would settle my stomach. There is nothing like the scent of moonshine being slowly cooked over a well-tended flame. I hated it. I loved it. I will never forget it.

Moa had mastered the art of making moonshine after many years of practice. As best she could recall, she had learned this skill when she was a child, while she was still a slave. Moa was not only a manufacturer, she was also a consumer. In her day, she could hold her liquor better than most men. I guess Papa got his liking for liquor from her, although he could not hold it quite as well as she could. Even in her later years, Moa took a little nip at night to help her get to sleep.

Moa was a hard, strong, tough old woman who had survived a lot of hardships, including spending most of her adult life without a husband. When Moa was quite young she had been married to a man by the name of Phifer. They were married for a number of years and had several children. They stayed together until he was run off because he had gotten in trouble with some of the white folks, which was easy to do. All you had to do was say or do something the white folks objected to. Sometimes you didn't have to say or do anything at all to get in trouble. Sometimes just being black was enough to get into trouble. In any event, he had gotten in trouble. Oftentimes, the only way to get out of being crosswise with white folks was to get dead or to get gone. I guess getting dead did not appeal to him so he chose to get gone. He left all of a sudden, on foot, in the middle of the night. He didn't have time to pack much for his trip for fear the law was hot on his trail. He only took a few articles of clothes and some food with him. Moa helped him pack. He didn't even tell Moa which way he was headed. North or south, no one knew. I suppose at the time he left, he didn't know which way he was going either. He only knew that he had to leave, and he had to do it quickly.

It was a long time before Moa heard anything about him. When he left he had followed the creek south to Andalusia. While Andalusia was only forty miles away, the white folks never caught up with him. Nor did he ever come back to his family. Moa used to refer to him as "one scared nigger." As far as she knew he never made any attempt to come home. That was the end of Mr. Phifer. Word came back to Moa years later that he had taken up with another woman and started a new family down there.

Moa never saw him again. She did not like to talk about him very much. Whenever we tried to bring him up in conversation she would stop us short and change the subject.

Moa never married again but she did fall for another man. Mr. Willie Hall, Papa's daddy, and my great-granddaddy. They had several children, including Papa. Willie Hall wanted to marry Moa but he wasn't able to do that. You see he worked for a mean old white man. If you didn't do everything the white folks told you to do you would be in trouble. This case was no exception. Willie Hall worked for this white man. He lived on his property, and he had to do as he was told. The old white man had a decent-looking young black woman who worked for him in his house doing the cooking and cleaning. Apparently she was doing other things for him as well. It was no secret. And as old folks used to say, what's done in the dark will come to light. And sure enough it was not long before that old white man's deeds caught up with him. The woman was in the family way. She did not have a husband or a boyfriend so everyone knew the baby belonged to the old white man she worked for. The white man told Great-grandpa Willie that he had to marry the black woman and rear the baby. At first he refused because he wanted to marry Moa. After a long discussion, Moa finally convinced him that he would be better off alive and married to a woman he did not want and raising that white man's baby than dead. Dead he could not be of any use to anyone. And dead he would surely be if he did not do what he was told.

So, reluctantly, he did as he was told. He married a woman he did not love. That happened to a lot of black people in those days. It was normal everyday business for the white landowner to have sexual relations with the black women who worked for him. Some tried to hide it and some didn't. There were a lot of light-skinned black people in those days. Like it or not there was not much that could be done about it. It was typical of the times.

After the loss of first her husband and then the loss of Great-grandpa Willie Hall, Moa never thought of getting married again. She learned to be stronger than any man. She had to. She was a survivor and she learned to make it on her own. Even though Moa and Great-grandpa Willie were never able to live together as husband and wife, he never abandoned her. He was always there for her when she needed him. He did what he could to support his children too, Papa and the rest. His wife understood the situation and never gave him much hassle about helping out. After all he had helped her out of a bind as well, and she was understandably grateful to him for doing so.

While Moa's adult life was a struggle, her childhood had been worse. Moa was a great storyteller. She told heart-wrenching stories about her childhood. Moa was born into slavery. It's hard to believe that my great-grandmother had been a slave and lived to tell about it. I heard the stories firsthand—from her lips to my ears. I still tear up when I think about it. The first few times I heard Moa tell the stories I didn't want to believe them because they were so horrible. I would ask how she made it, how she survived. Moa would reply, "I had no choice but to make it."

Her stories of life as a slave were filled with beatings, hard work in the cotton fields, sugarcane fields, and orchards. The lack of freedom was the hardest aspect for me to imagine. She was not free to speak, think, sleep, drink, eat, sing, or do anything of her own free will. It was always at the will of the master. She was property, chattel owned by another human being. Moa said that at least her mama and papa were allowed to get married, or jump the broom as they called it. Drucilla and Ed Henderson were Moa's mama and papa. Moa also spoke of a younger sister, named Viola. She seldom spoke of any other relatives; maybe those were the only ones she knew enough about to speak of.

She recalled that the plantation where she was born had rows and rows of shacks for the slaves to live in. She called them the quarters, after hearing someone else call them by that name. The slaves all lived together in those shacks, related and unrelated alike. There were few real family units like hers, with a mama, papa, and children. There was no need for the family unit. If there was a family, it might not stay together very long. Families were bought, sold, and traded from plantation to plantation, work farm to work farm. Sometimes they stayed together but more often they were separated never to hear from their relatives again. Moa often said that when she died she knew she was going to heaven. She said that being a slave was hell, and she had already been there, and she didn't care much about going back.

Moa lost her entire family on one such trade of Negroes. She recalled the occasion when dozens of slaves had been sold from the plantation on which she lived. She, along with her entire family, was sold with that group. They were all gathered together early one morning about daybreak. It was late spring and the morning air was still cold. They had been assembled to begin the trip to their new plantation home. They were going to make the trip on foot. At least the slaves were on foot; the white overseers escorting them to their new location were on horseback. The trip was scheduled to begin early. After hearing the news that they had been sold, the slaves needed only a few moments to pack their meager belongings. They were allowed to take everything they owned to their new home, but they didn't own much, maybe just a few scraps of clothing.

They headed out on the road all bunched together. Moa said that she felt like they were being driven like cattle. If one of them stepped out of line or fell behind, they were hit sharply with a whip by one of the overseers on horseback. The going was rough for all of them, especially the women and children. They traveled by the light of day and slept in the woods by night. Not much food was brought along for the trip, and no water was carried at all. The only water they had to drink was what they found in the creeks and gullies along the way. It was common for a slave or two to get lost by the wayside either intentionally or by accident. Moa's mama and papa took turns carrying her younger sister Viola who was too small to walk on her own. Hunger and thirst were their constant companions, accompanied by the sharp crack of the whip in the distance.

The going was slow. After a few days of walking, everyone was tired and Moa had difficulty keeping up with the group. On about the fourth day, she tripped and fell into a ditch beside the road. For a few minutes she lay there stunned. When she realized what had happened she was afraid to move, afraid that she would be beaten for falling behind. She must have lay in the ditch motionless for hours. By the time she got the courage to move she was all alone. Not a soul remained. No Mama, no Papa, and no Viola. No one was left but Moa.

Moa was more afraid than ever and she didn't know what to do. She was too exhausted to try to run and catch up with the others and she was afraid to turn back. They had been walking for days and she had no idea where she was. She decided to leave the trail and proceed through the woods. She pushed herself through briars and bushes, stumbling now and then over tree roots and stumps. Soon she had scratches and insect bites all over her body. She walked all day through the woods, not stopping until dark. By this time she was even more exhausted. She was hungry and thirsty too. The sack with food in it was being carried by her mama. She wondered where her family was and what they were doing. She wondered if they had missed her and whether they had tried to find her. She had never been without her family before. In fact, she had never been alone before. She began to cry, but there was no one to hear her. She sat down to rest for the night by a large stump. She prayed to God that she would survive the night without being eaten by some creature from the dark woods. She also prayed for food. It had been more than a day since she had last eaten. That night she slept alone in the woods.

She woke up the next morning in the woods still alone but with a new resolve. She had to survive. She had to find her family. She had to find someone. She no longer worried about getting a beating from the overseer. In fact she would welcome it; she just didn't want to be alone any more. After walking for a few hours she saw a clearing in the woods in which she spotted a small farmhouse. Even though she had never been there before, there was something familiar about the place: farm animals in the yard, an old barn, smoke drifting up from the chimney of the house. These were things she had seen before. Moa used to say she felt like an old stray dog circling the house, hoping to find some scrap of food. By this point she was nearly overpowered by hunger. She was no longer afraid of anything. She just wanted food and rest.

Before she could get her bearings a tall gangly white woman appeared from the side of the house. Apparently they frightened each other. The woman yelled, "Who are you child and what do you want?"

"I'm Mary," Moa replied, "and I'm lost and hungry."

"Where you from child" the woman asked?

"A long ways from here," Moa replied. The woman told Moa to wait outside and soon returned with a plate of food. Moa ate hungrily; it had been days since she had eaten. The woman asked Moa where she was headed. Of course Moa had no idea which way her family had been headed, and she didn't know where she was. The woman asked Moa if she wanted to stay there with her a while. Not having anywhere else to go Moa agreed.

The woman summoned her husband who fixed a place in the barn for

Moa to sleep and a place for her things, which consisted of one dress other than the one she was wearing. Moa soon settled into life with the white woman and her husband, but she never forgot about her family. She stayed and worked for that white family for a number of years. She was no longer a slave, but she was an indentured servant of sorts.

Moa never saw her mama and papa again. She never heard what became of them. She thought her sister Viola was lost forever also. But about forty or fifty years later she heard tell of a Viola who lived some twenty miles from her. This Viola was her long-lost baby sister. They had grown up only twenty miles apart. She often wondered what things would have been like for her if she had stayed on that road years before. Would she have been separated from her family at a later date? Would she still not know what became of her parents and baby sister? Would her life have been any better, any worse? She would never know if she had made the right decision to lie still in that ditch. She never knew if her mama and papa had died as slaves or as freedmen.

Even after slavery officially ended, Moa said things weren't much better for black folks. Many of them continued to live on the same plantations and farms where they had been slaves. Where else could they go? It's no wonder Moa turned out to be such a strong woman. If she was going to survive she had no choice.

Since she was born a slave, Moa never had a birth certificate, so there was never any written record of her age. But she certainly lived to be well past 120 years old. Her time finally came and she died in the early 1970s. I was about eleven or twelve years old. And although I loved her very much, and I knew I would miss her, it was hard for me to cry for her when she died. I knew deep down inside that she was finally on her way to heaven. Hell, where she had been for more than 120 years, was over for her. I always thought that Alabama was a better place because she had lived; I know that I am a better person because of her. The family matriarch was gone. God bless Moa.

Four Bales Are Not Enough

Papa, Mama's daddy, worked all his life as a sharecropper for one white family or another. In the 1930s and 1940s most colored folks were share-croppers, and Papa was just like everyone else. There was not much else for them to do in order to earn a living. In those days colored people didn't own any land of their own. How could they? They never earned enough money to own much of anything. The land that they lived on was usually owned by the white folks that they sharecropped for. And the old shacks they lived in were just a few pieces of lumber nailed together with a tin roof to keep some of the rain out. Most of the old shacks had dirt floors. If your house had a wooden floor, you were considered to be living pretty high on the hog.

Papa always seemed to be deep in debt to John Grant. John Grant was the white man that Papa sharecropped for. Year after year Papa tried his best to get out of debt. But no matter how hard he tried, he never suc-ceeded. He was never able to grow enough crops or earn enough money to get out of debt. In return for living on Mr. Grant's land, Papa had to give Mr. Grant half of everything he raised each year. Papa had to give him half his corn, peas, beans, tomatoes, okra, watermelons, and cotton. Cot-ton was the major cash crop of the area so that's what Mr. Grant really wanted, but he never turned down any of the food that Papa had raised to feed his own family. It didn't matter what the crop was, Mr. Grant was happy to take half of it off of Papa's hands. Not that Mr. Grant needed the food. He didn't. He was a rich man already, but he took half of all the crops anyway. Papa used to say he took half just because he could.

Each year would start out the same. In the springtime, which was planting season, Papa would be forced to borrow money from Mr. Grant for seeds and planting materials. Even though Papa would have earned a little money the previous year from selling his crops, it would have been long since gone by the time planting season came around. So, in order to plant a new crop, Papa would have to borrow money for the bare necessities to get his new crop going. He knew full well that he would have to pay Mr. Grant half of everything he grew just for living on his property, and now, after borrowing additional money for seeds, he would also have to pay Mr. Grant a portion of what he earned from the sale of his half of his crop. It was a vicious circle. No matter how hard Papa tried, he could never make a profit. He was in the hole before he even got started each year. He always ended each year still owing money to Mr. Grant no matter how good his crops for the season had been. He had to feed himself and four children with his share of his crop, and his share was never enough to make it from one harvest season to the next without having to borrow more.

Papa's situation was not unique. Almost every colored person in the South was faced with the same situation. In fact, there were a number of poor white folks who were also caught up in the vicious sharecropping circle. Essentially, there were those who had, and those who had not. All the colored folks fit into the "had not" category. Each year Papa would plan not to be caught short and not owe Mr. Grant extra money at the end of the season. Each year he failed. If he could only get one big crop to come in he thought he could make it out of the cycle of debt. But there was always something in the way of making that really big crop. Some years he failed to make it because there was not enough rain; other years there was too much rain. Some years the crops were plagued by insects and plant diseases. There was always something to keep the crop production down and keep Papa in the hole.

There was one year, in the late 1930s, when everything seemed to be falling into place for Papa. He still had to borrow money from Mr. Grant for seed, but not as much as he normally did. So things were looking up. Papa planted everything that year in large quantities. He planted more than enough vegetables to keep the family going all summer, and he planted enough to put some away to keep the family going the next winter as well. Papa and his mule also planted several acres of cotton, more than they had ever been able to plant before. Papa was the only adult in the family, and the only help he had was his mule and four small children. Even so, he was able to plant a bumper crop of everything.

That year the whole family worked hard all spring and summer tending the crops. Even the smaller children could be found in the fields, hoe in hand, chopping cotton and weeding the vegetables. No one was spared the hard work. Every hand was needed to help out, no matter how small that hand was. Everyone pitched in and helped, even Mother Nature. She provided just enough rain to ensure a good crop. She provided the right amount of sunlight, not too much, which would burn and wilt the crops, not too little. This year, everything was falling into place for Papa and his family. Even Mama and the other children sensed that there was something different about this planting year. Even though they were still quite young, they were aware of the things that went on around the house and fields. After all, the children played an important role in the work.

After several months of hard work planting, hoeing, and tending the crops, it was finally time to reap the rewards—finally harvest time for the vegetables. Everyone got excited about harvest time. Papa and the children were happy to see the vegetables ripening on the vines. Fresh vegetables were a welcome addition to their diet. The past winter they had eaten dried meat and old potatoes from out of the smokehouse and the potato beds outside. Mr. Grant was also happy to see the vegetables ripen, but not for the same reasons that Papa and his family were. Mr. Grant and his family had eaten like royalty all winter long. He was a man of means and he never had to worry about where his next meal was coming from. No, Mr. Grant was happy for a different reason, money. He seemed to be able to smell vegetables ripening on the vine from miles away. Whenever vegetables got ripe and ready to eat, Mr. Grant was always close by to make sure he got his half. But it sure was a lot easier for Papa to give away half of a bountiful crop than half of a sparse crop. For the first time in years it looked as if his family would not have to go hungry through the winter. Even after giving away half of the harvest to Mr. Grant, it looked as if there would still be enough food to last through the winter.

Papa, Mama, and the other three children began canning and preserving their portion of the vegetables in preparation for the winter. Mama and her sister Susan had learned to can vegetables from their Grandma Moa while Papa was off in jail serving his year and a day. Knowing how to can and preserve food was a fine art, especially in those days when everything was feast or famine. There was a feast in the summer months when vegetables were ripening on the vines, and there was famine in the winter months when there were days when no food could be found. So the girls began to put food away for the coming winter. The vegetables were so plentiful that year that they were able to sell a few, even after giving Mr. Grant his half. For the first time in a long while they had a dollar or two to buy things that they could not raise, such as shoes and clothes. Papa was even able to raise a few more hogs. He had always raised one or two, but this year he had six pigs, more than he had ever been able to feed at one time. The tide seemed to be turning. The family had meat and vegetables to eat and a couple of dollars hidden away. Yes indeed, things were looking a little better.

The vegetables were not the only crops that did well that year. Papa's cotton crop was coming along well also. The weather had been good all year. Even the worms and bugs that usually attacked the cotton crop were on their best behavior. Hardly any of the crop had been lost to the pest infestations. Papa and the children had given that cotton crop months of tender loving care, and it had paid off. By the time cotton-picking season arrived, everyone was ready. Papa, the children, and Mr. Grant were all eager to see the size of that year's harvest. Papa and the family wondered how much money they would be able to make. They were hoping and praying to get out of debt to Mr. Grant, at least for a year. They would have done anything to just break even with him. Mr. Grant on the other hand was just anxious to get his half of the cotton crop.

Papa and the children began the hot, arduous task of picking and baling the cotton. It was long, hard, slow, back-breaking work and everyone had to help. It took the family almost three weeks to pick the several acres that they had planted. Up one row and down the next, they picked every plant clean. They were careful not to leave any cotton on the plants, because cotton left on the plants was like money left to rot in the fields. So each long cotton row was picked and then picked again to make sure that nothing was left in the fields. Papa and the family toiled sunup to sundown. They watched the small burlap sacks that they used for picking slowly grow into a large mound of cotton. The work was performed under the watchful eye of Mr. Grant, who came by every couple of days just to see how things were going. Actually, according to Papa, he came by to make sure that none of the cotton owed to him was being sold without his knowledge. Not that he needed to do that. There was only one cotton gin in town. Any Negro who sold cotton knew it would be reported to the white landowner he sharecropped for. There was absolutely no way a colored man could cheat a white man, even if he wanted to.

After several weeks of hard, hot work Papa's family had picked all the cotton plants clean. Everyone, even Mr. Grant was surprised at the final tally. Papa and his four small children had planted, raised, and picked four huge bales of cotton, more than they had ever produced before. This was quite an accomplishment for a family so small. Four bales of cotton, along with all the vegetables and hogs they raised was indeed a miracle. Papa couldn't remember ever doing so well before. Things had indeed looked up for them.

Like clockwork, Mr. Grant soon came around to collect his half of the family's cotton production. Mama said that Papa almost cried as he watched Mr. Grant haul away his half, his two full bales of cotton that the family had worked so hard to produce. Papa knew that there was nothing to be gained from crying. He knew that work and only work was how he was going to make a difference for his family. Sharecropping, giving half of your crop to a white landowner just for the privilege of staying in an old rundown shack, was the way it was. It was the way it had always been, and as far as Papa knew, it was the way things would always be.

In spite of his discouragement, Papa was composed as he watched Mr. Grant haul his two bales of cotton away. Papa packed his two remaining bales of cotton onto his wagon, hitched up the mule, and headed to town to the cotton gin. It was time to sell his crop. Papa's mind was not on the road as he drove into town. Instead he was thinking about the possibilities that lay ahead of him if he actually made a profit from the cotton. There were so many things that his family needed. He thought about the price of cotton. Would a bale of cotton sell for more or less than last year? The price of cotton changed every year, and during cotton-picking season the price changed every day. Papa wondered why he even bothered daydreaming about the price of cotton anyway. He knew full well that the owner of the cotton gin was going to pay colored folks just what he wanted to pay them for their cotton. The market rate for cotton was only there for the white folks, not the colored folks.

When Papa got to town he slowly pulled in line behind five or six other wagons. Both colored and white folks were lined up, all waiting to see what a season's hard labor had brought them. The white landowners were there to see how much richer they had become. The colored folks were there to see how much deeper in debt they would be. Would they earn enough money to feed and clothe their families for another winter? Soon it was Papa's turn. After Papa's cotton was weighed, the man at the gin counted out eighty dollars to him. He had earned forty dollars for each bale of cotton. Who can imagine earning only eighty dollars for a year's salary? While it is extremely hard to imagine now, that eighty dollars was a lot of money for Papa and his family; he had never earned so much on one crop before. It was hard for him to contain his excitement. But would eighty dollars be enough?

For a brief moment, Papa felt like a rich man. Papa took the eighty dollars and began making his rounds through town. His feeling of being rich faded quickly. He owed money to practically every merchant in town. He had been buying things on credit all year in hopes of a good productive cotton season. The productive cotton season was over, and now it was time to pay up. Merchants were all too willing to let colored folks have things on credit, especially if they were sharecroppers and hard workers like Papa was. Papa would enter a merchant's place of business and count out the money he owed them. Papa kept very good records and was quite aware of what he owed, but that made no difference. In those days all colored folks were thought to be ignorant whether they were or not, and they were constantly cheated out of the little money that they had. Even though they knew exactly how much they owed the merchants, there was nothing they could do about being cheated by them. If they wanted to stay out of trouble and continue to have a place to trade when they had no money at all, they did nothing. They simply went from merchant to merchant and paid what the merchants claimed they owed.

By the time Papa finished making his rounds to all the white merchants in town, he stopped by the side of the road to count his remaining money. When he checked, he had less than twenty dollars left in his pocket. Twenty dollars wasn't much for a year's work, especially when he had four hungry mouths at home to feed. And Papa's bill paying was not quite over yet. He still had to pay Mr. Grant for the money he had borrowed from him during the year. Even the seeds that had produced the bountiful cotton harvest had not yet been paid for. Papa was dismayed. He thought back on all the hard work that he and his small children had done to raise that remarkable crop of vegetables and cotton. He had raised the largest cotton crop ever, he had less than twenty dollars in his pocket, and he was still paying bills. Soon the hot rays of the sun beaming down on him encouraged him to move on. With a "giddy-up there, mule," he continued his journey home.

On his way he stopped off at Ol' Man Grant's house to settle up with him. When Papa got there, he asked Mr. Grant what his year's debt amounted to. Mr. Grant went inside and quickly returned with a notebook. After figuring for a moment or two, Mr. Grant told Papa that he owed him a total of twenty-six dollars. This was, of course, six dollars more than Papa had left to his name. Papa told Mr. Grant that after making his rounds to the merchants in town, he didn't have quite that much money left. As usual, Mr. Grant took what Papa had and told him not to worry. He told him that he would have a bigger crop next year and they could settle up then.

Papa returned home tired, discouraged, and of course penniless. He couldn't believe it. This year had not been any different from the others at all. They were all the same. He had hoped and prayed so hard that he and his family would get out from under Mr. Grant's debt for at least one year. But it was not to be. All his hopes and prayers had been in vain. Papa and his children had done all they could to earn more money that year. The days and the rows of cotton had been so long. Papa and his family had had an outstanding year, but they were still in debt. They had learned a hard lesson that year. They had raised more vegetables and more pigs than they had ever raised before. They had grown more cotton than they had ever grown before. Four bales of cotton were unheard of for a family their size. But four bales were not enough.

Mama's Medicine

We didn't get an opportunity to visit a doctor very often when I was growing up because we had no money for that. We had to be seriously ill to actually see a doctor. The only regular health care we had was from the county nurse who was sent out about every three months to check on poor rural folks like my family. She was a doctor on wheels of sorts, and the only kind of doctor we ever saw. My brothers, sisters, and I hated to see her coming. We couldn't figure out why some white woman could care about the health of poor black folks. I guess she didn't really care at all; she was just doing her job. Even so, we hated to see her coming.

We could smell her coming from a mile away, and when we got wind of her, we would scramble like ants and run for cover. We all despised her, because needles were almost always involved with her visits. Part of her job was to vaccinate us.

When the nurse showed up, we ran. The slower ones, such as me, always got caught first. She would routinely give us an exam of sorts, checking our ears, eyes, and throats, and listening to our hearts before she would stick us with those needles of hers. I really hated those shots; I think we all did. The nurse always left a first aid kit with some basic supplies, such as bandages, alcohol, and iodine, along with a few drug samples. I thought she left these few items to remind us of her visit.

The county nurse was not our only health care provider. Mama was a great doctor; with thirteen children, she had to be. No matter what the ailment was Mama had a remedy or cure that had been passed down for generations. Most of them sounded rather peculiar but they usually worked. For example, Mama's remedy to stop cuts from bleeding was strange. As I recall, she would put a spider web onto the wound. Strange though it may seem, immediately after she applied the spider web, the bleeding would stop.

Mama's cure for the mumps was a smelly one. She would drain the oil from a can of sardines and then would rub the sardine oil on our swollen throats. I am not sure if the fish oil really reduced the swelling or if we just felt better because of Mama's attention. In any case, mumps had its benefit because we got to eat the sardines.

Mama had an excellent remedy for insect bites and stings. She would draw the pain of the sting straight out by applying a poultice of tobacco. Relief could be felt in seconds. The only thing I hated about the tobacco remedy was how Mama got the tobacco. There was always some old person around with a mouthful of chewing tobacco or snuff. And when we got stung they would reach in their mouths, grab a wad from their gums, and slap it on us. I found that distasteful.

Mama's cure for colds was one of our favorites. She always had a jar of moonshine around the house and she would combine some moonshine with lemons or peppermint. Her usual dosage for a cold would be a couple of tablespoons several times a day and a double dose at night. It may not have done much to cure the cold, but we sure slept better.

For backaches, Mama made pills from rosin, which is the sticky sap found oozing from pine trees. She would take the sap, which smelled like turpentine, and form it into pill-like rolls that we'd take by mouth. They really worked to relieve backaches and sore muscles. Most of those old remedies were quite effective. The county nurse, along with Mama's medicine, did wonders for our basic health care. But even they couldn't cure some of our health problems. By the grace of God most of us stayed pretty healthy—with the exception of me. I was haunted with major health problems all through my childhood.

I was born with rickets, a childhood disease caused by a lack of vitamin D in the diet. This condition impairs the body's ability to absorb the calcium needed to produce strong, healthy teeth and bones. In children, as in my case, this can lead to severe deformities in the bones because of their softness; in that case corrective surgery is necessary. This disease is rare in the United States but quite common in underdeveloped countries.

By the time I was born in 1959, there were still a few hundred documented cases in the United States each year. I would often think, "I have twelve sisters and brothers, and all of them are healthy. Why me? Why am I the only one stricken by this devastating disease?"

While my disease was difficult to diagnose, Mama said that she knew all along that something was wrong with me. By the time I was twelve months old, unlike all my sisters and brothers before me, I could not walk and was not even close to it. Money was not available for me to see a specialist, so the only care I had for several years was from the county nurse and an old country doctor's remedies. Eventually, the county nurse put my family in contact with a group called the Crippled Children's Clinic. When I was finally diagnosed, I was already past three years old and just trying to take my first steps. I don't know what was worse for me, the disease or the treatment. As I recall, they were both pretty bad.

The Crippled Children's Clinic was comprised of doctors, specialists, who donated their expertise to poor crippled children, like me, who had no money to pay. A social worker, Sally Smoke, a kind and gentle woman, was assigned to my case. I was afraid of her at first because she was a big lady. She was a middle-aged overweight white woman. However, she was always there to talk me through the things that were going to happen to me and to serve as an intermediary for my family and the clinic doctors. We needed an interpreter because it was difficult to understand the gravity of my situation.

The doctors held a clinic about once every two months at an old abandoned schoolhouse in Andalusia, about forty miles south of Greenville. Mama took me to that clinic every two months. She always found a way to get me there, which was hard to do because we did not always have transportation. Daddy worked out of town a lot and, for the majority of the time, Mama and I were on our own, but thanks to Mama we never missed a clinic date.

Attending that makeshift clinic was a terrible experience. The old school was located on a large hill, off the main road right after you entered the city of Andalusia. There was a large classroom set aside for all the poor families and crippled children to register before seeing a doctor. After registering, I could see at least fifty children in as bad or worse condition than I was all lined up in rows and rows of chairs, waiting to see the two or three doctors who had volunteered their time and expertise. I felt like I was the main attraction at a freak sideshow, which was humiliating. I imagine the other children felt the same. It was a tough experience for a child: the all-day trip, the traveling, the sitting, and the waiting. After hours and hours of waiting, Mama and I would be called back to the examining room, which was actually another classroom. The doctors would examine me and decide what experiment they would try on me next.

I can recall the years and years of pain and suffering. I would not wish my childhood pain on anyone. I am a firm believer, however, that we can endure what we have to endure. Therefore, I did what I had to do. Mama used to say that the Lord never puts more on us than we can handle; however, I often thought that I had reached my limits.

The first type of experimental treatment tried was calcium therapy. The experts of the day felt that massive infusions of calcium would cure my deficiency and put me back on the road to good health. They were wrong. The calcium did nothing to harden my soft bones. I can remember being given large quart bottles of pure liquid calcium that tasted horrible and would burn my throat as it went down. The smell of it alone would make me sick to my stomach. Smell or not, I had to drink it because I was told it would make me better. It was so potent that it would harden in the bottle before I could consume it all. I often wondered what it was doing to my insides if it was becoming as hard as a rock just sitting in the bottle. I was forced to drink about a quart of that stuff each week. Even though the calcium therapy failed miserably, I took it for more than a year before the doctors finally realized that it was not doing anything to help my disease.

The next treatment they tried on me was even more horrible than the calcium. After one fateful visit to the clinic, I was fitted for braces. Because my body was not absorbing vitamin D, my teeth and bones were soft. The bones in my legs were so soft that they would bend under the weight of my small body. Because of the bending, I was extremely bowlegged. As I aged, I didn't grow up, I grew out. All of my height was absorbed in my bowlegs. So when the calcium didn't harden my bones, the doctors decided to try and straighten the soft bones, but that didn't work either. I wish they had known the braces weren't going to work before they forced me to wear them for so many years.

The braces were extremely painful to wear. They were constructed of a metal frame that had leather straps attached from one end to the other, about every six inches or so. They also had special shoes attached. They were boy's shoes. The braces ran from my feet, all the way up to my hip and were rigid at the knee. While I could walk in them, I couldn't walk very well. The metal construction made them heavy and not being able to bend my knees didn't help much. Each day I would be exhausted from carrying them around all day. Even nighttime did not bring any relief for me because I had to wear them to bed. Once I got into bed and under the covers, I had to stay in the same position, on my back, all night because the braces were so heavy that I could not turn over in bed while wearing them.

Attending school was also difficult. My older brothers and sisters helped me out a lot. One of them would always be around to lend a hand. They would actually carry me on and off the school bus. Since I couldn't bend my knees, I couldn't get on the bus by myself. They also protected me from the taunts and harassment of other children who were cruel to me. I could never have survived without the tender loving care of my older sisters and brothers.

Recess was the worst time for me in school. It was awful to sit and watch the other children run, jump, and play. In fact, it was pure torture for me. I can remember, on several occasions, when I would remove my braces at recess and go outside and play with the other kids in my stocking feet. The joy was always short lived because once Mama found out that I had taken off the braces I would be in deep trouble. Mama spent a lot of time worrying about and caring for me.

Daddy was just the opposite. For the most part, he treated me as if I were not ill at all. He was very disciplined and strict with me, just like he was with the rest of my brothers and sisters. He told Mama that I had to learn to carry my own weight around the house. So, carry my weight I did, plus a few extra pounds with those heavy braces. At the time, I resented Daddy a little for his approach to my illness. Now I realize that his treatment prepared me for the world I now live in. Now, in everything I do, I carry my own weight. Daddy taught me how to do that early on.

Now and again Daddy did something special for me because of my condition, like the time he built a banister so I could get up and down the front steps without assistance. My brothers and sisters helped me navigate all the obstacles that confronted me at school. But around the house it was a different story. They would have helped me at home as they did away from home, except at home I wanted to be able to help myself. I tried much harder to cope at home, away from the pity and judgmental eyes of the teachers and the other children.

Three steps led from our small front porch to the ground. That's not much of a climb for most people; even toddlers can negotiate three steps. But with my braces, which would not allow me to bend my knees, those three steps might just as well have been the Grand Canyon. But only for a while. I soon figured out a way to get down those steps on my on. I would sit on the porch floor and slowly inch my way across the porch and down the steps. I would go feet first, butt second, and hands last. I looked like an inchworm. It took me about thirty minutes to get outside. I would be so exhausted by the time I made it down to the ground that the thrill of going outside would be all but gone. And even though I was able to scoot down the steps on my own, it was a different story trying to get back up them. The truth is I couldn't get back up, at least not on my own.

After Daddy had watched me half-walk and half-crawl and sometimes simply fall down the front steps many times he put a short banister on the front of the house just for me. Boy oh boy was I happy when that happened. No more sore bottom, no more splinters in my hands from those rough wooden steps. I quickly learned that if I hung on to the banister just right, I could maneuver myself down the steps in an almost upright position like normal people do. This was a dramatic improvement. Don't get me wrong. The banister did not make getting down the stairs easy; it only made it possible. I would hold on to the banister and lean backward as far as I could. Then I would slowly slide my unbending knee forward and down the first step. Gravity would propel my second leg forward, fast. As I moved my hands slowly along the banister, I was able to slowly lower my second leg onto the step below. The only thing I had to worry about was hanging onto the banister. Letting go was a sure way to fall headfirst onto the ground.

After I got really good at going down the steps, I managed to find a way to go back up, all by myself. Independence is a wonderful thing, wonderful indeed. At the age of ten I was finally able to do what most toddlers can do at two. But I didn't worry about the late blooming, nope not at all. Thanks to Daddy and my banister I was just as proud as any two-year-old who had learned to go up and down the stairs. It felt great being able to go in and out of the house without asking for help.

When you can't do things for yourself, something as simple as getting in and out of the house, up and down the steps can mean a lot. That banister was only a few scraps of lumber and a couple of well-placed nails, and I doubt that anyone else in the family ever gave it a second thought either after it was built. I thought about that banister a lot. It gave me freedom and independence for a time. And it demonstrated my daddy's compassion, something not often seen.

After a number of painful years, the braces were judged to be as miserable a failure as the calcium treatment had been. Neither treatment worked, but the braces had been particularly difficult for me. They had been painful and demoralizing. I did get one benefit from wearing the braces. I had the opportunity to spend endless hours on my schoolwork. I couldn't run, walk, or play, but I could read, and I learned to do an awful lot of that. While I didn't particularly enjoy reading, it helped me pass the long lonely days sitting alone in a corner. Reading eventually became a welcome companion.

The only thing remaining that the doctors had not tried was surgery. Mama was not eager to consider surgery because the success rate was less than 50 percent. That is, there was a fifty-fifty chance that I would end up in a wheelchair for the rest of my life. Mama did not like those odds. The surgery was indeed radical for the time. The plan was to saw both of my leg bones in half, remove several sections of bone from my hips, and graft those sections of bone that were removed from my hips into my leg bones. Then my leg bones would be put back together with pins and screws and everyone would pray that they would heal enough for me to walk. Mama hated that plan and so did I. She refused to risk my never walking again on the radical experimental surgery. The doctors had made promises before with the calcium and the braces. They were both miserable failures. The stakes were getting higher.

By the time I was a teenager, having spent my entire life in pain, I was willing to chance the surgery. By that time the odds were a little better, about sixty-forty, that I would be able to walk after the operation. I wanted help for my condition, but I didn't want Mama to blame herself if things went wrong. So I made the decision on my own to have the operation.

Surgery was torturous. I had three separate operations. During the first, my right leg and right hip were broken. Bone grafts from my hip were installed in my leg, along with a number of pins and screws to put me back together. My right leg grew four inches overnight. Of course it didn't actually grow. It was longer because a section of my hip bone was added right into the middle section of my upper leg, after my leg had been sawed in half to accommodate the new addition. I spent seventeen agonizing days flat on my back in Mobile General Hospital. Mama never left my side. The preparation for that first operation was grueling. The day before the surgery, I was in the x-ray room all day. They took over one hundred x-rays, from every angle imaginable. On the night before the surgery I prayed all night. I prayed that I had made the right decision. I prayed that I would be able to walk again. I didn't sleep an hour all night because I was so scared. When they came in to get me for surgery early the next morning I was a nervous wreck; they gave me a couple of shots to make me sleepy and calm my nerves.

By the time I was wheeled into the operating room I was barely awake, but I was still aware of what was going on. While they were hooking me up to all sorts of machines and gadgets, and strapping my arms and legs down to the table, I could see another table out of the corner of my right eye. It was covered with a green surgical cloth. The nurse removed the cloth to reveal a collection of tools: saws, hammers, screws, and drills, just like in a regular tool kit. The sight scared me so badly that I fainted. When I woke up, my first operation was over. There are no words to describe how bad the pain was.

After the surgery, my left leg was fitted with a built-up shoe because my right leg was so much longer. The pain of recuperation was unimaginable. I spent six months on crutches and wore a protective brace on my leg for nine months. Miraculously, after a year, I could walk. I could walk on my own and my right leg was straight. The horrifying thing was that I had to have the same procedure done on my left leg and hip unless I wanted to walk around with one straight leg and one bowleg, not to mention one leg four inches shorter than the other. I had no choice. I had made a decision and I had to stick to it. I had to move forward with the next operation.

The second surgery was just as painful as the first. And the recuperation time was another full year. But after two years, I could walk, and I had straight legs, which seemed like a miracle. After a couple more years passed, I thought that I was healed. While I still had severe pain every day, at least I looked better. But I was in for another surprise. The doctors told me that some of the pins and screws in my thighs had to be removed. "Oh no!" I thought. "Not again." I didn't think I could live through another operation. But again, I had no choice. I don't know if I would have agreed to the surgery in the first place if I had known that I would have to endure three separate operations. This time, they operated on both legs at the same time. I remember asking God what I had done to deserve such pain and torture. I don't remember getting an answer. I had to use crutches for another two months. I still have some hardware in my body, enough in fact to set off the metal detectors at the airport. Maybe it could have been worse, but I don't see how.

My days of surgery are not yet over. I have been told that I must have knee replacement surgery on both knees. I have also been told that knee replacements only last for about twenty years and I am too young to have it done now. No matter, I am not looking forward to it anyway. I have never had a day in my life that was pain free. I know now that I never will. I have learned to live with the pain.

When I think about my childhood rickets, I no longer ask "Why me?" Why not me? The fact that I can walk at all is a testament to my perseverance. And I still have much to be thankful for. I am thankful for Miz Smoke, for all the teams of doctors who volunteered their time, and to the faceless strangers who donated the many thousands of dollars needed to pay for my treatment. But most of all I am thankful for Mama's medicine and that she never left my side.

II
The Work

The Pecan Orchard

My entire family worked from season to season in the agricultural fields and orchards where I grew up. With each change in season came a change in where we worked and what we did in the field. Wintertime meant picking pecans in the pecan orchards around the county. I thought this type of field work was best mainly because it provided a break from work in the broiling hot midsummer sun. I also liked pecan-picking time because it occurred around Christmas. With thirteen children in one family, just buying enough food was a struggle. During the summer months all the money we earned was contributed to the family fund to provide food, shelter, clothing, and the bare necessities. And in Mama's house, there was always a savings fund, "for a rainy day," she would say. As far as I was concerned, every day was a rainy day. All the money had to go toward the good of the family. Even so, we were often allowed to keep some of the few dollars we had earned to have a special Christmas.

I remember one particular trip to the pecan orchard as vividly as if it were yesterday. I had been going to the orchard for as long as I could remember, but this was my first outing as an actual picker, a picker on the same level as my parents and my older sisters and brothers. During my other trips to the orchards I was too young to work; so I would just sit quietly and coldly on a quilt in the sunniest corner of the orchard; occasionally my mother or one of my siblings would check on me. Yes indeed. This trip was different. This time I would earn my own money.

I was awakened early that morning by the soothing sound of wood crackling and popping in the stove. I poked my head out from under the covers to see if anyone else was awake yet. Immediately the cold air hit me in the face. The roaring flame in the wood-burning stove did not put a dent in the cold morning air. I could see my breath freezing in front of my face. In the middle of last summer I had wished for winter; right now that felt like a rather silly wish.

I could hear a racket in the kitchen and smell the faint aroma of pork. It was still dark outside, but Mama was already up making breakfast. Pork was a typical part of the winter morning breakfasts. It had not been long since hog-killing time, and pork would be a staple on the menu until well after the first of the year. I never got tired of eating pork. We usually ran out of pork, and meat in general, before I got tired of eating it.

By now my sisters and brothers had begun to stir. One by one they were slowly getting out of bed and getting dressed. I was excited about going to the orchard today and I didn't want to be the last one out of bed. Until today I had been too small and too young to pick up pecans. I didn't want to spoil my first real job by being late. I jumped out of bed onto the freezing cold floor. The cold went right through my bare feet and I felt as if they had frozen to the floor. I leaped twice and was in front of the stove, jockeying for position with my sisters and brothers for the warmest spot. In a couple of minutes the backs of my legs, indeed my entire backside, were very hot—so hot, I thought I was being cooked like the pork that I could smell frying in the kitchen. At the same time that my backside was burning up, my front was still frozen. I turned around to warm my front and give my backside some relief from the scorching heat. This turning ritual continued every two or three minutes until I was toasty warm all over.

Only then did I begin to get dressed. Mama yelled from the kitchen, "Better put on another layer of clothes, Peggy, it's going to be cold out there today." It was hard for me to imagine how it could be colder outside than it was in the house. The nights were so cold in that old house that spilled water would freeze on the floor before morning. Nevertheless, I heeded Mama's warning and put on more layers of clothing. I had on so many clothes that it was difficult to bend over, and bending is essential for picking up pecans.

Daddy was noticeably absent from the pecan orchard ritual because at this time of year he was up North, where black men could find regular work in the factories. They did a lot of piecework so the white men could be home with their families at Christmas and such. Daddy had some distant relatives in Indiana and he stayed with them while he worked part-time in the factories. The work never lasted more than a couple of months. During that time he would send a few dollars home. His few dollars never seemed to amount to much more than the family was making in the orchards. Each time Daddy returned from one of his trips up North, he would keep at Mama until spring about moving the family up there. Mama always won this argument. She would convince him that poor black folks in the South fared better than poor black folks in the North. As far as I was concerned, poor black folks everywhere were just poor black folks. In any case, because Daddy was away, most of the orchard work was left to Mama and the children.

Breakfast was ready by the time I finished getting dressed. It consisted of fatback, syrup, and hot biscuits. Hot biscuits and syrup have always been a favorite of mine, and the fatback, well, it was pork season. I had no sooner taken my first bite of food when I could hear the sound of a vehicle in the distance. "The truck is coming, the truck is coming," yelled my sister. Everything started happening so fast. It seemed as if only minutes had passed since I had first peeped out from under the covers and already it was time to leave for the orchard. We finished breakfast, grabbed our coats and hats, and ran outside. I could see this old, dirty beige truck slowly approaching the house. There were homemade wooden rails attached to each side of the truck reaching high above the cab. I guessed those rails were for hauling cargo that could be piled much higher than the truck was originally built for. The cargo this morning was colored folks headed to the orchards.

The truck was being driven by an old bearded white man, Willie Zed Gafford. He and his wife, Miz Emma Lee, were typical wealthy white folks. They seemed to me to own all the land in the world. They certainly owned acres and acres of pecan orchards along Highway 31, the major road in Greenville. The highway ran north and south from Mobile to Birmingham. In Greenville, directions were given in relation to the main road: north, south, east, or west of Highway 31. The Gaffords, for example, one of several white land-owning families in the area, had fields and orchards east and west of 31. The Standoffs, for whom my family sharecropped, owned land east of 31.

The truck had arrived and my entire family piled into the back, which was already half filled with black folks from down the road. I recognized one of the older black women as Miz Evie Akins, a friend of Mama's from Bolling, which was a community a couple of miles south of where we lived. It was common for the Gaffords to have two or more families working in an orchard at one time.

Miz Evie, I remembered, had been on some but not all of our other trips to the orchard. Her family was just as poor as mine. Mama, Miz Evie, and five or six other older black women got together after church on Sundays, as well as during the week in the orchards and fields. They were all members of the Eastern Star, a religious group that was just for women. They liked the group a lot. The organization had lots of secrets, because the women never talked about what they did in the Eastern Star if any of us children were around. But that was no matter to me; I had more important things on my mind anyway.

The truck was full now and we were on our way. The sun was beginning to peek out just above the horizon. The wind was blowing fiercely and we clung to each other in the back of the truck in an effort to keep warm. The cold air burned my throat and lungs. My nose was beginning to run. I couldn't remember ever being this cold before. The thought of staying outside in the cold air all day was wearing away at the enthusiasm I had felt going off to my first day of work in the orchards. I wasn't sure I could make it. I hadn't picked up one pecan yet and I was already thinking of getting home at the end of the day.

After a couple of miles, the truck pulled into the country store owned by Mary and R. B. Pope. Like other prominent white families in the area, the Popes owned property, but the store was their real moneymaker. Everyone shopped there because it was the only store for miles around. Since most black folks had no transportation other than shank's mare, a store within walking distance was a blessing. For folks who couldn't get to the Popes' store, Mr. Densey, R. B. Pope's cousin, owned what we called a rolling store. Actually it was a large panel truck packed with every kind of merchandise: shoes, clothes, food, cloth, stamps, and so on. Almost anything you needed was available from Mr. Densey. From country house to country house he traveled, selling as he went. Of course, if you could catch a ride to town, you could purchase any of the items sold at the Popes' store or on the rolling store for about half as much. But catching a ride to town was hard to do. That's why Mr. Densey's rolling store was so profitable. The Popes' store was to be our only stop before reaching the orchard. The Gaffords stopped by the store so their help could pick up supplies before beginning the day's work.

The store was a large, white, one-room wood frame building with a gas pump at the front door. On the left side of the door was an old run-down shed that looked like it had once been used for repairing cars. Now it housed a lot of old tires and wooden soda bottle crates. My folks, like most black folks in the area, had a credit account at the Pope's store. It seemed as if no one ever had cash to buy anything with. Mama also cooked Sunday dinners and washed clothes for Mary Pope and her family. Any supplies needed for the day could be bought on credit. All of us knew that we would stop back by the store at the end of the day after we had been paid for our work. Some of the hands were now buying food for lunch on credit. I wanted to be all grown up, and it seemed to me that buying food on credit would just about get me there. As usual Mama had packed a lunch for the entire family. A store-bought lunch sounded a lot more appetizing to me than a cold fatback biscuit. I recall Mama suggesting that I eat the packed lunch and save all of my earnings so that I would have more money left at the end of the day. I insisted on setting up an account and she let me do so. Although she knew she was right and that I would almost certainly be sorry later, she never wanted to raise a fuss in front of white folks.

The store was filled with goodies. There was one counter in the middle of the store that made a complete square. The wall at the back was stocked with an array of canned meats, fruits, and vegetables. The wall on the right had bags and bags of flour, cornmeal, and sugar. Next to the sugar were countless bottles of soda pop. There was a table on the left side of the store with a large wooden hoop. Under that hoop was a huge round of cheese; that cheese was the first thing you smelled upon entering the store. All the breads and cakes and other sweet treats were near the door on the left. I went all out. I bought a honey bun, a can of sardines, and a slice of cheese, all on credit. On the counter was a large homemade wooden tray filled with little tablets, each with a different last name inscribed on it. Miz Pope pulled out a tablet that had Allen written on it, made an entry, and put the tablet back into the wooden box. Then she handed me a small brown bag that contained the goodies I had bought for the day. As I left the store I remember feeling the warmth emanating from the potbellied stove near the door. The stove was surrounded by empty rocking chairs that seemed to call out for someone to sit a spell. But they were surely not calling for Negro bottoms to sit in them. I could never recall seeing a black person sitting in any of those chairs, only white folks.

After we were back in the truck, we rode for another mile or so before we arrived at the orchards. Row upon row of trees towered above us. Standing among the trees made me feel so small. They stood elegantly, silently, like soldiers standing at attention. Most of their leaves had fallen; the few remaining ones swayed gently in the winter breeze. Mr. Gafford jumped from the cab of the truck and dumped a double armload of burlap sacks in the middle of the orchard; then in a flash he was gone. We were on our own. We started at the north end of the orchard and worked our way south, each person picking from his or her own tree. We had all day to pick up as many pecans as possible. The going rate for pecans was three cents a pound. Of course, the white folks were getting sixty cents a pound in town. I got my burlap bag and went to work. I worked very hard, picking up pecans one by one. The ground was littered with leaves almost the same color as the pecans. You had to search for the nuts between the fallen leaves—and the cow manure. Willie Zed Gafford had allowed his cows to graze in the orchard and cow manure was everywhere. This was back-breaking work. Time passed slowly. In the cold damp air my nose ran constantly. By ten o'clock, when the winter sun began to beam down on me, I realized I was overdressed. I took off one layer of clothes, which cooled me off and made moving around a bit easier. After a few hours I decided that a little cow manure never hurt anyone, and at three cents a pound the heavier the burlap sack the better, even if part of the weight was from cow manure. Dragging a heavy sack through the orchard was difficult, so I changed sacks each time I had collected a few pounds.

Finally after what seemed an eternity, it was time for lunch. The sardines, honey bun, and cheese were a delicacy, and the scene was so tranquil that I momentarily forgot I was in the middle of a pecan orchard, surrounded by trees, leaves, and hundreds of mounds of cow manure. I was exhausted, and the brief rest to eat was a gift from heaven. But I had forgotten that it was still cold outside. Work generates heat, and after sitting still for a while to eat I was reminded of that reality. By the time I had put back on my discarded clothing and was warm again, lunch was over. It was time to go back to work.

I kept a close eye on my sisters and brothers as we worked our way through the orchard. I kept a particular watchful eye on my sister Ediffie. I had heard the many stories of her being able to pick more cotton, more peas, more beans, and yes, more pecans than anyone else in the family. I had heard that she could pick more than all my brothers. I didn't believe this, so I watched her closely. Ediffie worked quickly. Her hands moved so fast it was hard to keep track of them. She never seemed to stand still. Bend and pick, bend and pick. One sack became two, and two became three, and so on. I began to believe that the things they said about her were true. She was fast and she was going to make a lot of money today.

The second half of the day was slower and harder than the first. My back and knees ached, and picking up each pecan was torture. My hands were so small that I could only pick up two pecans before having to put them in the sack. If I tried to pick up more than two, I would drop them and have to start all over again. An almost-empty sack was too heavy to carry. I was dead tired and physically and mentally battered. All I wanted was to go home. Even cow manure under my fingernails didn't bother me anymore. The sound of that old truck returning to the orchard was magical. As the truck grew near everyone began gathering their sacks of pecans, their work for the day. Mr. Gafford parked the truck in the middle of the orchard. He reached inside and grabbed a large scale with a big hook on the end. "Time to weigh up," he yelled. The scale had a big white face with black numbers, like a big clock. It was common knowledge that the scale was rigged. In Mr. Gafford's favor of course. At home Mama complained bitterly that the scale was off, but no one would dare complain about it in front of the white folks. My sister Ediffie told me that we got our own justice to a certain extent because the sacks also contained bits and pieces of twigs and branches and leaves. And in my case, cow manure.

Everyone moved slowly toward the truck with their sacks in tow. Mr. Gafford reached in his shirt pocket and pulled out a pencil and a tablet of paper. As he hung a sack over the hook to be weighed he wrote in his tablet. Name, pounds, name, pounds, and so on. As the sacks were being weighed, I could hear my sisters and brothers bragging about the hundreds of pounds of pecans they had picked up. I wasn't worried. I knew I had not done badly for my first turn as a pecan picker. But my biggest accomplishment was simply surviving the day. And then it was my turn. Name, Peggy, pounds . . . thirty-five. Wow! I had actually picked up thirty-five pounds of pecans. I was proud of myself. And I know that my sisters and brothers were proud of me also. My name was finally written in the book. Soon we were all done; everyone had had the precious cargo weighed. We all got in the back of the truck for the trip home, home by the way of the Popes' country store to settle our accounts.

Before entering the store we all gathered near the door. Mr. Gafford was standing again with his tablet and pencil. This time also with a fist full of what I thought was an awful lot of money. He was calculating the day's earnings. A line formed in front of him and one by one he paid the hands for the day's work. Soon my turn came. After writing for a few seconds on his table, he placed a dollar bill and one shiny new nickel in my palm. This was my first payday and I had earned over a dollar. I was thrilled.

I went into the store and got in line. This line was to settle up for the lunch I had bought on credit earlier that day. A fire was still burning in the old potbellied stove near the door. The rocking chairs that were empty this morning were now filled with old white men wearing dirty overalls, rocking and chewing tobacco. They were filled with the same kind of men I always remembered seeing in them. And just as I had suspected this morning, there was not one Negro bottom among them. I walked slowly toward the counter, and as I reached it, I saw Miz Mary standing behind it. She may once have been tall, but now the large hump on her back tilted her forward and made her look short. She was old and palsied but her right hand was steady enough to hold a sharp pencil tightly. When it came to money, white folks always had a sharp pencil and a steady hand. "Okay," Peggy she said. "That will be thirty-five cents for the sardines, twenty-five cents for the honey bun, and ah yes, fifteen cents for the cheese. That's a total of seventy-five cents." I opened my hand to reveal the dollar bill and the nickel. I was not sure how much money I would be left with after paying my bill. She removed the dollar from my hand and replaced it with a quarter. I had a whopping thirty cents left. I slowly backed away from the counter in disbelief. I could not believe my eyes. I had worked from dawn till dusk and what did I have to show for it but a runny nose, thirty cents, and cow manure under my fingernails.

No one ever said a word to me about spending my money before I had earned it. Even Mama, whom I expected to at least say " I told you so," held her tongue. I guess everyone figured that I had learned a lesson on my own. Indeed I had.

The trip home was short. By the time we arrived, the sun had started to set. The fire in the stove had long since gone out and the house was cold once again. It only took a few minutes for my brother Floyd to get a fire started. Without sitting down for even a minute, Mama went straight to the kitchen to get supper started. I know she had to be tired. But she uttered not a single complaint. In no time the smell of pork was wafting through the house again. Before supper was ready and before the house could be warmed by the newly made fire, Mama called us all into the kitchen. On the table was an apron, outspread in the center. Without a question we placed the day's earnings in the apron. Mama counted the money and tied most of it up in a handkerchief, which was placed under her mattress for safekeeping. The remaining money was divided among us, each child getting to keep a little for the day's work. We all had Christmas dreams. But the larger dream was that one day we would buy our own land and have our own house. The total earnings for the family that day was less than twenty-five dollars, and "one day" seemed a long way off. That dream was, indeed, a long time in coming. But eventually it did come true. After many years we bought our own land and built a house on it. My day in the orchard was my first contribution to

The Allen family home once stood in the middle of this pecan orchard. The old wood frame house, now long gone, was located to the left of the photograph. The property was owned by a white man named John Standoff. Because we were share-croppers and lived on this land, we were not paid for picking the pecans in the orchard. Why? Because Mr. Standoff said so.

the family dream. I had become a part of the Allen team. When we finally bought our land, Mama planted two pecan trees on the new property, maybe as a reminder of how we got there: a reminder of that old cold house in the middle of a pecan orchard where the Allen family dream finally came true.

My Hoe

Daddy was really tough on us kids as we were growing up. Sometimes he was difficult for no apparent reason, at least none that we could see. Mama always said it was because he had had such a rough childhood. To us he was just mean. Sometimes it seemed as if he enjoyed it. None of us escaped his wrath, not even me. Why should I be any different from any one else? Just because I was the sickly one didn't seem to matter much to him at all. He was as hard, or in some cases harder, on me than on the rest of my sisters and brothers.

In addition to working in the fields of all the white folks in the area, we also had a field of our own to work each year. We raised peas, beans, watermelons, cucumbers, tomatoes, corn, sugarcane, okra, sweet pepper, hot pepper, strawberries, and more. If it grew out of the earth, we raised it. I often thought that the only reason we kids were born in the first place was to tend the fields. But having so many kids was also a liability. Sure, there were many more hands available to help out in the fields but at the end of the day there were many more mouths to feed. Whether a baker's dozen of children was a blessing or a curse, it was a reality in my family.

I remember one summer when Daddy was on a particularly savage rampage. He could not stand to see any of us idle for even one minute. He had heard that an idle mind was the devil's workshop, so we always had to be doing something. If we did not have any work, he would find something for us to do. Our fields and gardens were the cleanest in the area. Not a sprig of grass was allowed in the fields, nor a weed in the garden.

We hoed everything. Old black folks in the neighborhood used to scoff at Daddy for hoeing corn because that was unheard of. Nobody hoed corn except Charlie Allen; he hoed everything. In the summers when all our other work was done, Daddy had us go outside and hoe corn just to keep us busy. Everybody knew that was crazy because no benefit could ever come from hoeing corn. Corn was a hardy plant and it would grow just fine with or without grass around it.

I had to hoe with everyone else. Being small, weak, and sickly was no excuse for missing work. Every hoe we had was big and heavy. I was only about three and a half feet tall; the handle of the hoe I was using was at least five feet long. It felt as if the hoe weighed as much as I did. I did try to hoe with it, but it was too heavy, too long, too awkward. The blade of the hoe was made of a heavy metal; I suppose it was iron. It was rectangular in shape and even without the large wooden handle it would have been quite heavy. The handle was a long wooden pole. Many hands before mine had worn the once-rough pole to a smooth, almost slick, finish. The pole was thick, too large for me to get a hand around it. Even using both hands I could barely get enough of a grip to pick the hoe up. Because I was short, my grip on the hoe was little more than two feet off the ground. Just lifting the heavy tool was a chore, let alone trying to hoe with it. It was a pendulum and I was the fulcrum trapped in the middle. Each time I picked up the hoe it would be either top-heavy or bottom-heavy; one end or the other would hit the ground without any guidance from me, swinging my small body along with the dominant end.

My older sisters and brothers tried to help me with my row of corn but I quickly fell behind. I couldn't keep up and I refused to quit. I didn't want to go back to the house and admit that I couldn't pull my own weight. And I didn't know what Daddy would do or say. Maybe he would let me quit but again, maybe not. So I hung in there. I gave it all I had, which wasn't very much. The work was hard for everyone, for me it was brutal. The sun was hot and there was never any shade in the fields. I took a number of breaks, that is if carrying water for everyone else to drink can be considered as taking a break.

The end of the day couldn't come soon enough for me. Hoeing was long, hot, back-breaking work, but that was a typical day for us. I went to bed that night tired and sore all over. My tiny hands were swollen and covered with blisters from gripping the handle of the hoe. Since no one else complained about blisters, I didn't either. That night, I over-heard Mama telling Daddy he shouldn't make me hoe in the fields any-more: The work was too hard, the hoe was too large, and I was too sickly. "Everybody has to pull their own weight," Daddy replied, "everybody, even Peggy."

I knew then that Mama had lost the argument and tomorrow would be just like today had been. I would have to work in the fields hoeing with my sisters and brothers. Mama had tried to help me but as always when Daddy got something in his mind that was it. He reminded Mama that he didn't get a break when he was growing up just because he was small. I decided the best thing I could do was go to sleep. I had to look forward to another long, hot day of dragging that heavy hoe around. I had best get some rest.

I was up the next morning, before the sun. We all were. I could hear the rooster crowing in the distance. I could also hear the familiar sound of a file being dragged across the blade of a hoe or some other farming tool to sharpen it. Daddy always sharpened the tools early in the morning. This was a signal to us kids that we would be working in the fields. That piercing sound of metal against metal was more than a signal to wake up. It was a brutal reminder that today would be like yesterday, and that last night's dreams of a reprieve from hoeing, were just that, dreams.

As usual, Daddy had all the tools sharpened and ready for us to use before we were ready for work. By the time we ate a quick breakfast and headed outside, the newly sharpened hoes were lined up in a row leaning against the workbench where Daddy had sharpened them. One by one my brothers and sisters took one of the hoes and headed toward the fields. I steeled myself for another long day of torture, dragging that heavy hoe around the fields and hauling water all day.

When I reached for my hoe I was shocked. The large heavy tool I had struggled with the day before was gone. It had been replaced with a hoe half its size. The handle was only about three feet long and about as big around as the neck of a soda bottle. So small in fact I could hold it firmly with just one hand. I could tell that the handle was not a store-bought one. I could still see the knotholes along the shaft. It had been made from part of an oak branch and trimmed down to fit the head of the little hoe. All the bark had been carefully removed from the handle, exposing the fresh green wood underneath. I could smell the freshness of the wood, as if it had been cut only moments earlier. The metal part of the hoe was much smaller and lighter than the one I had used the day before. Where had it come from? I didn't know quite what to think. After hearing Daddy tell Mama that everyone had to pull their own weight, I never thought he would try to make it a little easier for me to do so. He was hard on everybody, especially his own family. I don't know why he made the little hoe for me. He never said a word about it and neither did I. I don't know why he did it but I do know it made my work a lot easier. I was grateful, even though I never said so. Field work is never easy but having a hoe that I could actually pick up was a help. Maybe Mama's plea the night before had made an impression on Daddy. I'll never know for sure. I wanted to thank Daddy for that hoe, but I was afraid. To be on the safe side, however, I did thank God.

Crowder Peas

As a child, I had experiences with many different types of vegetables. Vegetables were just a part of everyday life. There were some vegetables, however, that I liked more than others. And there were some that I downright hated. Not because I didn't like the taste, it went deeper than that. Eating vegetables was something that I had to do. Our family had a lot of meals where there was nothing but vegetables on the table.

The crowder pea was one vegetable that I hated. Crowder peas were easy to grow; all you had to do was stick a seed in the ground and it would grow. Crowder peas flourished in the Alabama heat. With the family's help, Daddy raised rows and rows of crowder peas. Planting them wasn't too bad. They were planted in early spring when the weather was still cool. But by the time the little pea plants were about six inches tall, the weather had changed from cool to hot. And by the time the grass had to be hoed from around the tender young plants, it was extremely hot. At a very early age, I learned to distinguish a crowder pea plant from the numerous varieties of southern grasses growing in the garden. We all learned that lesson early. We knew there would be hell to pay if Daddy caught us hoeing down pea plants instead of grass, although we were often tempted to do just that.

By the time the pea plants were fully matured and began to have blooms, we would have hoed the grass from around them at least three times, and each time the sun was hotter as summertime crept nearer. I remember praying that the blooms would just dry up and fall off the plants. I prayed for this to happen year after year, but it never did. By mid-summer, that is to say, pea-picking time, we had a bountiful harvest of crowder peas. After providing TLC to the plants for several months, we now had to pick the peas.

Pea-picking days usually started early in the morning. Everybody in the house had to pick peas, and there were always more than enough peas to go around. Like picking most vegetables, everyone had their own row to start from. We had to be careful to pick them just right. They had to be full of mature peas, so we could not pick them too early. Peas that were already dry had to be removed from the plant as well, all under Daddy's watchful eyes. Daddy planted rows of peas that were so long you could not see from one end of the row to the other. The sun was always overhead before we had completed even half of one of those rows.

I was young and weak and could not last very long picking peas in the field. But that did not excuse me from going to work. There was a large oak tree in front of the house large enough to cast a shadow for thirty or forty feet. On pea-picking day, Daddy would place two large quilts on the ground in the shade under that big oak tree. Those quilts were the dumping ground for the peas after they were picked. It was also the dumping ground for me after I was worn out.

My brothers and sisters continued to pick peas. As they accumulated a bushel basket full, one of them would make the trip from the field to the quilts. They would dump the bushel of peas onto an ever-growing pile and return to the field to pick more. Once I had left the field my job was to separate the peas. I had to separate the green tender vegetables from the ones that had dried on the vine. The dry peas were placed in a pile all to themselves to be used in the spring as seed for the next year's crowder pea crop. Since I was the only one on the quilt, while eight or nine of my brothers and sisters picked in the fields, I was overwhelmed in no time. That pile of peas on the quilt grew by leaps and bounds. The pile was quickly taller than I was.

Separating the peas was not my only job; I also had to shell peas. When I think back on it I probably would have had an easier time if I had stayed in the fields and picked peas with my sisters and brothers. They couldn't possibly be as tired as I was. I didn't shell peas just for our family. I also shelled them for Daddy to take to the market. While most people bought the peas still in the hull, there was also a market for peas that were already shelled. I wondered about those lazy white people who didn't shell their own peas. I knew they had to be white folks because black folks did not have money to spend on such a thing.

Around eleven or so in the morning, Mama would come out to the quilt to see how I was doing. She would usually take all the peas that I had shelled into the house and wash them before putting them on the stove to cook for dinner. The large mound of peas would grow sometimes to the size of a small car, which is no exaggeration. The mound was so high that it could be seen from the highway. That was the only good thing about such a large pile of peas. Occasionally white folks would see the big mound of peas while they were just driving by and stop to see if they could buy some, which made me happy because I wouldn't have to separate or shell those that they bought.

After shelling peas for a few hours, my hands began to ache. I hurt from the tips of my fingers all the way to my shoulders. The green and purple hull of the peas had dyed my hands, which would take days to wear off. My thumbs were swollen to twice their normal size. Crowder peas are not the easiest peas to shell. The hull is thick and tough. With your thumbs you snap the hull at one end, being careful not to tear the snapped end off the hull as you would normally do with green beans or snap beans. Once snapped at one end, you find the stringy vein running the entire length of the hull. You pull that vein from one end of the hull to the next, which makes it easier to open the pea. Starting at one end, you pry the pea open, alternating one thumb and then the other. Then using your thumb, you drag all the peas from the hull. This is easy for the first fifty to a hundred peas. But after shelling a bushel or so, your hands swell like you've been boxing without gloves, and they feel like it too.

By early afternoon, when the sun was at its hottest, all the rows of peas had been picked. One by one my brothers and sisters slowly returned from the field, bringing with them their last bushel baskets of peas. And one by one they added their final bushels to the pile of peas. They had spent the entire day in the blazing sun, bending and stooping, while I sat in the shade. How could I have ever thought my job was harder than theirs?

The day's work wasn't done just yet. Those peas still had to be taken to market. Floyd and Sonny helped Daddy pile most of the peas in the back of Daddy's old truck for the trip to town. Daddy soon left for the market to sell the day's goods. All that was left behind was a couple of bushels of peas for the family.

That night for dinner we had crowder peas and cornbread, not much of a dinner after such a hard day's work. I hated eating those peas that we had labored over for so many hours. The meal that had taken all day to acquire was gone in minutes. But we were all tired and hungry and it was peas or nothing. So we ate the peas. The next morning came too soon, as mornings always did. Crowder peas took a little time to mature, so we didn't have to pick them every day. That did not mean we did not work in the fields every day. We did. There was always something to be done; if we weren't hoeing, we were harvesting. If the peas weren't ready, we picked some other vegetable. The peas were ready to pick about every three days. Then we would go through that whole painful ritual again. It took at least that long for my swollen thumbs to heal.

Today, when I see fresh crowder peas in the supermarket, I avoid them. I can buy the frozen ones with no hesitation. But when I get too close to fresh, green crowder peas, my thumbs start to ache. I am not sure if it is actually my thumbs that ache or if it is just the painful memory.

Hog-Killing Day

One of the more memorable experiences from my childhood occurred during the fall. The blistering hot summer days were gone; the cold days of winter were not yet upon us. If the summer had been good to us with vegetables, then there would have been enough food to raise a hog or two. When we did not have enough corn to share with the hogs, we would feed them the husks. They preferred the actual corn, but they were not picky eaters. The number of hogs we had as we headed into the winter months was directly proportional to the abundance of our summer crops. When food for the family was scarce, the hogs suffered as well. It was hard enough to feed the family through the winter; trying to keep the hogs well fed would have been downright ridiculous. But we needed the pork during the colder months in order to survive. Pork was usually the only meat we got besides a chicken or two. We went to the meadows and grassy areas of the fields to pull peanut grasses and clovers to supplement the hogs' diet.

Slopping the hogs was a dirty chore, and it was hard work carrying food and water for such a long distance from the house. In the winter I had to remind myself that come June I would be glad the hogs were so far away from the house. The stench of a pigpen is almost overpowering during an Alabama summer.

Nothing about hog-killing day was haphazard. Every minute was carefully planned. Every task had someone assigned to it; every person had a chore. My daddy was meticulous in everything he did, and he had hog-killing day down to an art. He ordered us around more like hired hands than family but that was just his way. Of course not even Daddy was as proficient at hog killing as my great-grandma Moa. She was the real expert; Daddy just thought he was.

I remember being awakened early in the morning while it was still dark outside. It was early fall and although the morning air was not cold there was a slight chill in the air. While I was getting dressed, I could see that Mama, Daddy, and all of my sisters and brothers were already up and busy. Several neighbors were also stirring about outside. A quick trip to the kitchen revealed an assortment of knives, and pots and pans of all sizes. But no breakfast. We always had breakfast, except on hog-killing day. Everyone, including Mama, was too busy to bother with cooking. Instead of a pan of fried pork on the stove, there were four large boilers of hot water, no food at all.

One look out the kitchen window and I soon forgot about breakfast. A large fire was burning outside under the big black washpot. I ran outside to investigate. We called it the washpot because Mama used it to heat water for washing the clothes. Sure enough there was water in the washpot. There was also a large mound of firewood near the pot. The mound of wood was much larger than I remembered from the day before. We were going to use a lot of wood today. My brothers must have worked for hours to accumulate such a sizable stack of firewood. Now I knew Mama was not going to wash clothes on hog-killing day, so the water had to be for something else. I would soon find out its purpose.

The sun was beginning to come up now, shedding light on the busy scene unfolding in front of me. I had not noticed that my brothers were missing from the yard until I saw them walking toward the house. Calvin, Sonny, and Floyd were carrying small branches with green needles that they had cut from pine trees. They placed the branches in a pile near the washpot and quickly left for the woods to get more. They repeated this ritual until they had accumulated a large mound of fresh pine branches. The unmistakable smell of turpentine lingered in the cool fall air.

About twenty feet from the washpot was a large barrel. A hole had been dug in the ground and the barrel was placed in the hole at about a forty-five degree angle. After my brothers had made a mound of pine needles near the washpot, they began to place the pine needles into the barrel an armful or two at a time. In the distance, behind the barrel, I could see Daddy and an old black man about twice Daddy's size working near the crib, a barn of sorts with a wooden floor. Many years ago Daddy had built this crib, which he used for numerous purposes, such as storing tools, plows, and farm equipment and storing meat for curing. They had fastened a wooden tackle with a metal hook on each end to one of the corner posts of the crib. A closer look revealed that it was the same tackle that had been attached to the plow and the mule this past summer. The tackle was about a half of a foot over Daddy's head, and he had to stand on tiptoe to reach it. After securing the tackle to the crib, Daddy had dug a hole beneath it. The hole was about twelve inches deep and about the size of a foot tub.

The water in the washpot was beginning to boil. Daddy beckoned to Sonny and Calvin. Without a word being exchanged between them and Daddy, they began filling the barrel with the boiling water. They carried buckets of hot water about twenty feet or so from the washpot to the barrel. As Sonny and Calvin filled the barrel, Daddy told Floyd to go into the house and get the rifle. Soon Floyd returned with a .22 rifle and a handful of shells. The walk to the pigpen seemed long when you were carrying a heavy bucket of food or water to the pigs. This time Daddy was carrying a rifle and a bucket, but the bottom of the bucket was barely covered with shelled corn. I had no idea what that was for. We all followed slowly behind Daddy, my brothers and sisters, Mama, and the neighbor folks who had come to help out. The large man who had been helping Daddy earlier had two burlap sacks thrown over his shoulder.

We were soon at the pigpen. Daddy began hitting the side of the bucket that held the thin layer of shelled corn. The pigs, responding to the noise, crowded around the feeding trough, all four of them vying for position. Now I knew what the corn was for. Banging the side of the feed bucket was the way we always called the hogs in at suppertime. It was a surefire way to get them all to gather up close. The decision of which pig to kill would have been tough for me, but it wasn't for Daddy. He said out loud, as if he could hear my thoughts, "the big one." He poured the handful of corn into the feeding trough and all four pigs went for it at once. Daddy loaded the rifle with a single shell. He placed the barrel of the gun about six inches from the head of the largest hog. Without warning, to me or the pig, he pulled the trigger. The pig fell to the ground. Just like that it was over; the hog was dead. I had thought it would be fun to watch this part of the process but I was wrong. It was no fun at all. I wished I had stayed near the fire. The power of a single gunshot to drop such a large animal was purely amazing. I regretted having seen it. Daddy handed the empty rifle to my brother and jumped into the pen followed by several other men. The large pig was partially lifted, partially dragged out of the pen and placed onto the burlap sacks lying on the ground. Each man grabbed a corner of the sacks and began dragging the lifeless pig toward the waiting washpot and barrel.

The men lifted the pig and slid it into the barrel hind feet first. He was allowed to sit there for only a moment and then he was turned over so that the hot water and pine needles covered his other side. Meanwhile small buckets were being used to dip boiling water from the washpot and pour it over the pig. The remaining mound of pine needles was now placed on the ground, just below the mouth of the barrel. The men then reached into the barrel, grabbed the pig by his front legs, and pulled him out and onto the bed of pine needles. The pig lay on one side, completely surrounded by men with knives. I thought they were going to cut him to pieces right there. Instead, a slit was cut into the hind legs of the pig, somewhere close to the bone near the foot. Then, the men carried the pig to the crib with its waiting tackle. The tackle was lowered to meet the pig and the pig was raised to meet the tackle. The hog's carcass was heavy, and the men struggled with this part of the job. The two metal ends of the tackle were inserted into slits in the pig's hind legs. And then slowly as if they were drawing a bucket of water from a well, the men raised the pig to a height of about six feet. There he was, hanging head down against the crib. I noticed a trickle of blood dripping from the single gunshot wound in its head. The blood was slowly dripping into the hole that Daddy had dug beneath the tackle. Daddy approached the pig with a large knife and once again I thought he was going to cut the pig to pieces. Instead, he turned the blade of the knife parallel to the pig's body and, starting up high, near where the tackle was attached, began to scrape the hair from the hog. Each scrape of the knife revealed clean white skin beneath the hog's dirty red hide. It was hard to believe it was the same animal. It was also hard to believe that the hair was so easy to remove. I guess the hot water and pine needles played a part in that. On the straight, flat parts of the pig, the knife moved smoothly, removing hair all the way. It was not so easy in the folds, bends, and turns of the animal. For those tough spots hot water was drawn from the washpot and poured over the pig. Then the knife was again scraped against those spots. The hot water did the trick. Soon the pig was as clean and white as a sheet, from hind hoof to snout. (As I recall hot water was just as effective in removing feathers from freshly killed chickens.)

I waited anxiously to see what would happen next. Daddy grabbed the same bucket that he had used earlier to put corn in the trough and placed it in the hole under the pig's head. He then stooped down, and holding the pig's head in his left hand and a knife in his right he cut the pig's throat from ear to ear. Immediately, blood poured from the cut into the waiting bucket. I had been waiting to see the pig get cut, but this was not what I had expected. Nor wanted. Daddy had performed this ritual numerous times; it was routine to him. To me however, it was as if I was seeing the pig die all over again. I couldn't help feeling a little sorry for the animal, though I knew that if all the hogs were allowed to live through the winter, my family might not have survived. So it came down to him or us. I realized that, even at a very young age. But I still did not like being so close to what was happening.

Finally, the time had come to cut the hog to pieces. Daddy began by placing a large sharp knife in the hog between his hind legs. He cut the hog right down the middle, from his hind legs, down past his stomach, and then to his neck where his throat had been cut. You could see all of the hog's insides—everything was exposed. I asked Daddy if I could touch some of the pig's innards. I just wanted to know what it felt like. I am not sure what I expected, but the pig was still warm and it gave me the willies.

Daddy quickly removed the bucket, which was partially filled with blood, and replaced it with the large washtub. As he cut the insides of the pig away from the backbone, they slowly dropped into the tub below. Everything fell. Now there was only a shell of a pig hanging on the tackle. The tub, which contained all of the pig's insides, was taken to one of two homemade tables near the crib. The shell of the pig was removed from the tackle and taken to the other table. The men went to work right away on the pig shell. They first cut off both hams, which are some of the best parts of the pig. Then they cut off the shoulders. They proceeded to cut the pig into so many different parts and pieces that he was no longer recognizable as a pig. One thing in particular was notable to me. There is a thick layer of fat that covers the entire pig's body. They cut this layer of fat away from every part of the pig except for the hams, shoulder, and head. They then cut that fat into quarter-size pieces. By the time they were finished, there were about two five-gallon buckets of the fat pieces from just that one hog.

While the pig was being cut into many pieces, some familiar pieces like pork chops and ribs began to emerge. Mama and Daddy were at the other table working with the pig's insides, separating the heart, liver, and finally the intestines. Food was scarce and not one part of the pig would be discarded. We used every part but the squeal. The intestines (called chitterlings or chitlins) seem to stretch on and on forever, being connected only by a thin membrane. Daddy began cutting the intestines into pieces about one and a half to two feet in length.

It was time to clean the chitterlings. This was done by taking a section of the intestines, dipping one end into warm water to fill it which loosens the contents (pig poop). Then we would hold each end out stretched in front of us and alternate raising one end and then the other, rinsing the contents. We would stand over a hole that had been previously dug near the end of the field, let go of one end of the intestines, and allow the contents to drop into the hole below. Daddy wanted everything clean, a major task when working with chitterlings. To say that cleaning chitterlings is a dirty job is an understatement. The smell was pretty bad too. This dirty job was usually reserved for the children. I hated it; everyone did. When all the chitterlings were cleaned, the holes were covered and filled in with fresh dirt by my brothers. You could hardly tell what was in them. You could hardly tell, but you knew. It was hard to tell if chitterlings were actually ever clean because you could never get rid of the smell. Clean or not, chitterlings smell bad. Thank God that dirty job went fast.

The day after hog-killing day was not as exciting as the day before. There was still lots of work to do, but fewer disgusting sights to see and fewer people around to do the work because no one was there except the family, Mama, Daddy, and us kids. Breakfast, however, was more excit-

ing. Today we all had fresh pork for breakfast; Daddy had a little something extra scrambled with his eggs. To him it was a delicacy; to me it was
quite disgusting, so much so that I won't tell what it was. It almost made
me sick to my stomach to think about it. Trust me, you don't want to know.

While the men had done most of the work yesterday, today was mostly
work for the women of the house. We had to make the lard, cracklins,
headcheese, and sausage. The lye soap would be made later on an as-
needed basis.

The washpot that had been used to heat water yesterday would be used
today for a different purpose. Today we would use it to make the lard and
cracklins (pork rinds). A large fire was built under the washpot just as
yesterday. Today instead of water, we dumped the quarter-size pieces of
fat from the two five-gallon buckets into the washpot. The meat was allowed to cook, fry if you will. Because it was mostly fat with very little
lean, this procedure resulted in a sizable amount of grease and lard for
cooking. The meat had to be stirred constantly. It was important not to let
it stick to the bottom of the washpot; if it stuck, it would burn. It wasn't
a matter of just burning the meat or cracklins; if the meat burned, the
grease would also burn. We didn't want to have to cook food with burnt
grease for months. Stirring was a time consuming and tiring job so we
took turns, being careful not to get scorched by the fire or splattered by
the hot grease. It was a difficult chore. After a few hours the cracklins
were done. The two buckets of fat produced about five gallons of lard and
about two gallons of cracklins. There would be enough cracklins to eat
by themselves or to cook with cornbread for a couple of months. Cracklin
bread tasted good with collard greens. I also liked to eat cracklin bread
with fresh buttermilk, fresh from the cow out back. There would also be
enough cooking fat for a large part of the winter. We stored the lard in
five-gallon cans under the cabinet in the kitchen. Surprisingly, it never
spoiled or went bad no matter how long we kept it. Lard lasted forever,
and we used it for things other than cooking. I remember that Daddy
once used lard for a rattlesnake bite on our dog Bozo. Daddy said the fat
would draw the poison out of the wound. I am not sure if the lard was a
true snakebite antidote, but Bozo lived, so maybe the lard did work.

Mama also made the sausage. She mixed bits and pieces of both lean
and fat meat into a large pan. She added her own collection of spices and

peppers to the mix. It looked horrible. She put it all into a hand grinder. The grinder mixed everything into a kind of mush. Unfortunately, with such a large family, the sausage would not last long. Meat was plentiful for a while, but only for a short while.

Mama also made the headcheese. They called it that because the primary ingredient was the fat and meat from the head of the hog. It was almost pure fat. It tasted great, but to see it being made was more horrible than watching sausage being prepared.

Hog-killing days were special. Not the watching or the participating. Those parts were disgusting. But when hog-killing time came around, we knew there would be meat on the table for a little while.

The Cotton Field

My first memories of the cotton fields weren't too bad. I guess because in those first memories I wasn't actually doing any work. In fact, as I recall I wasn't doing very much of anything. Thank God I was too small to pick cotton for a time. Nonetheless, I was in the fields even when I wasn't working. Whenever we went out to fields, whatever type they were, we went as a family.

While cotton was not the primary cash crop in Greenville it was a very popular crop. Cotton was cheap to grow too. The seeds were relatively inexpensive and the fields, once planted, did not require a lot of work until picking time. They required no work for the white folks because that was all left to the colored folks. The young cotton plants had to be hoed on occasion to remove the grass and extra cotton plants. They used to call that chopping cotton, which was an art. You had to know just how many excess cotton plants to chop and how many to leave. If you did this job wrong, you could actually ruin a cotton field. However, most colored folks were very experienced at chopping cotton and my family was no exception. We all knew how to do the job right. Knowing cotton was something that had been passed down reluctantly from generation to generation. Before I ever picked my first boll of cotton, I knew about chopping cotton.

Work in the cotton fields began rather early in the year. The cotton plants were planted, hoed, and chopped long before the hot summer sun of the cotton-picking season began. Some white farmers in the area owned large heavy equipment, but most of them relied on Negro power. In many cases, Negro power was cheaper than a tractor. By the time cotton-picking season began, all the black families in the area were already committed to working in the cotton fields of one white family or another. Cotton picking was hard work and the farmers wanted to know early just who they could count on to do the work. Sometimes there was not enough colored help to go around. When times got hard there would be some poor white families working alongside black folks in the fields. But this was a rare occurrence. Things had to really be bad for black folks and white folks to work in the fields together. Most white folks, even poor white folks, just wouldn't hear of it. Even when we worked the same fields, we seldom did it at the same time. It was too humiliating for the poor white folks. Black folks didn't really mind much who they worked beside. They just wanted to make as much money as possible for food and essentials.

Cotton-picking days were long. I can recall the entire family working from sunup to sundown performing back-breaking work. For my first few years in the fields I watched the work from afar. My sister Jan, my younger sister, Diane, and I were allowed to sit on a quilt under a shade tree in the middle of the cotton fields until we were old enough to help out with the work. And while we sat on the quilt, we were the keepers of the water there in the shade. Water was essential for anyone picking cotton all day. Most folks couldn't last more than thirty minutes or so without a drink. In any event we were never left alone on the quilt for very long. Occasionally Mama or one of our older siblings would come check on us. Or someone would walk over to get a drink of water.

I remember one time in particular that it was good to have people checking up on us regularly. We, the ones who were too small to work, had taken our usual position on the quilt under a shade tree. My brother Floyd walked over to check on us, at least that's what he said. I suspect that he merely came for a drink of water. Either way, he arrived just in time to rescue us from the fangs of just about the largest rattlesnake that I have ever seen, before or since. The snake was actually sharing the quilt with us and he was only a couple of feet away. I have no idea how we missed seeing him before Floyd showed up. Floyd got us all off the quilt and out of harm's way, then he returned with a hoe to take on the snake. It took him several minutes to kill the snake by chopping off its head. Each time he chopped at the snake, the snake struck at him. It was back and forth, touch and go for a while but Floyd eventually got the best of him. He totally severed the snake's head from the rest of its body. After the incident with the rattlesnake, I never felt really comfortable in the shade again. But working in the field wasn't much safer, and it definitely wasn't more comfortable.

By the time I was seven or eight, it was time for me to help work in the cotton fields. There was no more sitting in the shade on a quilt. I had to pick cotton, which was much worse than I had suspected. The sun was hotter and the rows and rows of cotton much longer than they appeared. And as for the pay, it hardly seemed worth the effort because we were paid by the pound. Cotton is lightweight. You had to pick a lot of cotton to get a pound, and you picked it one little cotton boll at a time. But our family was large and in a day, we could pick a lot. Some of my siblings were better than others at picking cotton. My sister Ediffie was one of the best. She was very good with her hands and she worked fast at everything she did. She could pick more cotton than some of my brothers. It was commonplace for her to pick more than a hundred pounds of cotton in a single day. A few cents a pound wasn't much, but when you could pick a hundred pounds like Ediffie could, it would add up. Ediffie was just as good or better at picking cotton than she was at picking up pecans. She simply worked miracles with her hands. Picking cotton, picking pecans, it made no difference to Ediffie, she was the best.

My first efforts at picking cotton didn't amount to much. On my first day, like everyone else, I was given a large burlap sack to fill with cotton. Those burlap sacks sure were common for picking things. I often wondered as a small child just where white people got so many burlap sacks; they were everywhere.

My instructions were to pick each cotton plant clean, and I was told only to put the cotton, which included the seeds but no sticks or bulbs, into the sack. That sounded simple enough. It was simple until you factored in the one hundred degree heat, the rattlesnakes, and the spiny thorns on the cotton plants themselves. I don't know what it was about rattlesnakes and cotton fields, but they seemed to go together. Everywhere there was a cotton field to be picked there were a few rattlesnakes around to keep things interesting. We were lucky that no one was ever bitten. There were, however, a lot of close calls. I can't recall how many times I actually had an opportunity to look at a snake eye-to-eye.

On a normal day of picking cotton, we would come within an arm's length of at least two to three snakes. Even so, I tried to do my best. I must admit that my best was not very good. It seemed as if my cotton rows went on forever. Mama would just tell me to do my best, and not to try to compete with my sisters or brothers. Mama knew that I could not do much, but she made me feel that my pound or two was just as important a contribution to the family as Ediffie's one hundred pounds were.

I did not finish a single row on my first day. I couldn't. I know for sure that I spent at least thirty minutes on my first plant alone. I was trying to follow the instructions to pick the plant clean. By the time my first picking day was over, my small body was wet with sweat, and my little fingers had several dozen pin-size pricks from the thorns on the cotton plants. My hands were also cut in several places. The bleeding had long since stopped, but the pain was still fresh, and I was dead tired. Picking cotton was the hardest work I had ever attempted in my short life. I probably hadn't covered more than thirty yards or so, and I probably had only about five or six pounds of cotton in my burlap sack, which was not much for a day's work. Nevertheless, I had made a contribution. At the end of the day, my earnings as well as Mama's, Daddy's, and all of my sisters' and brothers' were placed in Mama's apron, to be counted and added to the family funds.

We would go from cotton field to cotton field and repeat this same ritual all summer. We would pick cotton all day for pennies, after which the entire family would pool whatever earnings we made. Very seldom were we allowed to keep any of our earnings for ourselves in the summer time. The family always needed the money.

All the cotton fields in the area were basically the same. The only difference was the length of the rows. Even the owners were all the same because they were all white, although they weren't all wealthy. Most of them were, but not all. There was one cotton farmer in particular who was without a doubt the poorest cotton farmer in those parts. They called him Mr. Brownie. You could tell by what they called him that he was poor. He was the only white man that other white folks refused to call by his surname. They called him by his first name just like they did colored folks.

Mr. Brownie never had much of a cotton field. He was too poor to even hire black folks to pick his cotton for him. And the ones he did hire, he would end up not paying. Our family never worked for him. Daddy called him a "white nigger" because white folks treated him as bad as they did black folks.

All my family's experience with cotton was in either one white man's cotton field or another. Cotton was one of the few things that Daddy would not plant and grow. He refused to do it. Even though there was money to be made in cotton, not picking cotton, but growing it, Daddy always thought that it was somehow sacrilegious for colored folks to grow cotton. I must say that I agreed with him. Daddy's beliefs did not do us a lot of good, however. That is, it didn't keep us out of the white folk's cotton fields. It just kept us out of one of our own. Thank goodness cotton-picking season did not last all year.

While my first memories of the cotton fields, watching from a quilt in the shade, were not too bad, my later memories were horrible. When it came to cotton, I took after my daddy. He hated cotton fields and so did I.

The Strawberry Patch

One of the many things that Mama did to try and earn money for the family was growing strawberries. She always had a strawberry patch, and from as far back as I could remember strawberries were growing somewhere around the house. Strawberries were her pride and joy, and rightfully so. Of the many fruits and vegetables we grew, Mama took the greatest pride in her strawberries. She loved them and she put her heart and soul into every plant. Strawberries can produce a bountiful harvest if they are tended just right, and they were a really consistent income-producing crop for years. Even though the number of berries we raised was relatively small in comparison to the other produce we grew to sell like corn, peas, beans, potatoes, cucumbers, and such, they were almost worth their weight in gold. While everyone loved the taste of strawberries, only a few well-to-do white folks were able to afford to eat them. Strawberries were a delicacy. Mama grew strawberries but we couldn't afford to eat them.

Strawberries were a delicate crop and required a lot of tender loving care. Of course Mama made us kids provide a lot of that care as well as attending to the other vegetables and crops. Each year she would plant a new strawberry crop, right from scratch. We had to spend all spring and summer tending and caring for them. It was hard work, but in the end it was always well worth the effort.

I remember when Mama first got interested in growing strawberries. The family had been working for a white farmer south of town. We had tended his strawberry patch for a couple of years. We worked for him off and on from early spring planting his strawberries, through the heat of the summer, hoeing them, tending them, and eventually harvesting them. It was amazing to see the small seedlings grow into a mature plant that produced a large delicious fruit at the end of the season. It was a wonderful sight to behold. At the end of the season it was also rather amazing to see the amount of money the farmer got paid when he took the strawberries that my family had raised for him to the market to sell. He was making about twenty cents for a pint, and about forty cents for a quart of strawberries. In those days that was a fortune, especially for such a small item. He was making more from just a few quarts of strawberries than he was paying my entire family for a couple of day's work tending to them. It didn't take Mama long to figure out that growing strawberries for herself would go a long way toward feeding the family. Selling one quart of our own strawberries brought in more money than picking ten pounds of cotton. It was a no-brainer; even poor, uneducated black folk could figure that out. And she already knew the family could raise strawberries; we had just done a great job of that for someone else.

So the next spring, in addition to working in other fields, Mama went to work for herself raising strawberries. At first she started out on a small scale. Strawberries were planted in very early spring. The farmer we worked for would order the young tender baby plants in late winter through a mail order catalog. He would literally order thousands of them. Even though he had many plants left over from the previous year, he always wanted to supplement his crop with fresh new hardy plants. By the time the plants arrived through the mail several dozen would be in such bad condition that the farmer didn't want to waste time planting and nurturing them. Or rather he didn't want us to do that. So after a long hard day in the farmer's fields planting the tender new plants, Mama would gather up all the discarded plants and bring them home. She planted them all out back in one big mound of earth that she watered, fertilized, and pampered for several weeks. After a lot of care, a couple dozen of those old dying plants survived and this was the beginning of Mama's first strawberry patch.

Mama treated those first few plants like gold. In a way, they were almost worth as much. That first year, we worked two strawberry patches, the white farmer's and Mama's little patch. When it was time to hoe the plants, we hoed the white man's plants by day, and we hoed Mama's small patch at twilight. When it was time to gather pine straw to surround the young plants to keep the fresh blooms and small berries from touching the bare ground, we gathered pine straw for the white farmer by day, and we gathered pine straw for Mama's plants afterward. When it was time to pick the farmer's huge ripe berries, we picked his strawberries by day, and we picked Mama's strawberries at twilight. It was hard work but Mama never complained, and for fear of her wrath we never complained either.

We alternated our strawberry patch duties with our other field work. While we did not work in the strawberry patch every day, we were certainly working in the fields every day. One field or another, it really didn't matter. It was all the same. It was all very, very hard work. Except that the work we did in Mama's strawberry patch was for our benefit alone. No white farmer paid us a pittance and then took the produce to market. Mama had a bountiful harvest the first year. In fact, she earned more money from the sale of her own strawberries than the whole family earned working the strawberry fields for the white farmer. Mama turned out to be a pretty good businesswoman.

After the success of that first little patch we were on our way. Mama soon became an expert at growing strawberries. Year after year she planted a new crop of berries. And each year her patch got larger and larger. Strawberries eventually became one of my family's staple crops. As the patch got larger, the strawberries got bigger and sweeter as well. We were not allowed to eat any of Mama's strawberries, but I secretly took enough to know that they were very tasty. I imagine my brothers and sisters did too. The crop was too valuable for us to eat; Mama tried to sell every single berry. The only strawberries she allowed us to keep were those that were damaged or too small to sell. We never got even a taste of the large juicy berries, at least not with her knowledge.

Birds were a real problem. Sometimes they would go through a large portion of the patch and take a single bite out of the biggest, reddest strawberries, ruining them for sale. Those were the berries we were allowed to eat. Mama would cut off the damaged portions and make the most delicious strawberry pies. She also made great-tasting strawberry preserves and jams. It seemed that everything Mama made with her strawberries was delicious.

Mama not only made strawberry treats just for us kids, she also made a treat of sorts for grownups too— her famous strawberry wine. Mama would make five gallons at a time. Even though I wasn't supposed to know anything about the wine, I did. All the kids knew about it. It would have been very difficult to hide anything from all us kids. With thirteen of us underfoot, we were literally everywhere. And we saw, smelled, and tasted everything. There was absolutely no way Mama was going to be able to keep a wine-making operation secret. In fact, my brothers were regular consumers of her wine. They even began small, secret wine-making operations of their own. The wine they made was not nearly as tasty as what Mama made; and hers had more of a kick to it. It would have had a bigger kick except my brothers Calvin and Sonny would take a quart of Mama's wine while it was still fermenting and replace it with a quart of nice clean well water, I suspect Mama knew what they were doing but she never let on if she did.

Mama's strawberry wine was very good. I learned how to make it myself. I have included Mama's recipe below, just in case anyone wants to give it a try.

Mama's Strawberry Wine Recipe

Ingredients

    3 lbs. fresh strawberries

    2½ lbs. granulated sugar

    2 tsp. citric acid

    1 gal. boiling water

    yeast and nutrient; pectic enzyme

Process

First, make sure the strawberries are fresh. Wash them well and place them in a container. A clean plastic bucket will suffice. Using a large wooden spoon, crush the fruit as fine as possible to release the juices. Pour one gallon of boiling water over the crushed fruit and stir well. After the mixture cools to about lukewarm, add the pectic enzyme.

A day later add the yeast and nutrient. Cover the contents with a clean towel and tie a piece of string or elastic around the top to ensure that the bucket remains covered. After about five days, strain the juice into the two and a half pounds of sugar. Stir well until it is all dissolved. Pour this mixture into a one-gallon dark glass container. Don't fill the mixture to the top, and fit an air lock. Hold the remaining mixture to the side in a separate smaller glass bottle. In a day or so the fermentation process will begin. It will continue to ferment vigorously for five or six more days. The smell alone lets you know that the process is working. Once the fermentation stabilizes, use the remaining small portion of juice reserve to top off the gallon bottle to the base of the neck. Leave the gallon bottle in a warm place until the fermentation ceases. This will probably take about four or five weeks.

At the end of that time, you can then rack (siphon) the wine into another bottle. After two or three weeks, rack the wine again. Each time you rack the wine, it gets clearer. When the wine is sufficiently clear after several weeks, it is time to bottle it.

The operation is complete.

Mama used to make strawberry wine each year with the strawberries that she was not able to sell, put into delicious pies, or make into jams and jellies. She wasted absolutely nothing. She shared her wine with friends and family. We kids were not allowed to drink wine but that did not stop us. Whenever we got the opportunity, we would sneak into wherever Mama was hiding the wine and pilfer a taste or two. It always tasted extremely good.

Throughout the year Mama would also make wine out of other fruits. If it wasn't strawberry season, it was some other fruit-bearing season. And Mama made wine from most of those fruits.

Nothing went to waste around our house. Not even old strawberries that were not fit to sell. Mama became very good at growing strawberries and she grew a yearly crop for many years. Of course we were there to help out. The few dollars that she got from the sale of the strawberries really made a difference in our lives. Sometimes the strawberry money meant there would be meat on the table where there otherwise would have been none. There were other times when the money meant a desperately needed pair of shoes for one of us. As a small child, I never got enough strawberries to eat. I wasn't allowed to because we really needed the money. Now, when I visit the supermarket and see those large containers with delicious red strawberries beckoning to me to buy them, I can't help but smile and think of Mama's strawberry patch. That succulent red fruit played an important role in my family's survival. I have fond memories of strawberries.

Gee Haw

As I recall we always had large fields of our own where we grew food. We grew most of what we ate. There was no such thing as going to the store to buy vegetables and such. In fact, we bought very few food items from the store. Most of the manpower used to work in our fields was just us kids. After all we couldn't hire help; we were the hired help. The only assistance in the fields at all came from Daddy's mule. He always had a mule, which was, without a doubt, the hardest-working member of the family. It was his task, along with Daddy to plow every inch of our fields. And that was no easy task. There were acres and acres to plow. Tractors had been around for a while, but no black folks in the area could afford to buy a tractor. Only a few black folks could afford to buy a mule. Daddy was one of those few.

Owning and caring for a mule was hard work. A mule was only productive in the planting season, but he had to be fed and tended to all year long. Feeding the mule was the kids' job. The mule's lot as we called it was located about a hundred yards away from the house. Daddy had fenced in an area for him that had a shallow branch running through it. The branch came in handy because carrying food for the mule was hard enough. To have to carry water for him also was downright torture. He could drink several gallons of water every day. It was a good thing for us that the branch supplied water most of the year. It did, however, occasionally go dry in the middle of the hottest summers. It was then that we had to carry water. Nevertheless, the mule earned his keep, water and all.

The mule's work began in the early spring, in late February and early March. That's when the fields had to be made ready for the planting season. It was tough getting that ol' mule going in February. It seemed as if he knew he was in for a long, hard, hot planting season. He was a difficult and stubborn old thing. Whoever invented the phrase stubborn as a mule must have been talking about Daddy's mule. The darn thing had a mind of its own. I can't say that I blame the mule at all for being stubborn, especially after watching Daddy hook him up to a plow for the first time. It had to be torture.

Daddy had plows in three sizes, large, medium, and small. I never understood why he needed more than one. They all seemed to do the same thing. Basically the plow was a wedge-shaped piece of metal. It had two wooden handles attached to the back end. The metal wedge, pulled through the earth by the mule, would separate the soil and open a trench for planting seeds. The handles were there so Daddy could guide the plow into the ground while walking behind the mule. The front of the plow was a wooden piece with a tackle that attached the plow to the mule. The mule also had a bridle in his mouth. The bridle was attached to a rope on each end. The rope led from the mule's mouth back to Daddy who would be standing behind the plow. When he was plowing, Daddy would usually keep both hands on the plow handle. He usually let the rope, which was attached to the bridle, just lie across his shoulder. Since he couldn't hold onto everything, the plow handles seemed to be the most important. The bridle was used to encourage the mule to walk in the direction Daddy wanted it to go. The mule always needed a lot of encouragement. Watching Daddy and the mule was like watching a prizefight. You never knew who was getting the best of whom. Most of the time it looked as if the mule was winning the fight but you couldn't tell Daddy that.

Daddy would hitch the mule up to the plow early in the morning and set out for the fields. In the early spring there would still be a chill in the air when they got started. As the mule struggled to pull the plow you could see the mist and condensation as his warm breath hit the cold air. The mule and Daddy shared a language of their own in the fields. In order to get the mule going in the morning, Daddy would start with "Giddy up there, mule." Sometimes this phrase had to be repeated several times to get the mule started. Occasionally it would also have to be followed by a sharp slap on the mule's rump. Once the mule got started he was good to go. That is until he reached the end of a row. Getting the mule to stop was usually simple enough. Most of the time a firm "Whoa, mule" would do the trick. Getting him turned around and started back in the other direction on a new row was a challenge. Daddy had to pick the plow up out of the earth while at the same time pulling on the mule's bridle to get him to turn. It was hard work. The plow was heavy, and it was not easy to keep picking it up out of the ground, especially when it was full of dirt. From afar it looked like they were doing the two-step, right there in the middle of the field.

That mule always seemed to know just what to do to upset Daddy. Plowing fast was one of those things. The mule wanted to plow just a tad faster than Daddy wanted to walk, which naturally caused a problem. Daddy had to get the mule stopped and started all over again, just to slow him down. This drove Daddy crazy. I always thought that mule was walking fast on purpose. I think Daddy sort of believed that too.

Another problem with plowing using that ol' mule was keeping the rows straight. Once the mule got going he wanted to go his own way. His own way may have been back to the lot and branch for a cool drink of water. It was hard to keep him, and thus the plowing, in a straight line. Daddy had a couple of other commands for that. When Daddy wanted the mule to go a little to the left he would yell "Gee!" When he wanted him to go a little to the right he would yell "Haw!" Believe it or not the mule understood the directions. Of course understanding and doing are two different things. The mule would have good days and bad days. And on bad days he would simply refuse to cooperate. When the mule was in a bad mood, you could hear Daddy yelling at the top of his voice. "Gee! Gee mule! Haw! Haw mule!" The fight was on.

To say the least, Daddy and the mule did not get along very well. It always surprised me how the two of them could fight so much yet get so much work done. And they did get a lot of work done. In one day, Daddy and that mule could plow several acres of land. By no means were we all standing around watching Daddy and the mule do all the work, not at all. There was an assembly line going at all times. The mule was always first. He would be followed by the plow and then Daddy. Daddy would be followed by one of us, dropping seeds of some type into the freshly plowed trench. Usually the younger children would plant the seeds. Of all the work, dropping seeds was one on the easiest jobs to be had. The person planting the seeds would then be followed by someone with a hoe or rake to cover the seeds.

By the end of a long hard day, the fruit of our labor could be seen. There would be several acres of perfectly plowed field, most of which would already be planted before the sun went down. Despite the fact that Daddy and the mule seldom wanted to gee or haw at the same time, they always managed to work together. The rows plowed by Daddy and the mule would be as straight as the ones on the white folks' farms, which had been plowed by a tractor.

Running Beans

I hated running beans when I was a child. Some folks call them running beans, some call them pole beans, and they may be called by a host of other names as well, but they are all the same to me. No matter what they were called, I hated them. My intense dislike for running beans had nothing to do with the taste of the beans. One bean tastes pretty much like another to my mind. I had another reason for hating running beans.

They were a special breed because of how they grew. And I guess that is how they got their name. Most peas, beans, and such grew from a simple plant, which when mature had an average height of between a foot and a half and three feet. But running beans grew a little differently because they never stopped growing. They grew on a vinelike plant, on and on for dozens and dozens of feet. One single plant could actually have an end twenty yards from its root. And therein lies the problem. You could let the branches of a plant run along the ground for twenty yards only to have the beans on the plant die and rot right there on the ground. This is where Daddy got ingenious. Over the span of my childhood he devised a number of different methods to lift the vine off the ground and thus save the plant and the beans from certain ruin. While I loved my Daddy, I must admit that most of his plans were of poor design. At least that was how it appeared to me. But his idea for saving the running beans was different. It actually worked.

Daddy had tried various schemes for saving every single bean. Then he hit upon his teepee method. After much practice, Daddy got this method down to an art. He started out with his mule in the early spring. Sometimes there would even be frost still on the ground when he and that old mule got started. Daddy and his mule would plow and prepare at least ten extremely long rows. These rows were set aside; they were intended only for planting the running beans. After the rows were prepared, one of my brothers would have to walk behind Daddy and his mule with a hoe, leveling off the high tops of the freshly plowed ground to make a more suitable row for planting. This was a tough job and only my brothers were strong enough to handle it. My brother would then be followed by one of my sisters with another hoe. This time the hoe would be turned upside down and a hole would be pressed into the fresh soil with the handle of the hoe. This job was not quite as difficult as actually forming the rows, but traveling up and down rows with a hoe turned upside down soon became tiresome. Even feathers get heavy if you have to carry them long enough. The holes were usually about four inches deep and about eighteen inches to two feet apart. My job was to walk behind my sister who was punching the holes and drop four or five bean seeds in the holes. But the job still was not finished. I was followed by another sibling with yet another hoe covering over the newly planted seeds with soil. These may seem like simple tasks. But imagine doing them over and over and over . . .

After the planting was done, we waited for two or three weeks to see if our seeds would come up. I say we waited, but during planting season, we never waited for anything. Once we finished planting running beans we were off to plow and plant some other crop in some other distant field. When the beans finally came up we were able to see how well we had done our jobs. For example, at this point it was easy to tell if I had dropped too many or too few seeds in the holes several weeks earlier. Once the plants grew to about twelve inches in height, Daddy would install his teepees for saving the plants. He and my brothers would take a trip to the woods closest to the edge of the fields. They would cut dozens of oak branches, all about an inch or so in diameter and about five feet high, and haul them back to the bean field. At this point Daddy would take two of the branches and stick them in the ground, straddling the bean plant one limb on each side of the plant. He would then cross the two limbs at the top and fasten them together with wire. This formed a triangular shape similar to an Indian teepee. Daddy would go through the entire bean field constructing teepees over each and every plant. When he finished, the entire field was littered with dozens and dozens of little teepees. The field was amazing to look at from afar. It looked so planned, so organized.

I can recall many times going out in the middle of the bean field in the late evening. I would lie flat on my back in the shadow of a teepee and daydream. I imagined that I was a little Indian girl, resting comfortably among the teepees in a large Indian village. I was surrounded and protected from all harm. It felt great to visit my imaginary village. But I was always snatched back to reality. I was only a poor little colored girl working in the middle of a huge Alabama bean field, with my Mama, Daddy, and twelve poor little sisters and brothers. That was the real world.

Once all the teepees were in place, towering over the young bean plants, as if by magic, the plants knew what to do next. They would grab hold of the limbs and climb. They would twist, turn, and crawl skyward along the limbs as if heaven itself was beckoning them upward. And as the beans climbed skyward, they would begin to flower and blossom, giving birth to small sprouts of beans, all high off the ground and safe from ruin and decay, just like Daddy had planned it. And in no time flat those small spouts grew and matured into thousands and thousands of good old running beans just dangling on the vines and ready to be picked.

Now came the really hard part. Picking those beans was grueling, hot, hard, back-breaking work. Daddy hardly ever helped with the picking. He usually left that part of the work for my sisters, brothers, and me. The bean-picking days were hot and long. And unfortunately for us, the rows of beans were even longer. It would have been pleasant to daydream about the days, just a few weeks earlier, when I could lie on the ground in the cool of the late evening and pretend to be a little Indian girl, a girl who was surrounded by dozens and dozens of teepees in a large Indian village and had not a care in the world. But there was no time for daydreaming. There was always too much work left to be done. The many rows of beans were always so long and so heavy with beans that we were seldom able to pick all the beans in a single day. Even with all our hands helping, it usually took two or three days to pick the entire field. After a couple of days there were more beans ripe on the vines and ready to be picked, and we would begin the three-day picking process all over again. The running bean harvest seemed to go on forever.

Most years of planting, tending, and harvesting running beans were about the same, and the hard work was constant. There was one summer in the bean field, however, that I remember vividly. That year started out like most, with Daddy and his old mule readying the field for the beans. As usual my brothers, sisters, and I did our part by leveling the newly plowed rows, punching holes into the fresh earth, planting the bean seeds, and finally covering them over with dirt. And this particular year, like most, Daddy decided to use his teepee method to save the harvest from spoiling. Several weeks after the planting, the beans had sprouted and were tall enough for Daddy to start building the teepees.

This year Daddy decided to make a small change in the way he constructed the teepees. Hoping for an even larger crop, Daddy decided to add additional space for the beans to run. After all, they would run and grow forever if they had a surface to travel on. So, this year after Daddy had installed the dozens and dozens of teepees over the small plants, he went one step further. He connected all the teepees together at the top with a long string of wire, barbed wire. The teepees were connected together right at the spot where the two limbs crossed. It looked pretty neat.

Only a few weeks after the teepees were installed the beans began to climb skyward. Once the beans reached the tops of the teepees, they grabbed hold of the barbed wire and ran along it as well, just like Daddy had predicted. Everywhere the beans ran, they blossomed, and everywhere they blossomed, they produced beans. Daddy was right. Adding the additional wire increased the bean harvest that summer threefold. Of course having a larger bean crop meant we would have to spend even more time in the fields picking beans. No one looked forward to that additional time in the blazing hot sun. I know I did not. That didn't matter. Whether I wanted to spend the extra time in the field or not, it was something that had to be done. So we got started.

Early one morning I was awakened by the sounds of pots and pans clanking in the kitchen. I turned my head to look out the window and saw that it was still dark outside. I was still tired from picking beans the day before. It couldn't possibly be morning already, but it was. Soon the noise of pots and pans gave way to the smell of pork cooking in the kitchen. Mama was already up cooking breakfast before daybreak. I tried to close my eyes and go back to sleep but I knew there was no use. Once Mama was up and stirring, she would be demanding the same of us. And once we set foot out of bed, the day of hard work was on.

Before I could close my eyes, Mama was yelling for us to get up. We knew we had a long, hard day ahead of us, and no one was eager to get started. Soon we were all up, dressed, and fed. And by the time the sun came up over the horizon we were headed for the bean field. We must have been a sight: a dozen colored folks walking single file at dawn, carrying buckets, pails, or baskets, anything to hold our bean harvest. By the time the sun was high overhead, the family had already picked several bushels of beans. We had accomplished a lot but there was still a lot of work to be done. I worked hard as always, doing all I could do to pull my fair share of the weight. I tried everything to help out. I was only six or seven, standing about three and a half feet tall. I could pick the beans on the lower end of the teepee, but there was no way I could reach the beans near the top. It was slow going. I wanted to be able to be left alone on a row of beans to pick like my sisters and brothers. But because I couldn't reach most of the beans, I always had to have help. I hated that.

After picking beans for several hours, I had an idea. If I could climb up on the limbs that formed the teepees, I could reach the beans all the way on the top of the poles, and if I could reach all the beans, I could pick on a row alone, just like my older sisters and brothers. I began climbing the limbs. Each time I got to a new teepee, I would climb just a little higher than the last one. Mama saw what I was doing and warned me to stop. Like most children, I heeded her advice for a while, but as soon as she turned her head I was climbing again. I reached a limb that had a lot of knots on it where Daddy had cut off smaller branches. Those knots were perfect for hand- and footholds. I began to climb, picking beans as I went. I was having great success and before I knew it I had climbed all the way to the top of the teepee, towering above everyone in the field.

All of a sudden I lost my footing on the limb and fell. It was a normal reaction to try and grab hold of something to catch myself as I fell, and that is what I did. I caught onto the wire that Daddy had strung between the teepees. The barbed wire. As I reached out, the palm of my left hand was snagged by the barbed wire, which tore deep into my hand and held me tightly, suspended above the ground. The barbed wire caught my right arm at my elbow. As gravity pulled me downward the wire tore into my flesh, raking a huge jagged gash from my elbow to my wrist. The pain was excruciating. There I was, dangling about three feet off the ground, held up by the piece of barbed wire that was embedded deeply into my left hand. The wound on my right arm was bleeding profusely. I screamed.

Almost immediately I felt hands around my waist. Mama gently lifted me upward until I was able to bend my left arm. Then, after several attempts, one of my brothers was able to release my hand from the grasp of the barbed wire. By the time Mama lowered me to the ground, I was already running. I took off like a flash. The pain was horrible, but the sight of all that blood—my own blood—was too much for me. Without stopping I ran full speed back to the house, leaving a trail of blood behind me. Only God knew where I was running to because I sure didn't. Everyone set out running after me. It was the first and only time in my life my short bowlegs outran everyone in the family.

Mama caught up with me as I reached the house. I didn't know she could run so fast. Mama had to literally tackle me in order to get me to stop running. By this time I was covered in blood. After Mama cleaned most of the blood away, she was able to see how badly I was hurt. It was pretty bad.

This was one of the few occasions that warranted a trip to the doctor by one of us kids. I had lost a tremendous amount of blood and Mama was even afraid that I might bleed to death. I didn't know anything about bleeding to death. I just knew there was tremendous pain. There was a half-inch tear in the palm of my left hand where blood gushed out each time my heart beat. And the jagged cut on my right arm was more than twelve inches long. I was wrapped in rags and rushed to the doctor. Several hours later I returned home covered in bandages. I remember hearing Mama scold Daddy for putting barbed wire at the top of the bean poles. She blamed him for my accident. I blamed him too for a while. But it wasn't his fault. All he was trying to do was increase the bean harvest as much as possible.

Though the puncture wound in my left palm has faded, the jagged scar on my right arm, from elbow to wrist, is still visible. And I still bear the mental scars of that day. I picked running beans many times after the accident, but I never again tried to pick a single bean that was out of my reach. Daddy never used barbed wire again on his running beans. Not that I would have noticed. I never got close enough to check.

So that's why I hated running beans as a child. I still do.

III
The Business

A Year and a Day

Daddy spent most of his life and all the time I knew him engaged in making moonshine. He had a number of close calls with the law, but he almost always managed to stay one step ahead of them.

I remember one close call in particular. It was a spring afternoon in the early 1960s. There was a slight breeze and a mockingbird could be heard trilling in the distance. Daddy had not been at the house all day. That was not unusual, especially on the weekends, which was when he usually made his moonshine. We kids were not supposed to know what he was doing, but of course we did know. Daddy walked into the house just like it was a normal day. It was late afternoon but long before dark. In an instant all hell broke loose. I remember seeing five or six cars pull into the yard on two wheels as they say, and all at the same time, following closely behind one another. Several were marked police cars. There were also a couple of regular cars that could have belonged to anybody. "What the hell is going on?" I heard Daddy yell. "It's the sheriff," Mama answered. She knew he had been at the whiskey still all day and figured he was caught for sure. The sheriff at the time was a mean, nasty ol' cuss who had been sheriff of Butler County for years and who had put many a poor black man in jail.

The sheriff knocked on the door and then entered before being asked to do so. "Where is Charlie?" "I am right here," Daddy answered quickly. "What do you want with me?" "Charlie," said the sheriff, "you are under arrest for making moonshine." "What moonshine?" said Daddy. By this time, the other white men, who did not appear to be lawmen, had entered the house and begun ransacking it, searching for the moonshine. I could hear someone yelling at us to tell them where the moonshine was. The search was intense. Tables, sofas, and chairs were overturned and tossed around the room. Cabinets and closets were searched while Mama, Daddy, and all us kids just watched in silent terror. I had never seen the police looking for moonshine, but I had heard about it. And we all knew the penalty for making moonshine was jail.

Before the sheriff had burst in I had been in the kitchen eating with my older sister Ediffie. During the commotion she had dragged me from the table to a box beside the stove. Ediffie was sitting on the box, holding me and still trying to make me eat. Who could eat with all that racket going on? I was trying to see what was going on and was not at all interested in eating. After what seemed like forever but was probably only a few minutes, the house was in shambles. Everything was out of place. I had seen Daddy carrying bundles when he entered the house, but I had no idea what had happened to them. I wasn't the only one. The men searching the house found absolutely nothing. The sheriff told two of them to go outside and look around out there. They searched the grounds without finding anything. They headed over the hill toward the branch, in the same direction Daddy had come from just a few minutes earlier. Things were not looking good.

In a few minutes the men returned. They told the sheriff, "We found the still." The sheriff began to grill Daddy. "Is that your still, Charlie?" "What still?" Daddy answered. They went back and forth like that for at least an hour. The entire time Daddy denied any knowledge of the whiskey still. The sheriff had no real evidence. All he had was a still on land owned by a white man. He had found no moonshine in the house or on the property. Everyone knew that Daddy made moonshine, but he had not been caught in the process. The sheriff knew he really had no case. Nonetheless, he eventually told Daddy he was under arrest for making moonshine. They put Daddy in handcuffs and placed him in the backseat of one of the police cars. He was going to jail though there was no real evidence against him. The men piled into the cars, and one by one they slowly pulled out of the yard and headed toward town.

Mama didn't know what to do. We were all in shock. The punishment for making moonshine was a long prison term. Most black folks who went to prison never came out alive. I could not help thinking I would never see Daddy again. We didn't have enough money to buy groceries, let alone to pay for a lawyer, which meant we would have to settle for the public defender. He was a well-known racist from way back. Everyone knew he hated black people. They also knew his black clients almost always went to jail. Guilty or not guilty, they went to jail. We thought Daddy would be another statistic.

Soon it was time for Daddy's trial. The courtroom was full. Folks, black and white, came from all over to see Daddy get sentenced to jail time. Mama and a couple of my older sisters and brothers were there also. They couldn't sit in seats on the main floor near Daddy. They had to sit up in the balcony where the black folks sat. The ground level of the courtroom, like most places, was for whites only. The sign on the door clearly said so, "Whites Only." The judge, jury, prosecutor, Daddy's lawyer, the sheriff, and all the witnesses against Daddy were white. The odds were not in his favor.

The trial began and the first witness was called to the stand by the prosecution. He was one of the deputies who had been at the house when Daddy was arrested. He was asked where Daddy was when he was arrested. "In the house."

"Did you find any moonshine on him?"

"No."

"Was there any moonshine in the house?"

"No."

"Was there any moonshine on the premises?"

"No."

"Did you catch Charlie at the still making moonshine?"

Again, he replied "no."

"Who owns the land where the still was found?"

"That's Mr. Standoff's land." Standoff was the white landowner Daddy was sharecropping for.

"So, the land you found the still on doesn't belong to Charlie?"

"No," replied the deputy.

The crowd began to get restless and started to talk among themselves. Both the white people downstairs and the black people upstairs began to whisper. The next deputy was called up to testify. His answers were the same as the one who had testified before him. No, he had found no moonshine on Daddy. He had found no moonshine in the house or on the grounds, and Daddy had been arrested at the house not at the still.

As the second deputy was testifying, murmurs from the crowd got louder. People laughed at his answers and some members of the jury were even shaking their heads. The prosecution's case was beginning to go south. By the time the last deputy had testified, the courtroom was almost out of control. The judge threatened to evict some of the onlookers from the courtroom or even throw them in jail. When the trial recessed for the day there were only two people left to testify: the sheriff and Daddy. Though things seemed to be going in Daddy's favor, the sheriff had a reputation for making "niggers" look bad. And it wouldn't be the first time a black man was convicted without any evidence. Everybody testifying against Daddy was white, and being white usually meant being right as well.

The courtroom was packed on the second day of the trial. The colored section was filled to capacity, and there was standing room only in the white section as well. Everybody wanted to see what was going to happen to Charlie.

The sheriff was the first to testify. The prosecutor asked him the same questions he had asked the deputies the day before. He, like them, could not put Daddy at the still when the deputies found it. Nor had he found any moonshine on the premises. The judge called for a recess. During the recess Daddy's lawyer took him into a back room to have a talk with him. To this point he had not done a single thing to defend Daddy. And his talk did nothing to change that.

"Charlie," said the public defender, "do you see what's going on out there? You are making a mockery of the court. You are making every white man who got up there to testify against you look bad. You can't make those white men look like fools. You got to live here with these white folks and you can't do that if you make them look like fools in front of all those people. The sheriff won't stand for it.

"Charlie," he said, "you need to go out there and own up to that still. You know and I know that the still was yours and you need to go out there and confess. If you confess, I will see to it that you only get a year and a day. In a year you can come back here and live among these white folks. But you got to confess to that still."

Daddy told the public defender, "I will not confess to something that is not mine. For all I know, that whiskey still is yours. It's as likely to be yours as it is to be mine. I will not take a year and a day for something that is not mine." Daddy's answers made his attorney furious. He tried to scare Daddy by saying that if he did not confess and was found guilty he could be sent off for ten to twenty years of hard labor. Daddy only said, "I'll take my chances with the jury."

After the recess the sheriff was called back to the stand to answer a few more questions and then he stepped down. The only person left to testify was Daddy. Everyone was afraid for him. He took the stand and was asked the same series of questions as the deputies and the sheriff before him. He did not take his lawyer's advice. He refused to confess to owning the still. His case was now in the hands of the jury. They were only out for about an hour. But that was one long agonizing hour, especially for Mama. The jury returned with a verdict: not guilty. All the black folks up in the colored section gave a resounding cheer. Mama and the family were overjoyed. The sheriff, on the other hand, was distraught. This was the first case he had lost against a black man. He would not find it easy to forget.

From that day forth, the sheriff watched Daddy like a hawk. It became more difficult than ever for him to make moonshine, but not impossible. Of course he continued to make it because, after all, that was our livelihood.

After Daddy narrowly escaped jail time, he made some drastic changes in his moonshine business. The most visible change was in the location of his still. His old spots in the woods near the creek behind the house were constantly being watched by the sheriff and his deputies. He moved his still many times before he finally settled on a spot. The final location he chose was a stroke of genius: Daddy put the still under the house. You see, the land that our house was located on was not level. While there were only three steps to climb going the front door, there were at least ten steps going out the back door. This meant that there was a lot of space under the house near the rear. Daddy took advantage of that space. Daddy was not very tall, so he did not need a lot of headroom. Mama had been using the space under the house for years. She had gotten Daddy to build a series of shelves under there so she could store canned vegetables. After Daddy's close call with the law, Mama had to share her space.

And how did Daddy get to and from his still? He knew that he and the house were being constantly watched, and he couldn't very well be seen coming and going from under the house. Daddy needed a way to get under the house without going outside. Daddy loved a challenge. In the center room of the house was a bedroom, the boy's room. In that room was a closet. And in the floor of that closet Daddy built a trap door. That location under the house became the final resting place for Daddy's still. He never had to relocate it again, and he made liquor there for many years. While the still is long gone, the trap door in the closet still remains. I know that many a daughter says this about her father, but I must say it as well. My Daddy was the smartest man I have ever known.

Many years later I learned that on the day Daddy was arrested, he had indeed been making moonshine. The box in the kitchen where my sister Ediffie sat trying to feed me had been turned upside down over three gallons of moonshine that Daddy had just brought into the house. What a difference a year and a day make.

The Recipe

To say that raising a family of thirteen children in rural Alabama in the 1940s, '50s, and '60s was difficult would be an understatement. My daddy did any and everything to ensure our survival. Most country folks could make moonshine, but the manufacture of good moonshine was an art, and in his own right my father was an artist, a professional. You don't have to take my word for his professionalism and expertise, just ask the sheriff. While I can divulge his recipe for moonshine, his care and touch for the art can never be duplicated.

Moonshine Recipe
Ingredients
    sugar
    cornmeal
    water
    yeast
    malt
Note: Ingredients may vary slightly from manufacturer to manufacturer. Daddy did an excellent job with the above.
Process
- Mix all of the above ingredients in a large container and allow it to ferment. The yeast helps in this process. The fermented mixture is called mash. Some call it sour mash; you will find out why when you smell the concoction.

This copper moonshine still is reminiscent of the one Daddy used to make whiskey. Courtesy of the Appalachian Cultural Museum.

- The mash is placed into an airtight container (the still) and cooked. The vapor resulting from the cooked mash indicates the quality of the moonshine.
- The mash can be reused a number of times; just add everything but the yeast and repeat the fermenting process.

While this process may sound easy, it is not, because there are a lot of variables to consider. Fermenting mash has an odor. Since the manufacture of moonshine is illegal in most places, the smell could be a dead giveaway. The location of the still is critical. Since water is a crucial ingredient for the process, locating your still near a stream, or branch, is a good idea. Water is used not only as an ingredient but also to help the condensation process and to keep the alcohol from burning. The burned flavor can ruin a run. (A run is one complete cycle of moonshine manufacture.) Keep in mind that the still itself should be airtight. Copper is a good metal for the still and the tube or coil portion of the still. Daddy always used copper because it was safe. He said lead poisoning was bad for business.

Big Meeting Sunday

Daddy had a variety of customers for his moonshine sales, Christians and heathens alike. His Christian customers were an interesting breed. They had many faces. They had their Sunday-morning-go-to-meeting faces, and they had their Saturday-night, shot-house, buy-moonshine-out-the-back-door faces. On some occasions, they meshed into a single face. One such occasion was big meeting Sunday at Old Elam Church. Old Elam was a Baptist church that sat a stone's throw from our front door. The church was so close in fact, that on big meeting Sunday, if we opened our front door, we could hear the entire sermon, each and every word. Old Elam Baptist was a small community church that was attended by most of the people in the Wald community. Our church, however, was Mount Ida Baptist, about four miles up Highway 31.

Daddy was not much of a churchgoer, but he saw big meeting Sunday as an opportunity to do business. And he tried never to miss a business opportunity. Big meeting Sunday was usually held in the hottest part of the summer, on the last Sunday in July or the first Sunday in August. Wow, was it hot. Daddy always said it was hot enough to fry an egg on cement steps. We never tested his theory of course; eggs were too hard to come by and our steps were made of old lumber.

On big meeting Sunday, folks would come from all around. The women would be dressed in their finest dresses. Even the men would dress up for the occasion. The children, some of whom had not worn shoes all summer, were dressed up too, including shoes if they had them.

Big meeting was a good opportunity to hear some powerful preaching, eat a delicious home-cooked meal prepared by the sisters of the church, and sample some of Daddy's moonshine. People came in droves to the big meeting. There were always three or four ministers on the program. Two would preach before the noon break for dinner, and two would preach after dinner. You could never predict how long any one minister would preach. If the spirit moved him, he could go for hours. And rest assured, if he had a paying, shouting audience, the spirit would move him.

The heat was relentless. And back then the tiny church had no air-conditioning. The only air stirring was the incidental breeze created by dozens and dozens of handheld fans being waved back and forth by the women in a vain effort to keep cool. All that cotton, lace, and nylon they were wearing was coming back to haunt them. Nor did the church have indoor plumbing. There were two outhouses, one for the men and one for the women, which consisted of a few pieces of lumber surrounding a deep hole in the ground covered with a splinter-filled seat. In the summertime, the stench from those outhouses was horrible. The only relief from the heat was the well, located about a hundred feet away from the outhouses. The well had a bucket and a single dipper to drink from. Everybody drank from the same dipper. Even in the summer, that well water was cool and refreshing, but that afforded small relief from the blistering heat of an Alabama summer. The congregation, Daddy always said, was just ripe for the picking.

Daddy would set up shop early on Sunday morning. He usually went shopping the Saturday before and bought all types of soda pops. He had something for everyone's taste: RC Cola, Coke, grape, root beer, and orange. He would then go to the ice house over on Government Street in town and buy several big blocks of ice. Mama was always telling Daddy that God was going to strike him down for selling whiskey on Sunday. Daddy always replied the day of the week didn't matter. He was selling to the same people he sold to on Saturdays.

By daybreak on Sunday morning Daddy was ready to go. He would take his two newest and shiniest washtubs and place them on a table in the shade under the big oak tree in the front yard. Everyone from the church could see them there. He would chip up the large blocks of ice and fill the tubs with ice and sodas. Then Daddy would go into the house to get dressed. He would put on his finest outfit. He was dressed for church even though he had no intention of setting foot inside the church. No, today was all about business.

By 9:00 a.m. folks started showing up for service. They came by car, bus, truck, and wagon. Some came on foot. By the time the first preacher got started, the church was filled to capacity with wall-to-wall Christians. No sooner had church started, than people began to take toilet and water breaks. Business was going to be good. The children were the first to get restless in the summer heat and want a drink break. Water from the well was never as satisfying as a soda pop, at least not to the children. So Daddy would start selling sodas right away. Soon the women began to come outside, stand in the shade for a break, then come over and buy a soda from Daddy.

The men, including the deacons, were a different story. They would walk over to Daddy's table where he was selling the soda pop, taking care that none of the churchwomen or children were there. They would casually ask Daddy for a drink. "A drink" was not to be confused with a soda pop. Daddy kept that kind of drink, the moonshine, about ten feet away, near his car. He deliberately kept it out of sight. He also kept cups and extra ice over there. When the women and kids came for soda, they would usually buy a soda, take a few minutes to drink it in the shade, and then go back inside the church to hear more of the sermon. Once the men came outside and got a drink, there was no going back inside for them. They would hang out near Daddy's car and drink liquor all morning. By the time the church let out for the big meeting meal, most of the men were already borderline intoxicated.

Most of the women would have been cooking all week getting ready for the big meeting meal. Everyone wanted to show off her cooking skills. As the preacher began winding down his sermon, the women who prepared dinner, or "boxes" as they called it, would start to slip outside. They wanted to get a jump on each other so they could claim the prize spots to put their boxes on the long wooden tables set up behind the church. During the heat of summer, the best spot on the table meant shade.

By the time the preacher dismissed the congregation the women were ready with their food dishes all laid out. Some of them had fed their families peas and cornbread all week just to be able to make a good showing with chicken or beef or pork for the big meeting. They were all poor, and they all knew it, but they wanted to show their best at the meeting. There were cakes, pies, and puddings. There was also chicken, fried and baked. There were beef roasts, pork roasts, and turkeys. You could look along the table and spot every type of vegetable grown in the area. Food was plentiful that day.

The congregation would form a long line, looking over the boxes and taking a sample from this one or that one or the other. A piece of cake from Miz Tessie, a chicken leg from Miz Maybelle, the choices seemed endless. But some folks' cooking you wouldn't eat under any circumstances. And big meeting Sunday did not change that. Mama always told us whose cooking we were allowed to eat and whose to avoid. Believe me, on big meeting Sunday, Mama knew best. I never could figure out why the forbidden food looked just as appetizing as the food we were allowed to eat.

After fixing a plate, most of the women and children would head over to Daddy's washtubs again to buy something cool to drink. Only a few folks settled for well water. The men, however, would still be sipping on cups of moonshine near Daddy's car. By mealtime the crowd was a bit larger than before. The deacons and the men from the congregation would have been joined by the morning preachers. And there was one other noticeable addition: Miz Rosie had joined the men. Miz Rosie always joined the men and the moonshine. In fact, she was one of Daddy's best customers on Saturdays and Sundays.

By the time folks were finished eating, it was time to go back inside the church for the last sermons of the day. Only about half the people stayed around for the afternoon sermons. The other half packed up their cars with their children, extra plates of food, and drunken husbands and went home. God was good on big meeting Sunday. Christians got religion, food, and moonshine, all at the same time. And Daddy, well, Daddy just got paid.

D. C. Harper's

Butler County was a dry county. It had been dry since almost the beginning of time. When I was growing up, there were more dry counties in the area than wet ones. Wet and dry had absolutely nothing to do with the amount of rainfall we received each year. Wet and dry were the terms to describe whether or not it was legal to sell liquor, not moonshine but regular, store-bought liquor. The sale of moonshine was always illegal in both wet and dry counties. While most of Daddy's customers were local people and establishments, he had a few customers across the county line.

Daddy's local customers ranged from the individual who only wanted a pint or two to the shot house owners who would buy several gallons of liquor each week. The shot house owners made a lot of money from Daddy's moonshine. While he sold liquor to them by the gallon, they sold it to their customers by the shot. The shot house was where regular colored folks could go for fun, discretely of course. They could buy a drink, sometimes listen to a little music, and consort with women of questionable reputations. There were different kinds of shots depending on what the customer could afford. There was a dime shot, a quarter shot, a fifty-cent shot, and for the big spenders, there was the dollar shot. If you had the money, the shot houses had the shot. And there were a number of shot houses around. In our small town, there were probably a dozen or so. Some of them did more business than others. By the same token, Daddy was not the only person in town who made moonshine. He was, however, one of the best.

One of Daddy's customers was located in Crenshaw County, which bordered ours to the east. Crenshaw County was wet, meaning it was legal to sell liquor. It was not really that far away; in fact, the county line was only about fifteen miles from our house. But crossing the county line to deliver moonshine was a challenge—and it took nerve. If you were caught, you had to deal with two jurisdictions and two county sheriffs. But Daddy was not deterred.

This Crenshaw County customer was D. C. Harper. D.C. owned a juke joint for white folks. Unlike shot houses, it was legal to sell liquor at a juke joint. D.C. had a really jumping establishment. White people would come from miles around to dance, party, and drink liquor. The little joint sat close to the road and on Friday and Saturday nights you could see cars parked all down the highway. The place wasn't that large but it was always packed with people. There was always a good time going on inside. D.C.'s customers drank all types of liquor, including moonshine. Daddy stayed busy trying to keep D.C.'s place stocked up.

Since D.C.'s place was a white juke joint, it was for whites only. That meant colored folks were not allowed to go in and party with the white folks. D.C., however, was an equal opportunity businessman. Just because he would not allow colored folks inside his juke joint did not mean he was unwilling to take their money. He was. Colored folks were allowed to go to the back door at D.C.'s place where they could purchase beer, wine, store-bought liquor, or some of Daddy's moonshine. They were allowed to buy the liquor, but they were not allowed to drink it on the property. They had to buy it and move on. Everyone knew there would be trouble if the colored folks hung around too long at D.C.'s place. There was always a steady flow of colored folks at D.C.'s back door. They were steady coming, and steady going, but definitely not staying.

If Daddy wanted to buy liquor from D.C. he would have to go to the back door to get it. But when he was selling moonshine to D.C., he was allowed to carry it in at the front door. Of course Daddy never bought liquor from D.C. But that was the nature of the business. It was acceptable for a black man to walk in the front door to sell liquor, but it was not permissible for him to walk in the front door to buy liquor. No matter, D.C. was a good customer of Daddy's.

The Delivery

Daddy spent most of his waking hours trying to figure out a way to make sure we had food on the table. He alternated his time between making moonshine and working in some white man's field, our field, or at some other low-paying menial job. There was never enough money to support the family, no matter how many different jobs he held. He kept trying, but no matter what Daddy tried to do to get ahead, he always came back to making moonshine. That was the only full-time job he could rely on. It was also something he could do any season, day or night. So when money was tight for us, which was almost all the time, Daddy would fall back on making moonshine to earn a few extra bucks. Folks were always willing to buy moonshine, whether times were hard or times were good. Even when there wasn't money to put food on the table, people would find a way to buy moonshine.

Now making moonshine was the easiest part of the job, aside from the risk associated with manufacturing it. There were always deputies searching far and wide for Daddy's still, but Daddy was too clever for them. At one time or another over the years Daddy had a still located in every hollow and every creek bed from Greenville to Georgiana, and that's the gospel truth. He always managed to stay at least one step ahead of the sheriff. Many of his stills were eventually discovered, but only after Daddy had already abandoned them.

Making the final delivery to customers was the hardest part. The sheriff was always on the lookout hoping to catch Daddy on a delivery run.

Everyone in the county knew who was making the moonshine and who was selling it. They just didn't know how and when the deliveries were made. Daddy got his deliveries down to an art. The sheriff tried everything to catch Daddy. Roadblocks and car searches were commonplace. It became a sort of cat-and-mouse game. But in reality it wasn't a game at all because the stakes were so high. If Daddy was caught he had an awful lot to lose, everything in fact. There were many men behind bars for making moonshine, some for only a year or two and some for much longer. Daddy did not want to join them. He had already come close to going to jail once before. So every delivery he made he was taking a chance with his life, and Daddy always took life very seriously.

Daddy planned everything ahead of time; he left nothing to chance. He checked and double-checked. He mapped out possible escape routes to take in the event that he was cornered by the sheriff on some delivery route. It seemed to me that over the years Daddy got smarter and smarter and the sheriff and his deputies got dumber and dumber. Sometimes I think they didn't really want to catch Daddy at all. I mean, the sheriff and all his deputies were moonshine drinkers themselves. Why on earth would they want to shut down their best supplier?

While there is nothing funny about the prospect of going to jail, there was in fact a time or two when Daddy had a funny run-in with the authorities. Of course such run-ins are only funny after the fact, and only when you come out on top, like Daddy always did. I remember one such run-in that Daddy had with a deputy sheriff.

The day started out in a typical fashion for Daddy. It was a hot summer Saturday afternoon. Daddy had been working hard all week at his regular job, as well as working late into the night at one of his stills making a huge run of moonshine. Every evening after he came home from work he would head off into the woods down below the house. While Mama and all us kids knew exactly where he was going and what he was doing, we never discussed his activities. Like clockwork, Daddy would return to the house late at night, go to bed, get ready for work the next day, and start the whole process over again. By the time Saturday came around, he was ready to make a number of deliveries. The week might turn out to be a rather profitable one, which was not always the case. He had made a good run and had almost fifteen gallons of moonshine to show for his efforts.

While Daddy had been known to deliver moonshine any and every day of the week, Saturday was the day he usually made more than one delivery. On this particular day, he had made a number of deliveries to his customers in the shot houses all around town. On the average he would drop off a gallon or two at each location, each time returning to his still to pick up more moonshine before his next delivery. He never wanted to have more than a gallon or two of moonshine at a time. I suspect this was because such a small amount would be easier to hide should that be necessary. During the deliveries earlier in the day, Daddy had noticed one of the local deputies had been following him, trying very hard not to be noticed. Daddy would simply wait until the deputy stopped following him for a spell, drop off a gallon or two of moonshine, return to his still to get more, and continue on his way. This went on for the better part of the day.

Most of the time the deputies took turns following Daddy around town, so as not to make him suspicious. Of course Daddy was always suspicious. He tried never to let down his guard. The deputy who was following Daddy on this particular Saturday was Deputy Murphy who was a rare character indeed. Let me explain him this way. If Greenville, Alabama, were Mayberry USA, then Deputy Murphy would be Barney, with the one bullet in his pocket. Murphy was the laughingstock of the county. Most folks wondered how he ever became a deputy sheriff in the first place. It wasn't for his genius, that's for sure. Murphy was a tall, slender, red-faced man. He was so thin that his uniform looked more like it was hanging on a clothes hanger instead of draped over the figure of a man. He had dark, stringy, slick hair. It was obvious that he used too much hair oil. Either that or he simply never washed his hair. Considering his body odor it is entirely possible that a lack of soap and water was the cause of his hair problem. Murphy was also a chain-smoker. You rarely saw him without a cigarette hanging from his lips. I don't guess his smoking really set him aside from the others because all the local deputies were chain-smokers. I suppose it went with the job. Murphy carried a gun but most folks doubted that he actually had any bullets in it. Murphy was by no means the top deputy on the force and everyone knew that, including Daddy.

On this particular Saturday, Daddy's last delivery was for one of his

big customers in Georgiana. It was about seven miles south of Greenville but still in Butler County, and still in the jurisdiction of the sheriff
and his deputies. Murphy had been following Daddy around all day but
hadn't stopped him. En route to Georgiana, Daddy noticed Murphy in
his rearview mirror once again. Murphy sped up and got right on Daddy's
bumper. He trailed him close like that for a couple of miles. Daddy was
hauling several gallons of moonshine in a secret compartment under the
backseat of the car and he didn't want to get pulled over for a search.

Suddenly Murphy speeded up and flew past Daddy on his left. In a
flash he was out of sight, still both headed in the direction of Georgiana
and Daddy's waiting customer. Daddy knew for sure that Murphy was
up to something, and sure enough, about a mile down the road there was
Murphy. He had used his police car to place a roadblock at a four-way
stop. There he was, out of the car, lights flashing, and gun drawn. Daddy
was scared to death. Everyone knew Murphy was a kook and not too
bright. A not-too-bright kook with a gun is a very scary thing. For a moment Daddy wondered if Murphy knew Daddy was carrying moonshine
and knew where it was.

Daddy rarely allowed anyone to travel with him on deliveries. This
time, however, he had picked up one of his old buddies for this last run
of the day. Now this guy, Mr. Lewis, wanted no part in Daddy's impend-
ing confrontation with the law and he wasn't shy about letting Daddy
know it. All he did was drink moonshine; he had no intention of going to jail with Daddy for hauling it. By the time they reached the roadblock, Daddy and Mr. Lewis were in a heated argument. Stop. Don't stop.
Run. Don't run. What should they do? As the car slowly came to a stop
they fell silent. Their argument was over. Murphy slowly walked around
to Daddy's side of the car. He had placed his gun back into his holster,
but his hand was still on his gun. No sooner had Daddy rolled down
his window than Murphy stuck his greasy-haired head into the car. He
began to ask Daddy questions: "Where have you been? Where are you
going? What are you doing?" and of course, "Are you hauling any moonshine?" They soon began yelling at each other, and they kept on argu-
ing for what seemed like an eternity to Mr. Lewis.

Finally, Daddy told Murphy to either arrest him or leave him alone. At
the same time Daddy was saying this, he was rolling up the driver's side

window of his car. The only problem was that Murphy's head was still in the window. In less than two seconds Daddy had Murphy's neck caught tight in his window. The color drained from his face and his eyes bulged. He struggled to catch his breath.

Daddy and Mr. Lewis began to argue again. Leave the car and run. Stay in the car and run. One thing was for sure, Daddy didn't want to choke Murphy to death. The punishment for running moonshine was nothing compared to killing a lawman, even an incompetent one like Murphy. So Daddy rolled down the window. For a second or two Murphy just stood there looking dazed, then he fell to the pavement, out cold. Daddy stuck his head out the window and saw that he was still breathing.

For several minutes Daddy and Mr. Lewis just sat there in the car. They were afraid to leave and afraid to stay. They really didn't know what to do next. Before they reached a decision, Murphy began to stir. He rolled around on the ground back and forth for a while and then he got to his feet. He peered in the window on the driver's side of the car and looked right into Daddy's eyes just inches away from his face, not saying a single word. Daddy looked right back at him not saying anything either.

Murphy stood up straight, slapped the side of his hip as if to check for his gun, and then slowly walked around the front of the car to the passenger side where Mr. Lewis was sitting. He stuck his head in Mr. Lewis's window and whispered, "What happened?" "I don't know," replied Mr. Lewis. Murphy slowly stood up again, walked gingerly to his patrol car, got in, turned off his flashing lights, and took off back toward town. Somehow Daddy was able to regain his composure and make his final delivery. Mr. Lewis got out of the car at that last stop and told Daddy he would find another way back to town. I don't suppose Daddy could fault him for that.

Daddy never heard anything about that incident from Mr. Lewis or Deputy Murphy. I guess they both had good reasons to forget about the whole thing. But Daddy never forgot.

IV
The Characters

Black Coffee

Mama Sally was an old, almost-relative who lived down in Bolling. She wasn't really related to us but she was kin of sorts. Mama had an Aunt Alma who was the sister of Mama's mama, Josie. Aunt Alma was married to Uncle Horace. Mama Sally was Uncle Horace's mother. As I said, almost kinfolk.

Mama Sally lived alone in a small wood frame house in Bolling, off Highway 31. Her house was down a bumpy, winding dirt road. Once you turned onto the dirt road off 31 you had to go past several other small houses to get to hers, including Uncle Horace and Aunt Alma's house.

My first memory of Mama Sally is of a very old woman. She seemed to be in relatively good health even though she used a walking stick to help her get around. She used that same stick for disciplining that old dog of hers. So I am not really sure if the stick was more for walking or for hitting, but you never saw her without it. She had a small yard and the only peculiar thing about it was that it was completely void of grass. There wasn't a blade of grass anywhere. I don't know how she kept it that way but it was obviously deliberate. In that part of the south, in midsummer, grass grew everywhere. There was one more peculiar thing about Mama Sally's house. Her well was right at the front door. Most wells were much farther away from the house than hers. I had never seen a well right at the front door before.

Once you saw Mama Sally's house and yard you knew right away that she had a green thumb. While there was no grass to be seen, there were plants everywhere. Her house was surrounded by flowers. There were baskets hanging from every free plank on the house. But she had more than potted plants. The yard was filled with trees and flowers of all sorts. She had every kind of fruit tree you could name: peach trees, plum trees, fig trees, apricot, pear, and apple trees. And in summer they would all be in full bloom. There was always the smell of fresh blossoms in the air or of fruits ripening on the trees all around her house.

Mama Sally kept a vegetable garden as well. Even though she was old, she did all the work in her own garden. Her garden wasn't very large but it was productive. The size of her vegetables was unbelievable. They were huge. Her carrots were eighteen inches long on average. She grew heads of cabbage the size of basketballs and that's no exaggeration. I don't know how she did it but she did. Her entire garden was protected from all the animals by a wooden fence that included a large wooden gate, with a latch. As I recall, the gate was extremely heavy. Of course it may have just seemed heavy because I was so small. Mama Sally used to keep a hoe propped up against that old heavy gate. I guess she kept it handy in case she wanted to work in the garden on the spur of the moment.

Mama would go about twice a month to see Mama Sally. While Mama was visiting, us kids would usually stay outside in the yard and play games. We had been visiting Mama Sally for years before I realized why we went to visit so often. I had thought it was strange that whenever we went to visit, she always had other company. She never seemed to be alone. I just thought a lot of people loved her and that's why she had so much company. I did find it strange that her company never congregated or sat and visited with her together. Everybody took turns. Sometimes when we would go to visit on a Saturday morning, it would be well past afternoon before Mama could get in to see her. If Mama had to wait a long time we would get restless.

It didn't matter much to Mama how restless we got. We did not leave until Mama had her visit. Once when I was about eight or nine I remember going inside with Mama on a visit. This time I paid attention; I actually eavesdropped.

Mama and I followed Mama Sally inside the small frame house into the front room. The room was tiny, but adequate for a single old lady. We all sat down, then after Mama and Mama Sally had exchanged greetings they drifted to one corner in the room. In that corner was a wood-burning stove with a small battered coffeepot sitting on top of it. There was a small table right next to the stove, which had an old tin on it. There were also several spoons, an old rag, a bucket of water, and a couple of coffee cups that were very old and stained. The cups looked like they had been around for as long as Mama Sally had, which was a very long time. I could see the small handle of the dipper hanging out of the water bucket. Ignoring the array of spoons on the table, Mama Sally removed the lid from the tin and reached inside with her bare hand. When she pulled her hand out, it was filled with ground coffee. With her empty hand she removed the lid of the small coffeepot and threw the coffee into the dry pot. Then she grabbed the handle of the dipper, poured two small dippers of water into the pot, and replaced the lid. She then took the old rag from the table, used it as a shield against the heat as she opened the door to the stove, stirred the coals, and closed the door.

Without speaking, she and Mama went outside on the porch for a few minutes. I followed them. They talked about flowers and trees for a while then went back inside the house. Again I followed. By the time we got back inside, the coals in the stove had started to burn enough to heat the coffee in the pot, which was still sitting on the stove.

Mama Sally took one of the dingy cups that had been sitting upside down on the table. With the same rag she had used to open the stove door, she lifted the coffeepot off the stove and poured a few tablespoons of coffee into the cup. She swished the coffee around and around in the cup, coating the bottom and insides of the cup with coffee, then turned the cup upside down on the small table. The coffee spilled right out onto the table and dripped onto the floor.

After a few seconds had passed, Mama Sally turned the cup right side up and looked at the coffee grounds stuck to the bottom and sides of the cup. She showed the inside of the cup to Mama and began pointing at and talking about the coffee grounds. I saw only a dirty cup that was in desperate need of soap and water, but Mama Sally saw a scene unfolding before her eyes. As she pointed, she described the scene to Mama, telling her about the people, places, things, and events she saw in the cup. Mama listened closely, nodding now and then as if she understood what Mama Sally was saying. Some of the people they were talking about were names that were familiar to me. But Mama Sally was not only telling Mama what those people had done in the past but also what they were currently doing and what they would be doing in the future. I marveled that all that information was inside one little cup. No wonder Mama would wait for hours to see Mama Sally. An old lady with all that vision was wonderful indeed.

Mama Sally, of course, was a fortune-teller, able to tell the future by reading coffee grounds in an old dirty cup. I am not sure what her accuracy rate was in predicting the future, but I know Mama swore by her. The only thing I can swear is that Mama Sally grew the biggest vegetables I have ever seen.

Shoot Me, Miz Joe

My family came in contact with a number of colorful characters. Most of them were family and friends. And as I remember, there were none more colorful than Miz Rosie who lived about a half mile from us. Her huge house was on the dirt road, right behind the railroad tracks. It was one of those so-called shotgun houses. You could look in the front door and see all the way through the house and out the back door. The house sat high off the ground on pillars. It was high enough for a short man to walk under it without bending. She and her husband, Mr. Spoke, lived there together on Mr. Buck Henderson's place. Mr. Buck was a wealthy old white man who owned a lot of land in the area. He also owned several fish ponds, one of which was right in front of Miz Rosie's house near the tracks. That pond was a favorite fishing hole of my brother Floyd and me. Mr. Buck would occasionally allow us to fish there for brim. On a good day, Floyd and I could bring home a five-gallon bucket filled to the top with brim. They were all good frying-pan size, about the size of an adult's hand. While Miz Rosie might be called a friend of the family, she was actually more a friend of Daddy's than Mama's. She was one of Daddy's best moonshine customers and drinking buddies.

To say that Miz Rosie had a drinking problem would be an understatement. She drank all the time. I believe I saw her drunk more times than I saw her sober. She could outdrink any man. I suppose she had a right. You see, she could also outwork any man. Miz Rosie was a very large woman. She was bigger and stronger than any man I knew. Most of the work she did was as a field hand. She picked cotton, chopped tobacco, whatever the men did. If it was hard work that only required muscles, she could do it. She also worked in the fields baling hay. She could pick up a bale of hay weighing in excess of two hundred pounds by herself and throw it on the back of a wagon. That woman was strong. She worked hard, drank hard, and prayed hard.

Mama didn't care much for Miz Rosie; actually I think she was a little afraid of her. I don't think she was afraid just because she was such a physically powerful woman. People said that Miz Rosie worked roots, and Mama didn't want to mess with anyone who messed with roots. Miz Rosie used to do little things to test Mama, like the thing with the flour. She came to the house one day and asked Mama if she could borrow a bowl of flour. She even brought her own bowl. Of course Mama loaned her the flour but she was puzzled because there was an old country store closer to Miz Rosie's house than our house was. And Mama knew she had an account at that store. Nevertheless, Mama gave her the flour anyway. The next day Miz Rosie returned the borrowed bowl of flour. Already suspicious, Mama hid the flour away in a special place. A couple of days later, she came back to borrow another bowl of flour and again she returned it the next day. Mama had given her the same bowl of flour that she had returned the first time. This went on about three or four times, passing that same flour back and forth. Each time Mama would give Miz Rosie back her own flour. After a while Miz Rosie just broke down and asked Mama if she was loaning her the same flour time after time. When Mama told her that she was, her only response was, "You're a funny woman, Miz Joe." Mama told us later that she might be funny but she wasn't dumb. I still don't know what Miz Rosie was doing with the flour, but Mama was sure that she was up to no good.

Mama had good reason to be suspicious of Miz Rosie. There had also been an incident with the dog. Miz Rosie had made a dinner box one Sunday for the big meeting at Old Elam Church. Our family had not gone to revival that Sunday. But Miz Rosie had made a plate from her box and made a special trip to give it to Mama. There was no way Mama was going to eat anything made special for her, not by Miz Rosie. Mama wouldn't let us kids eat some folk's cooking, and she definitely followed her own advice. Mama accepted the plate graciously. As soon as Miz Rosie went out the front door; Mama was out the back door with that plate of food. It was unfortunate that the dog was out back. Mama gave the plate to the dog and thought nothing else of it, at least not until the dog started barking and running around and around the house.

The dog didn't stop running and barking until well into the early morning hours of the next day. The next morning, when Daddy went out to feed the dog, he was dead. Go figure. Mama was sure that Miz Rosie's food had something to do with it, and after Miz Rosie's next visit, I was sure of it too. You see, Miz Rosie came to visit about a week later. When she got to the house she seemed surprised to see Mama. The first thing she said to Mama was, "You didn't eat that plate I made for you did you?" After the incident with the dog Mama stayed clear of Miz Rosie. She also warned Daddy to stay away from her. Daddy said she was just a moonshine customer and he wasn't worried. It was then that Mama put her foot down and told Daddy to keep all his "customers" away from the house.

Miz Rosie tried the same stunt with Mama and a box of snuff as she did with the flour. She and Mama both dipped snuff, and Miz Rosie started borrowing and returning snuff. This drove Mama absolutely wild. By this time Miz Rosie had worn out her welcome with Mama. The final straw came one day when Mama had been away from the house. She returned to find Daddy and Miz Rosie in the kitchen with a bottle of moonshine. When she saw Mama coming, she jumped up from the table and tried to get out of the house before Mama saw her. But it was too late. She ran out the front door, made a misstep, and fell flat on her face in the front yard. Mama was fit to be tied. And that is just what she wanted to do to Miz Rosie and Daddy. Tie them, with a rope around their necks, both of them.

But the Lord does indeed work in mysterious ways. When Miz Rosie tripped, she fell into a nest of fire ants, a big one. In no time she was yelling and screaming at the top of her voice. Daddy tried to pick her up, but she was twice his size and every time he got her almost up on her feet, she fell right back into the anthill. She was tossing and turning and rolling from side to side on the ground, covered with fire ants, unable to get up.

She was screaming for help. She was totally helpless. Like a typical child, I thought that was about the funniest thing I had ever seen in my short life. Miz Rosie wasn't laughing.

Mama, meanwhile, figured Miz Rosie was getting exactly what she deserved. I can't swear to it, but I thought I saw Mama laughing herself. After a little while Mama went inside and got the insect spray gun, the kind with a pump handle. We mainly used the gun to kill flies and mosquitoes. When Miz Rosie saw Mama coming with the spray gun in her hand, she started yelling even louder. "Help! Help! Shoot me, Miz Joe. Shoot me. Shoot me, Miz Joe. Shoot me." Mama did. Finally, Miz Rosie struggled to her feet and headed for home, half a mile down the road. Mama never had any trouble out of Miz Rosie after that. She was still one of Daddy's customers, all right, but she must have done her drinking at home. I know one thing for sure, she didn't mess with Mama anymore.

Mr. Steve

Mr. Steve, one of our neighbors, was tall, slim, very dark skinned, and walked with a severe limp. He had lost a leg, long before my time, and had been fitted with a wooden leg that seemed to be much too short for his tall frame. Many different tales were told about how he lost his leg. I don't know if any of those tales were true, but for sure he had a wooden leg. He and his family lived about a quarter of a mile down the road from us. His house was on a small piece of land, not large enough to grow much of anything of his own, but he did the best he could with what he had and he always seemed to have something planted in his small garden.

Mr. Steve's house sat at a fork in the road, an old dirt road that went winding through the woods for miles and eventually ended up in town. Mr. Steve was the primary sugarcane juice extractor for the area. People brought their sugarcane to him from miles around to have the juice extracted. Everyone in the area seemed to be good at doing something. I suppose sugarcane was Mr. Steve's expertise. People usually brought sugarcane to him in a wagon drawn by mules or horses. During the summer and early fall, it was common to see mounds of sugarcane piled up near his house. Some of the mounds were so large that they were almost as tall as his small tin-roofed house. Most of the power for the sugarcane operation came from a mule. Mr. Steve never got paid much money to make the juice for folks, because people didn't usually have much money. Instead they would mostly pay him by sharing the juice with him. He would normally extract the juice and charge a percentage of the juice for

Mr. Steve's mule circled around and around the sugarcane extractor, which drew the juice from the sugarcane stalks.

his work. Later he would sell his portion of the juice for the money to support his family.

The procedure for extracting the juice was fairly simple. The sugarcane stalks were cut down and the husks were removed. It was important to remember to cut the stalks of cane as close to the ground as possible. The portion of the cane stalks closest to the root was the sweetest. Extracting every possible drop of juice from each stalk of sugarcane was also important. After the cane had been harvested, Mr. Steve would cut the stalks into sections about three feet long. These sections were pushed into one end of the extractor. As the mule circled the device, the cane would be drawn inside. The cane was then pressed in a vice and the juice crushed out of it. The juice fell into a bucket waiting below; the empty shell of the cane fell to the ground and accumulated in a pile.

Sugar cane extraction had few hazards. One was the yellow jackets that, along with honeybees, were everywhere around the operation. They loved sugarcane juice as much or more than I did. Sometimes they would get caught up in the extraction device and become a part of the delectable juice. I saw it happen. But I wiped that thought out of my mind when I drank the juice. Another hazard was rats. They congregated around the mounds of discarded juice-free cane stalks. But the rats didn't remain around long after the stalks were removed.

The cane juice could be drunk as is. It tasted pretty good that way. But it was used primarily to make cane sugar and cane syrup. Syrup was a staple in my family's diet, as well as a lot of families in the area. On most days we ate syrup at each meal. Everyone loved syrup with biscuits, but my brother Floyd even ate it on cornbread. While syrup was great with hot biscuits and butter, we kids thought it was even better cooked in a pan on top of the stove until it hardened. That was the homemade candy Mama would make for us. Homemade candy was generally the only candy we got. There just wasn't enough money for store-bought candy. After all the juice was pressed from the cane stalks, the dry, juiceless shell would be fed to the farm animals. For those fortunate enough to have animals, it was always a struggle to find enough food for them. The goats and mules enjoyed eating the cane shells.

Daddy grew a large field of sugarcane each year for us. We had a lot more land to farm than Mr. Steve. Daddy took all our sugarcane to Mr. Steve to be processed, just as everyone else in the neighborhood did. Since we only lived about a quarter of a mile down the road, Mr. Steve would sometimes bring his mule and wagon to our house to pick up the cane. The kids would load the wagon for him. Daddy would pay him in juice, just like everyone else did. But Daddy would always take the cane shells home as well as the juice. He never threw away anything that we could use on the farm.

Working with sugarcane was only one of Mr. Steve's ways of making a living. I don't recall him ever having a formal job at all, but I do remember him always having something to do with vegetables.

During the summer months, Mr. Steve would make a trip to town every day to sell vegetables. Since he didn't raise many vegetables on his own, the vegetables he sold were usually received as payment from his cane juice operation. He always seemed to have something to sell. The trip to town had to be hard for him; Greenville was at least seven miles away. He made that trip each day with his mule and wagon. You could hear the *clomp, clomp, clomp* of his mule approaching from a long way off. His wagon was so old and tattered that you could hear the wooden planks in the bottom rubbing together as the wagon went by. It sounded as if it would fall apart at any moment, but it never did. You could just about tell the time by Mr. Steve's comings and goings. He headed to town around 5:00 a.m.; I could hear the clomping of the mule's feet on the roadway while I was still in bed. He always returned around 6:00 p.m.

My younger sister, Diane, and I loved that old wagon. We would hitch a ride on it at every opportunity, which was a lot. After all he passed by our house twice a day. We never got up early enough to catch a morning ride, but Diane and I would listen for him every evening and go out to the road to wait for him. When he got in front of our house there would be a loud "Hold up there mule," and the mule would stop. We would jump on the back of the wagon, and after a "Giddy up now," we would ride the quarter of a mile to Mr. Steve's house, only to hop off the wagon and walk back home. Mr. Steve did not fare well selling his vegetables; he returned most evenings with about as many vegetable on the wagon as he had left with in the morning. But some way, somehow, he always took care of his family.

Mr. Gary's Clothes

I have fond memories of Mr. Gary. That might seem strange to most people considering the fact that I knew very little about him. Actually, Mr. Gary was a man I saw only once a year. He was a visitor from the North they say. There were some years in fact that I did not actually see him at all. But without ever laying eyes on him, I could tell for certain that he had paid us a visit down South. By us, I mean my family and neighbors in the surrounding community.

Mr. Gary was a northerner, but I was told that he had not always been one. Like most colored folks from the North, he had southern roots. He and his family had at one time lived in our area, somewhere around Greenville. I heard he had many relatives who still lived near by but I never knew who they were. Many years earlier, he had moved north. He left Alabama in an effort to make a better living for his family. He had traded in the cotton fields, corn fields, and pecan orchards for the city life and the promise of a blue-collar factory job. Colored folks could actually make a living in the North. And from what people said, Mr. Gary had made a much better living than he could have if he had chosen to stay in Greenville. There were some factory jobs in Greenville, at the mill and such; however, they all belonged to white folks. Colored folks were relegated to field work or, at best, housekeeping jobs.

Mr. Gary came to visit in late summer or early fall of each year. It was normally just after school had started. I don't know exactly what he did for a living up north or whether he actually had one of those fancy factory jobs that folks talked about. I do know what he did for us—my large family and the other poor black families in the Wald community—because when he came down south, he never came empty-handed. In fact, he never came with an empty truck. He owned a truck, which he drove down to Alabama each year. While he drove several trucks down over the years, he drove the light blue one more years than most. I remember that old truck quite well. The truck body was light blue with an extremely long bed. It had a large blue and white camper attached to the bed. There was one small window vent on each side of the camper, and at the back of the camper, there was a small door, with an even smaller window right in the middle of it. The tailgate of the truck had been removed to facilitate the opening and closing of the camper door. It was apparent that the camper was used more for hauling than camping. Those windows and the door were so small that camping in that old thing would have been quite uncomfortable. I never heard of Mr. Gary doing any camping at all, only hauling. But in those days I never heard of any colored folks going camping. Most of us lived partially out of doors anyway. To actually go camping would have been downright dumb.

Mr. Gary's camper carried a precious cargo, all the way from the North. His cargo was neither gold nor money, but valuable none the less. His precious cargo was clothes. He would drive the several hundred miles from the North in an old truck with a camper on back that was filled to the brim with clothes. That camper was literally packed wall to wall with clothes. The darn camper would be stuffed so tightly with clothing that when he opened the door for the first time it would be like an explosion had taken place. Clothes would actually blow out of the camper door with a tremendous force because they had been packed in so tightly. How Mr. Gary got them all in the truck in the first place is anyone's guess.

Clothes were precious items for everyone in the neighborhood. New clothes were something none of the poor families could afford. In my family we got hand-me-downs from the white folks Mama and Daddy worked for. This was clothing that was tossed out after the white families had no further use for it. Most of the items were already worn past any further use. After the white folks would hand them down to our family, they were handed down again by my older sisters and brothers to me, the twelfth of thirteen children. Most people cannot imagine what clothing handed down that much actually looked like.

When Mr. Gary arrived in Alabama, his first stop was usually at Miz May Belle's house. They were a colored family almost as large as ours, and they were definitely just as poor. They lived about a half mile away from our house on a dirt road, near Mr. Steve's place. Mr. Gary almost always came when all the neighborhood children were in school. Maybe that was when he took a vacation from his job, whatever that job might have been. I don't know why he stopped at Miz May Belle's house first. I thought that Mr. Gary might have been distant relatives of theirs and that maybe he was giving them first pick at the clothes. I don't know. It didn't really matter much to us anyway who got first pick of the clothes because Mr. Gary brought more than enough for everyone in the neighborhood.

I remember all of Mr. Gary's trips down south to visit, but I remember one of his trips in particular. It was a school day in early fall, about the same time of year he usually came to visit. My family rode the bus the fourteen miles round-trip to go to the segregated school in Greenville. By the time the bus got to the Wald community, there were only a handful of families left on the bus. There was mine, Miz May Belle's, and a couple of others. As the school bus rounded a curve on the dusty dirt road headed for home, Mr. Gary's truck came into view. It was parked in Miz May Belle's yard directly in front of her house. I could tell right away that it was his truck. Not just because I recognized the truck, but by the cargo it had been carrying. I could see from the bus there were clothes everywhere. There were mounds and mounds of them scattered all over the yard. There were clothes on the bushes, tree branches, grass, and shrubs. There were armloads of them still piled up on Mr. Gary's truck where the tailgate should be. Even the ground was covered with clothes. The sight was breathtaking. It was Christmas in September. I was concentrating so hard on the clothes that were scattered all about the yard that I almost missed seeing Mr. Gary leaning against the rear fender of the truck. I was keeping my eye on those clothes, as if they might up and disappear if I even blinked. God I was so excited.

The already noisy bus got louder with the cheers at the sight of Mr. Gary and his cargo. Everyone was excited. I could not remember the last time I had gotten a new dress, blouse, or pair of pants. It could very well have been Mr. Gary's visit last year since I had new clothing. A new dress to me did not mean that it had just been bought at the store. It only meant that I had not already seen it worn completely to pieces by an older sister. "New" meant the clothes were new to the family.

Once Miz May Belle's kids got off the bus, it would be thirty minutes before my sisters, brothers, and I could get off the bus at home and walk back to have a go at the clothes. For a moment I was terrified that I might not get an opportunity to pick through the clothes and find that special outfit, that something just for me. But there was really no need for me to worry. There were plenty of clothes to go around. Enough for everyone to make a good selection. And there wasn't anyone in the neighborhood my size. I was so tiny that any clothes that fit me could not possibly fit anyone else. Even so I couldn't wait to get back to the clothes.

That five-minute bus ride to our house seemed to take forever. By the time the bus pulled up to our house, we were all standing in the aisles. We ran inside the house, dropped off our school books, and within thirty seconds we were headed on foot back to Miz May Belle's house, where Mr. Gary and the clothes were waiting for us.

My sisters, brothers, and I were so excited when we arrived back at Miz May Belle's, we began going through the mounds and mounds of clothes immediately. There was something for everyone. There were dresses, pants, skirts, shirts, and blouses. There were even jackets, sweaters, and coats, in all sizes imaginable. Even though our winters were mild, a new jacket was a welcome addition to any wardrobe. As we began to pick through the large selection of clothes, we began to make little individual piles of the items that we had selected. I, like everyone else, began to make a pile. I remember my first selection. It was a red cotton shirt. It had short sleeves and little white buttons down the front. It had a white collar with red trim. In my eyes it was beautiful. I had never seen anything quite like it. I know for sure that Mama would never have been able to buy anything like it for me. It must have cost a fortune new. I tried to imagine the pretty little girl who had once worn it. I couldn't imagine why she would ever give it up. I knew that I would never give up my beautiful red shirt.

For the next couple of hours my sisters, brothers, and I along with the rest of the community carefully went through the mounds of clothes spread over Miz May Belle's yard. Meticulously we picked different articles of clothing for ourselves. Our individual piles grew larger and larger. Before we had finished going through the clothes, Mama arrived to lend us a hand. She was even able to find a thing or two for herself. She never bought anything for herself. When money was available, she always thought of us kids first. Not to worry, however; Mr. Gary's cargo always had a piece or two that she wanted to take home as well. Mama was also able to find a pair of pants or two for Daddy. There were clothes enough for everyone, men, women, and children. It was just like one of the stores in town, except we didn't have to pay. By the time the evening was done, my family, as well as most of the Wald community, had managed to find enough articles of clothing to get us through the year until Mr. Gary came again.

When we finished collecting all our priceless articles of clothing, they were tied up in bundles. Some of the bundles were so large they were difficult to carry, but carry them we did. It was a happy, heavy trip back home with our new clothes. By the time the community of families left Miz May Belle's house, all the clothes were gone. There was not a single shirt, dress, or pair of pants left. Everything that Mr. Gary had brought with him had been claimed. Each and every piece of clothing was slated to be worn by a needy person until it actually fell apart. I know that is what I planned to do with my new red shirt. Absolutely nothing would go to waste. Even though the clothes that Mr. Gary had brought us last year were completely worn to bits they would not be wasted either. Mama made use of everything. The old clothes that could no longer be patched and repaired would be cut up into small pieces of cloth for Mama's quilting operation. The clothing that once kept our bodies warm would end up as beautiful quilts to warm our cold bodies on Alabama winter nights.

I never knew why Mr. Gary did what he did. Why would he make a long trip down south every year to bring secondhand clothes to the poor needy families in the community? What could he gain from such a trip? I don't know why he did it. But I do know that what he did was a blessing to the entire community. The clothes that he brought meant a lot more than words could say to a large number of people who had no means to buy clothing. The clothes that he brought were all secondhand, but you could not prove it by us. To my family and the other families in the area, they were all like new. The clothes brought dignity to a community that had little else. I often wonder how my family would have made it without Mr. Gary's generous helping hand. I thank God I never had to find out. Mr. Gary was a kind man, and I will remember him always. I will also remember that red cotton shirt, the one with the little white buttons down the front, and the white collar with the red trim. Mr. Gary blessed us all.

Please, Lord, Help the Bear

Mr. Willie Gregory was a nice old fellow from what I can remember. As I recall he was a kind gentleman never causing much of a stir or gathering much attention to himself. You could hear Mr. Gregory and his mule coming from nearly a mile away. *Clip, clip, clop, clop,* the slow stride of his mule could put you to sleep. But the *clank, clank, clank* of his rusty, ragged old wagon would wake you up again. Most wagons back then sounded like they were about on their last legs. Though in many ways they were a relic of the past, they were still a part of the everyday lives of poor people.

Like most black folks in those times, Mr. Gregory barely scratched out a living from one year to the next. He worked at odd jobs, grew vegetables, did just about anything to earn a little money. He was a tall man, and his skin was very dark. This was not surprising since he spent most of his time outdoors in the hot sun. He was very thin, so thin in fact that he might have been suffering from some sort of malnutrition problem. He was just pretty much like any other old black man except for one thing. His legs were extremely long and his torso was extremely short. From his neck to his groin couldn't have measured more than ten or twelve inches. This made him a really odd-looking fellow. He had been that way all his life. His friends and neighbors were used to how he looked and knew it made no difference to the kind of man he was. Mr. Gregory lived for many years with his brother Ruben. Ruben was well dressed and rather handsome, not at all like his brother Willie. There was never a hair or an article of clothing out of place. Ruben was a teacher and in those days a teacher was a person to be respected in the colored community, because there were still so many folks who could not read and write.

After the stock market crash of 1929 people lost their trust in the American banking establishments. Even poor folks who had very little money to begin with had no faith in banks. I guess those with the least were also the ones who had the most to lose if things went sour. Many folks, rich and poor, resorted to keeping their money at home or at least somewhere near home. There were always stories being told about folks burying their life savings in secret hiding places. While the stories might vary, the hiding places were generally the same: a secret place in a wall, a hidden spot under the floor, a special nook in an attic, or a hole at the foot of an old oak tree. There were also many stories where the hiding place turned out to be in a well. Why on earth would anyone hide a fortune in a well? To me a well was a good hiding place for a cool drink of water and nothing else. Apparently some folks thought it was also a good place to hide money.

Wherever there are stories about buried treasure there are stories about treasure hunters. And with the average salary for colored folks set at twenty-five cents a day, if that much, it was every colored man's dream to find some long-lost fortune of some long-forgotten soul. If nothing else it was something to dream of and just the thought could keep an old body going while toiling away at some hot, seemingly endless task.

Willie Gregory played a part in many of the local treasure-hunting stories, either as a storyteller or as an active participant. I remember folks talking about one occasion when he clearly played both roles. It was many years ago in early summer. Mr. Willie and a bunch of poor colored men much like himself were all just hanging out discussing what it might be like to be rich. Of course being rich to them was having more the fifty cents to rub together. This was in the days where most of them rarely had two pennies in their pockets.

There had been stories for some time about an old hermit who had buried money, his life savings, deep in the woods and had not been able to retrieve it before his death. The money was there just waiting for someone to come along and find it. A lot of folks repeated the story, but not many of them took it seriously, at least not seriously enough to go looking for it. But it is amazing what one can believe after mixing together hot sun and moonshine. After three or four drinks, the part of the story where the treasure was being guarded by a red-eyed devil had no power to deter them. So Mr. Willie and his friends made a pact to go home, retrieve digging tools, picks, shovels, and the like, and meet at the edge of the woods at dusk. Clearly the effect of the liquor had not worn off at dusk because they all appeared at the appointed time, ready to go to work.

After traveling a mile or so deep into the woods, led by Mr. Willie, they reached their destination. One by one they took turns digging into the sun-baked earth. They dug down one foot, then two, then three. They dug for hours and slowly reached a point where after taking a turn digging it was increasingly difficult to get out of the hole without help from the men up top. Though the men talked and joked among themselves, they kept a watchful eye on their surroundings. They never forgot that they were colored men with picks and shovels on a white man's land in the middle of the night. If they were caught, it would be very hard to explain to the sheriff what they were doing. Very hard indeed.

The digging went on. It was sometime after midnight when Mr. Willie found himself back in the deep hole taking his turn with the shovel. They had been digging for hours and still there was no sign of the buried treasure they were all so eagerly anticipating. After a while Mr. Willie stopped digging. He listened closely to the night around him. It took him a moment or so before he realized what was wrong. It was the silence. The loud laughter and chatter that had been going on all night between the men was gone. All he could hear was the call of crickets. Mr. Willie was afraid. He was afraid to call out to his friends and afraid not to.

After standing for what seemed like twenty or thirty minutes but was probably not more than a few seconds, Mr. Willie gathered enough courage to lay the shovel down and look toward the top of the hole where he had last seen his friends. His friends had vanished. Where could they be? They had left him alone in the hole without a single word. He slowly turned around with his eyes fixed upward in search of a friendly face but there wasn't one to be found. They were all gone; they had left him. When he heard a noise behind him at the top of the hole, he turned to see where the noise was coming from.

Mr. Willie did not want to believe his eyes. A huge dark figure stood at the top of the hole behind him. He had never seen anything like it. It was a large bearlike creature with two large red eyes. It appeared to have four legs, but it stood upright at the top of the hole on its two hind legs. The creature did not make a sound. Mr. Willie was scared to death. He didn't know what to do. He backed up in the hole until his back was firmly against the wall on the opposite side from where the large creature was standing. The creature watched every step that Mr. Willie took. To and fro, side to side, those big red eyes watched his every move.

He stood still for a while pondering his next move. But Mr. Willie knew what his next move had to be. He had to get out of that hole and head for home. He hadn't noticed right away but obviously the effects of the moonshine had worn off. He was thinking clearly now, clearly enough to be deathly afraid. He began to claw franticly at the sides of the hole in an effort to climb up the sides. The last time he had climbed out of the hole, he had had help from his friends; now he had only his fear and determination to give him strength. Each time he climbed part of the way out of the hole he would lose his grip on the soil and fall back down to the bottom. Each time he fell back in the hole, he would look up to see the large bearlike creature standing there, staring down at him with those big red eyes. Over and over again he tried to get out of the hole, and each time he landed right back where he had started.

After resting for a moment in the bottom of the hole he started once again to claw his way up the sides of the hole. This time he was determined to free himself. Right hand, left hand, right foot, left foot he inched his way up the side of the hole. Finally his right hand reached the top of the hole and he felt grass under his palm. Then his left hand touched grass. Mr. Willie pulled his short torso up and over the top edge of the hole and with his remaining strength he flung his legs up and over the top as well. He was out of the hole.

He lay there at the top for a moment catching his breath before he remembered that getting out of the hole was only part of his problem. For a second he had forgotten that there was a red-eyed creature waiting there for him once he reached the top. He quickly sprang to his feet and stared across the hole at the creature on the other side. As Mr. Willie began to back up, the creature moved slowly around the hole in Mr. Willie's direction. Mr. Willie turned slowly then took off like a flash of lightning through the woods. The trees and bushes were scratching and tearing at his clothes and flesh as he ran. He ran for at least a couple hundred yards before he stopped to catch his breath and see if the creature was still following him. Sure enough, he could see those large red eyes bouncing getting closer and closer to him. It was just as he had feared. The creature was chasing him.

Mr. Willie took two deep breaths of the cool summer night's air and started out again, running as fast as he could through the woods. He knew where he was when he started out, but he was clearly lost now. He wasn't paying a lot of attention to his surroundings as he ran and with good reason of course. He simply wanted to get out of the woods. At one point he attempted to jump over a fallen log, tripped, fell, and landed flat on his back. Before he could get up, there it was. The creature was staring down at him with those frightful eyes. Mr. Willie began to fight. He scratched and clawed and struggled until he was able to get to his feet again. Then he took off running.

As the sun began to come up over the horizon, Mr. Willie saw a clearing in the woods and for the first time in hours he recognized his surroundings. He was approaching Old Elam Baptist Church, the small, wood frame colored church that sat close to the woods. He half walked and half climbed to the church and sat on the steps. Surely the creature would not attack him there, not at the house of the Lord. He was safe at last.

That's how Mama found Mr. Willie Gregory early one Sunday morning in the early part of the summer, on the steps of Old Elam Baptist Church. Our house was just shouting distance from the church. Mama was up early that morning just as she was most mornings making breakfast for us kids. She looked out the front room window and saw a torn, tattered, and bleeding figure sitting on the steps of the church. She was a little afraid to investigate on her own but she felt she had to. Daddy wasn't home. He was on one of his many trips up north working in a factory trying to make money to send home to us to make ends meet. So it was just Mama and the kids, and somebody had to see what was going on at the church.

Mama left the house and slowly walked toward Old Elam. As she drew closer she recognized the tattered and bloody figure as Mr. Willie. She yelled out to him, keeping her distance asking if he was all right. Mr. Willie realized he was safe. He stood up and took a step toward Mama, who stopped dead in her tracks. Whatever he had been tangled with had gotten not only the best of him but also the best of his clothes. Mr. Willie was naked from the waist down. Mama slowly backed away telling Mr. Willie that she was going inside to get him something to put on.

She returned moments later with a pair of Daddy's old pants and a shirt. She balled them up in a tight wad and threw them in his direction. He quickly put them on and slowly walked toward the house. Bloody, tattered, and torn, he was a sight to see, and Daddy's pants barely reached past his knees. He slowly followed Mama into the house. He sat down at the kitchen table and allowed Mama to tend the wounds about his head and face. He asked Mama for a cup of coffee, and she obliged. As he drank his coffee he told the story of his terrifying ordeal. He began the story with the drinking earlier in the day and went on to recall every detail of what happened next. He was telling his story to Mama but at least eight additional pairs of ears were listening. All in all, it was clear that he felt very lucky to be alive. It was difficult to believe the story as he told it. But it was definitely not hard to believe that Mr. Willie had indeed been in a fight for his life with someone or something.

Mr. Willie and his friends did not find buried treasure in the woods that night, but they did find something. Mr. Willie's friends all told the same story of being accosted at the top of the hole by a large, red-eyed, bearlike creature. They all did what any man would have done under the circumstances. They ran like hell for dear life. Mr. Willie said he didn't have any ill feelings toward his friends for running off and leaving him in the hole the way they did. That may be. But one thing is for sure, he never went treasure hunting with that group of friends again.

Mr. Willie continued for many years in his search for the elusive buried treasure. I can't say for sure if he ever found any of the treasure that he searched for most of his life, but it would be a good guess that he never found a dime.

I think Mr. Willie has gone on to heaven now. He is probably wandering around up there with a pick and shovel in his hand looking for treasure with his new friends. I don't know if fights actually break out in heaven; maybe they do. But I am not worried about Mr. Willie; he can take care of himself. So if a fight should break out between Mr. Willie and some red-eyed bearlike creature, please, Lord, help the bear.

Miz Lady Bug

Miz Lady Bug was a strange and colorful character. She was a nice old lady and a friend of my family when I knew her. I am not sure where she got the name Miz Lady Bug, but that is what everyone called her. Her real name was Miz Pearlie Reed and she lived about a mile up the road from us. She and her husband lived together in a huge old house on Mr. Buck Henderson's place.

Miz Lady Bug's house sat high off the ground on huge stone pillars. It was a large wood frame house, with a porch that completely surrounded it. The roof was made of tin, like most houses were back then. And in the middle of the summer that old tin roof could be seen from miles away glistening in the sunlight. At some angles it shone so bright it was simply blinding. Instead of glass windows, the windows all had wooden shutters that had to be opened early each day just to let in a little air and sunlight. This worked fine for the summer months when the weather was hot, but it was a different story in the winter. In the winter it was much too cold to open the shutters. So they remained closed all through the winter months. This made the entire house cold, dark, and dreary for a large part of the year.

Mr. Buck owned dozens of houses all over our part of the county just like the one Miz Lady Bug and her husband lived in. But houses were not the only things he owned. Mr. Buck owned a lot of the people in the area as well, black people that is. Of course the colored folks who lived on his property weren't really slaves. But they were as close to being slaves as one could come in a time and place where slavery had been outlawed. They lived on his land in old run-down houses. They worked on his land seven days a week from sunup to sundown for practically nothing. Yes, they were pretty close to still being slaves.

Miz Lady Bug and her husband were only one of dozens of colored families who lived on Mr. Buck's land. They, along with the many others worked on his farm. I call it a farm but it was large enough to be referred to as a plantation. In fact, many of the poor colored folks who lived and worked on his land called it just that, the plantation. Dozens of shacks where the colored families lived, spotted his land. They all lived on and worked his land. Some of the colored families did sharecropping for Mr. Buck. The majority of the families just worked to maintain his acres and acres of crops, in addition to raising small gardens of vegetables on the side for their own families to eat. Mr. Buck's colored folks raised a wide variety of crops. He had enough Negro manpower to grow just about anything he wanted to, and for many years he did just that. His main crops were cotton, soy beans, and peanuts. They drew top dollar in their time. He also raised vegetables to be sold at the local markets. There were sweet potatoes, white potatoes, sugarcane, watermelons, and all types of beans, peas, and corn. Mr. Buck's farming business was a very profitable one. For him. Buck was from old money as they say. Money, land, timber, houses, and Negroes had been passed down in his family for many generations.

Miz Lady Bug was a kind soul and a very hard worker. She was also a large, strong woman. She stood about six and a half feet tall in her bare feet. She must have weighed over two hundred pounds. She was very dark skinned and had a hard, tired expression on her face most of the time. Her hands and her feet were huge. They were large like what you would normally see on a man, not on a woman. She was very valuable to Mr. Buck and his farming operation. Miz Lady Bug could do more work in the fields in one day than three or four ordinary men. And work she did. From sunup to sundown Miz Lady Bug was in the fields working, hoeing, chopping, picking, planting, and such. She would even be found baling hay in the middle of the summer to feed Mr. Buck's livestock for the upcoming winter. She could walk behind a wagon and toss up a two-hundred-pound bale of hay onto the wagon as if it was nothing. There were only two women who could bale hay like the men—Miz Rosie and

Miz Lady Bug—and they both worked for Mr. Buck. Miz Lady Bug earned her keep though it's not as if she had a choice in the matter. As long as she lived on Mr. Buck's land, she had to do as he said. And having hard-working Negroes was the only thing Mr. Buck ever had on his mind, that, and making more money of course. The two kind of went hand in hand: The more Negros he had doing the work, the more money he made.

Miz Lady Bug may have been hard-working and kind, but she was also a jealous soul. Her husband, Mr. Reed, was at least a foot shorter than she was. He probably weighed about fifty or sixty pounds less than she did too. Mr. Reed gave Miz Lady Bug lots of cause to be jealous. He was always flirting with one old colored woman or another. How he could do all his work and still find time for flirting, no one knew. But he managed. When Miz Lady Bug felt that some old woman was getting a little too friendly with her husband she would let her and him know that she didn't appreciate it. She had never been known to do much more than fuss and fume. Everyone thought her bark was much worse than her bite, and in the beginning that was the case. Her husband found out soon enough, however, that Miz Lady Bug had a pretty rough bite as well.

One night Mr. Reed had been out drinking and messing with another woman, some poor sharecropper woman in the area. When he got home late that night Miz Lady Bug was in a jealous rage. It was winter time and she had a fire going in the stove when he finally showed up. She had been waiting up most of the night for him to get home, and she started in on him right away, yelling and screaming to no avail. He just ignored her. She was so angry that she picked him up like a rag doll, carried him across the floor, and plopped him down, butt first, on the hot stove. She was much larger and stronger than he was. He struggled desperately to get up off of the hot stove but she held him down firmly until she got tired of hearing him scream. It was horrible. Some of the colored folks in the surrounding shacks said they could hear him screaming from miles around. When she finally let him up off the stove, his trousers were burned clear through. His legs and backside were horribly burned. He was really in a bad way. Folks said they don't know what was worse for him, getting burned or getting treated for his terrible wounds. Miz Lady Bug made a salve that contained pig's fat and baking soda along with a few other ingredients. She said the mixture would help draw the heat out of his wounds and heal him faster. Every day for several weeks she would rub the mixture on Mr. Reed's bottom. The baking soda in the mixture must have burned something awful because every day you could hear poor ol' Mr. Reed screaming at the top of his voice as the salve was being applied. This went on for weeks until his wounds healed. Mr. Reed had apparently learned his lesson, for a while anyway. Many months passed before you heard tell of Mr. Reed even looking at another woman. He had one heck of a reminder on his bottom of the consequences of infidelity. With a reminder like that it should have been hard for anyone to go astray again.

Nonetheless, after many months and a healed bottom, Mr. Reed's eyes began to wander again. This was a bad decision on his part. All the colored folks in the surrounding shacks were talking about it. He was not trying very hard to keep it a secret. It seemed as if Miz Lady Bug was the last to know that there was something going on. But even she eventually found out.

One day, in the middle of the summer, there were about a dozen hands working in one of Mr. Buck's fields. There was Miz Lady Bug, four or five other women, and about a half dozen men. They were all toiling away in the midmorning heat, hoeing and weeding the long, winding rows of vegetables. As the day went on, Miz Lady Bug could hear a couple of the other women talking quietly about her husband, but loud enough for Miz Lady Bug to overhear their conversation. Actually they were taunting her. They wanted her to know what they were saying about her husband and the other woman. It was obvious that Miz Lady Bug was getting upset. You could tell by the short, deliberate strokes of her hoe. One of the women, remembering how Miz Lady Bug had burned her husband's bottom on a hot stove for his transgressions, suggested they stop taunting Miz Lady Bug. Another woman wanted to do no such thing. She continued to taunt and harass Miz Lady Bug, up one row and down the next. She was relentless.

Suddenly all of the teasing came to a head. Miz Lady Bug took the hoe she had been using to hoe vegetables, raised it high over her head, and struck the woman who had been taunting her once across the head. The woman fell to the ground with a loud thud. Blood began pouring from her right temple as if a water faucet had been turned on. The woman crawled on her hands and knees between the rows of vegetables in a vain attempt to escape Miz Lady Bug's wrath. There was no use. As the woman crawled between the rows of vegetables, she was followed by Miz Lady Bug, who was mercilessly striking her with the hoe around the head and upper part of her body. As the woman tried to get away, Miz Lady Bug hit her with the hoe, again and again. Everyone in the field saw what was happening but they stood and stared in silence. They were paralyzed, afraid to say or do anything. No one lifted a hand to help the woman who lay dying in the field. It would not have done any good anyway. The woman was soon dead. Her blood soaked quickly into the dry soil.

Miz Lady Bug was arrested and taken off to jail. After a makeshift trial she was sentenced to spend many years in jail for her crime. But the fact of the matter was that the life she had taken was not very valuable in the eyes of white folks. "Niggers" were a dime a dozen and all Miz Lady Bug had done was take the life of another worthless "nigger." While the victim may have been worthless in the eyes of Mr. Buck and his kind, she was not worthless in the eyes of God and her family. Even so, the woman's life was not considered much of a loss to society. But "niggers" had to be taught a lesson. If you let one get away with killing another "nigger" without any punishment, he might want to kill a white man next, and that must not be allowed to happen. That is why Miz Lady Bug went to jail. Not because she had taken away something that was valuable to society, but because she was to be an example set for the colored folks left behind. Doing time in jail was hard enough in those days. Doing colored time in jail was, in many cases, not survivable.

Colored folks said she didn't spend enough time there for taking another human life. White folks said it was too long for just killing another "nigger." At that time, colored folks put a larger value on another colored life than the white folks did. Not to worry, though, Miz Lady Bug was sentenced to many more years than she actually spent in jail. You see, even though slavery had long since been abolished, life for Negroes was in many ways just as it had been when slavery was the law. So Miz Lady Bug was, in essence, still the property of Mr. Buck Henderson. She lived on his land and worked on his farm. She was his property and after a short time, he wanted his property back. Murderer or not, she could still do the work of three men in the fields, and work was really all Mr. Buck cared about.

So after Miz Lady Bug spent a short time in jail, Mr. Buck figured that she and the other colored folks on his land had learned their lesson. He went to the prison and told them that he needed his "nigger" back to work his land. It was that simple. All Mr. Buck had to do was promise to be responsible for what he already deemed was his rightful property. Of course he was willing to do just that. And in no time flat, Miz Lady Bug was back living in her same old house on Mr. Buck's farm, back working in Mr. Buck's fields, back being owned by Mr. Buck. Things were practically back to normal.

Miz Lady Bug's fate on Mr. Buck's plantation was no different from that of many a black man and woman, before her time and since. Though slavery had been outlawed, many blacks continued to be "owned" by wealthy white landowners. And their lives, welfare, and future depended on the whim of those landowners.

I came to know Miz Lady Bug much later in her life when she was no longer a jealous wife. By the time I met her, her husband was long since dead, and not by her hand I might add. Nor was she the same person who had so viciously attacked her persecutor in the middle of a field on a hot summer day. She was no longer the angry colored woman who had committed murder and gone to jail, not for her crime but for the lesson she would teach to other colored folks. Even though she was still a large woman, Miz Lady Bug, when my family knew her, was merely a kindly old soul. As an old woman, she had outlived her usefulness to Mr. Buck in the fields many years earlier. He had forced her to move from the large house that she and her husband had shared. She had been relocated to a little shack less than one hundred feet from the railroad tracks down at the bottom of a hill. This is where she lived until her death at a very old age.

I don't remember her as the jealous wife, the field hand, the murderer, or the prisoner who served time for murder. I remember her as the kind soul who sometimes watched me and my younger sister while the rest of the family worked in the fields. I remember her as the old lady who helped me pick syrup buckets full of huge yellow plums from the trees in her yard. I remember Miz Lady Bug as a gentle, caring, helpful old woman because that is what she was to me.

Get Off My Road

Miz Rachel Driggers was a strange old woman. The only job I ever knew her to have was that of the neighborhood midwife for black folks. She herself was the product of a black mother and a white father. When I first remember laying eyes on her she was already very old and wrinkled. Some of her wrinkles did not come from age. She had been born with some kind of a skin condition that made her skin look rough, like that of a reptile. Old folks said that before she was born, her mother mocked her after a turtle. Being mocked was the old folks' explanation when a child was born not quite normal. Whether Miz Rachel was mocked or not, I don't know, but I do know that her skin looked a lot like a turtle's. You would very seldom see the skin on her legs, arms, and hands; she kept them covered most of the time, in summer and winter. She was light skinned with very dark eyes. Her hair was white, straight, and stringy, and it looked like it had never really had a good washing. When I first met her, she had to be at least in her eighties.

She lived alone in an old rundown shack on a dirt road near Mount Ida Baptist Church. In her time, she had delivered hundreds and hundreds of babies. I know for sure that she delivered me and all twelve of my sisters and brothers. She helped Mama bring me into the world in that cold sharecropper's shack where my family lived in the middle of a pecan orchard. Mine was a difficult birth. I was born in the early morning hours. Mama, nine months pregnant, had worked in the orchards picking up more than two hundred pounds of pecans just hours before I came into the world. You would be hard pressed to find a black person in Greenville whom Miz Rachel had not delivered. Not just blacks mind you, she delivered most poor white folks too. People say that she had been a midwife since she was a little girl. Not many folks had money to pay her for delivering their children, so they paid her with what they had: a couple of chickens, a piece of pork, a bundle of collard greens, a basket of vegetables, whatever they had to give her. I was a money baby myself, but not all of my sisters and brothers were. She never turned anyone down. She always told her clients to pay what they could, when they could. And people did remember to pay. Sometimes as many as five years would pass before the mother of the child would find a way to pay Miz Rachel something.

Occasionally she would receive money for her services. A dollar or two really added up in those days, especially if you did not spend much money. Everyone said Miz Rachel was a miser. She never spent any money. Every dime, every penny, every dollar she ever earned she hid away.

Miz Rachel was very old when I knew her. She must have been born in the late 1800s. Surprisingly, she could read and write. Not very well, but that was more than most black folks. Not many black people her age could read and write at all. She also kept very good records as a midwife. She kept a large trunk in her old rundown house. Inside that trunk were birth records of the hundreds of children she had helped to bring into the world. There was book after book filled with records. Each page in the book had a space for mother's name, father's name, sex of the child, live birth or stillborn, county, state, and date of birth. There was even a space for names of other children in the home at the time of birth. Her records were more accurate than those at the county seat.

I remember taking a trip to her house once with Mama. Her house sat about two hundred yards off the old dirt road, surrounded by trees and bushes. It was midsummer, so the tree branches and leaves almost hid the house from view from the road. Her grass was tall and I remember thinking there must be dozens of snakes around her place. As we came closer to the house I could see a well where she drew her water. It had an old worn rope attached to a bucket. The rope looked as if it would break under the strain of a full bucket of water but it was clear that it was still being used. The well was located under a large tree. The lowest tree branches scraped the side of the well and an old rusty piece of tin lay across the top of the well. I assumed it had been placed there to keep things like branches, leaves, and stray animals from falling into the well. At least, that is what the cover over our well at home was for. Back behind the house was a little shed. Like the house, the shed had a tin roof. The little building was leaning slightly to its right. I asked Mama while we were approaching, what that little building was for. She said it was Miz Rachel's smokehouse, used for drying and storing meat. I didn't bother asking what the other small shed behind the house was for. I already knew that must be the outhouse; I was quite familiar with those.

Her entire yard was covered with junk and trash. There were mounds of tin cans and glass jars scattered everywhere. For an old woman she was in pretty good health, I guess from all of the walking she did to town and back to her house. That was about eight miles round-trip. She carried an old burlap sack with her everywhere she walked. As she walked, she would pick up all sorts of things, mostly junk and put them in that sack. And everything she picked up, she took home. This was evident from looking at her yard.

When she wasn't delivering babies, she had another job. She made brooms out of straw. Just ordinary straw grass growing alongside the road. She also had a milk cow. She milked that old cow daily and churned the butter. So on her long walks to town each day, she carried straw brooms, milk, and butter to sell. On her return trips home, she picked up junk and other treasures and brought them home to her yard.

By the time we got to the steps, Miz Rachel must have seen us coming because she came outside to greet us. On the front porch were two large wooden chairs that had been covered and upholstered with old rags and burlap sacks. The porch was rotten, and the left side had completely rotted and fallen off onto the ground below. Mama and I followed her carefully into the dark house, watching every step we took. Once inside I noticed that the windows had no glass in them, just wooden shutters. All the shutters were closed tight and very little light was coming through them. No air was getting in either. The midsummer heat inside the house was stifling.

She told Mama and me to take a seat, but there was no place to sit. The house was full of clutter. A couple of shapes in the dim light looked like they had once been chairs; now they were piled high with paper, rags, and just plain junk. The walls were covered with junk as well. There were all types of paper nailed and glued to the walls. Every inch of the walls was covered with some form of paper. Miz Rachel went over to one of those walls, pulled a bundle of paper off a nail, and handed the wad of paper to Mama. While they talked my attention wandered to the large stone fireplace in the corner. The stone must have been too heavy for the wooden floor because it had sunk about six inches or so into the floor. It was summer and the fireplace was full of ashes. I wondered if the ashes had been there since last winter. It looked as if they had been. I could see through an open doorway into another room that appeared to be the kitchen. There were bottles, cans, and jars scattered all over the floor and on a makeshift table in the corner. There was absolutely no order to the house at all. I remember thinking, how could she keep such order in her birth record books and such disorder in her house. She and Mama talked for a few minutes and then we were on our way. We were only inside for a few minutes, but by the time we got outside, Mama and I were wet with sweat. Miz Rachel had not perspired a bit. Not a single drop. I guess she had been living in that old hot house so long she was used to it. I was glad to get out of there.

After we left, I asked Mama about all the old jars and tin cans. Mama wasn't sure about the cans, but she said Miz Rachel used the glass jars to store food in. She never had electricity, so storing food was a problem for her. She would put food in the glass jars and pack lard and pig fat around the food. Then she would bury the jars outside in the ground. That old rotten food would stay buried sometimes for years. But she would still dig it up and eat it. Mama said she didn't know why that food didn't kill Miz Rachel. I don't see why it didn't kill her either. Apparently she was accustomed to eating that rancid food as she had done it all her life. She also ate a lot of poke salad, which is a wild vegetable. There was always some growing near her house. It grew near our house too but we never ate any of it.

I know for sure that Miz Rachel occasionally got a decent meal. And boy, for an old lady, could she ever eat. As I said, she walked everywhere she went. Rain or shine, summer or winter, it didn't matter, if she wanted to go some place she walked. Early Sunday mornings about once a month, you could hear her coming down the road. You could hear her before you saw her because she was always singing hymns in a loud voice. She was on her way to Old Elam Church near our house, and she would always stop by our house on her way, always early on Sunday morning, and always at breakfast time. Like clockwork, Mama would set a plate for her. I remember peeking out from around the corner just to watch her eat. It was amazing. She could really put the food away. I always hated for her to drop in like that because the food she was eating was usually the kids' breakfast. Mama would always tell us to be nice to her. She would say she owed Miz Rachel more than we would ever know. I guess she was still paying her off in some way for helping to bring all of us into the world. I still didn't understand why owing her was a good reason to feed her our breakfast.

Miz Rachel didn't earn much money for delivering babies, but she did earn a few dollars for her brooms, milk, and butter. When her white father got old and ill, he asked her to come and take care of him. His white children didn't want to be bothered. She tended him for months. She told Mama that one day when he was near death, he told her that he wanted her to have his money for taking care of him. He said he would leave his house and land to his other white children. He told her where to go outside under a tree to dig. She dug up a jar full of money. She took it home and reburied it in her own yard. She never told Mama how much money her daddy left her. She only told her that it was a lot. It did not appear that she spent any of the money on herself, not by the way she lived, ate, or dressed. It was hard to figure how her daddy had much money to leave her anyway. He had spent a large part of his life selling homemade baskets. He sold them by carrying them around on a cart drawn by a donkey. Nevertheless, whatever he had, he gave to Miz Rachel.

Miz Rachel was a deeply religious woman. She was always at one church or another. She loved to hear good preaching. In those days a lot of people would get happy and shout when the sermon was good. When Miz Rachel got happy or was pleased with the sermon, she had her own way to show her excitement. When the preacher made a good point or said something she agreed with, she would acknowledge it by yelling at the top of her voice, "GET OFF MY ROAD."

"Get off my road" became her trademark. In her time she probably walked ten thousand miles, all on the roads around Butler County. She brought hundreds of babies into the world, most of whom walked the same roads she did. She sold hundreds of brooms, pats of butter, and gallons of milk. She was a good and decent old woman.

I found out many years later that the trip I took with Mama to Miz Rachel's house was a visit to borrow money. That wad of paper she pulled from the wall of her old rundown shack and gave to Mama had contained money. At the time it was money my family desperately needed. The money she gave Mama went to pay the property taxes on our land. We were close to losing our property though I did not know it at the time. She was a miser when it came to spending money on herself, but she was a godsend to the community, helping everyone who needed it. Mama was right, we owed Miz Rachel a lot, a lot more than we could ever repay. Even now when someone says or does something that I agree with I remember Miz Rachel, and I find myself saying under my breath, "Get off my road."

Mr. Will

Mr. Will, a white man, had a reputation among black folks as an evil old cuss. He hated them, all of them. He was proud of it too. He liked to brag to his white friends about how he mistreated or beat some poor "nigger" close to death. They say that he was also member of the Klan and bragged about that as well. I don't actually know if he was a member of the Klan. I do know that black folks in the area thought he was, and they were afraid of him. He was a large man. You almost never saw him without his big tan cowboy hat with a dark band around it. The other thing you never saw him without was his gun. He wore a holster around his waist with a revolver hanging from his right side. It hung low and reminded you of John Wayne. He was a very intimidating figure of a man. Daddy said he wore the gun just to scare colored folks but that he didn't scare him. Daddy was not afraid of any man, black or white. Mama always said Daddy was crazy that way. In addition to his sidearm, Mr. Will also always carried a whip around all the time like he was driving a herd of cattle or something. I never understood why he needed so much protection. Mr. Will cast a very big shadow in our parts, and it was said that the best way for black folks to get along with Mr. Will was to stay out of his way. But that was easier said than done.

You see, he owned several hundred acres of land. When you owned a lot of land it took a lot of manpower to work the land and fields, mostly black manpower. But Mr. Will's most prized possession was his country store. The store was located in an ideal spot to get a lot of business, black business and white business. It was right on Highway 31 about halfway between Greenville and Georgiana. You couldn't miss it, even if you wanted to. It was in a great location. That store was his pride and joy. He loved it, and he spent a lot of time in it.

Even though Mr. Will hated black folks, he did not hate their money. He loved Negro money, that's why he took so much of it away from so many Negroes. Most black folks in the area had a credit account with Mr. Will. They had to; no one earned enough money in those days to pay cash for anything. Credit was how Mr. Will made a lot of his money. Once you got a credit account with him, you always had a credit account with him. No black man's account was ever paid in full. Oh you could pay all you owed to Mr. Will, but you never paid him in full. Your account continued to grow whether you bought anything or not. And no one dared to contest a bill. No one ever contested a bill and lived to tell about it. No one except Daddy.

Daddy cared about as much for white folks as they cared for him, and that would be not much or none at all. As a matter of fact, most white folks around home called Daddy a biggidy "nigger." Daddy said they called him that because he had respect for himself. In the early 1960s white folks were all too happy to relieve a black man of his self-respect. Daddy did not trade at Mr. Will's store. He had traded there in the past but the two of them had had a run-in some years before. At that time Mr. Will had been on a rampage for the past several weeks. He had been treating black folks even worse than normal. He struck one man down with his whip for saying something he did not agree with. He was downright cruel. Daddy had decided he was fed up and was not going to do business at Mr. Will's store any more. Of course word got back to Mr. Will about Daddy's decision to stop trading with him. Word always got back to white folks about what blacks said or did. There was always some Negro more than willing to tell all on another Negro for the favor of a white man. Mr. Will sent word to Daddy that if he was going to stop doing business with him, he had better come in and pay him what he owed him or there would be big trouble. Whenever you did not do what white folks wanted you to do, there was always big trouble.

Mama warned Daddy to just send the money that he owed Mr. Will and not take it to the store himself. She even tried to take the money for him. Of course Daddy would not hear of it. He kept saying he was a man just like Mr. Will, and he was going to be treated like one. Mama was afraid for him to leave the house, but there was no stopping him. Mama reminded Daddy that Mr. Will carried a gun and could kill him dead in his tracks without any consequences, but Daddy insisted. He was going to Mr. Will's store and pay him off. Or at least he was going to try.

It was late one Saturday afternoon when Daddy decided to go to the store to pay off the balance of his bill at Mr. Will's store. He thought there would be trouble and against Mama's advice he had placed a revolver in his right front pants pocket. I am not sure what he intended to do with it. Mama said he had a death wish. No black man went up against a white man with a gun. When he got to the store it was crowded, full of the usual Saturday afternoon crowd. White crowd, that is. Old white men used to just sit around Mr. Will's store all day, just sitting, smoking, playing checkers, and talking the day away. When Daddy entered the store, he could see four old white men sitting at a table in the back of the store. They were laughing and talking when he walked in the store but that stopped the moment he stepped inside. It was so quiet you could hear a rat pee pee on cotton and that's pretty quiet. Mr. Will was sitting in a chair behind the counter smoking a pipe. When he saw Daddy come in the store he stood up.

Daddy walked slowly toward the counter. Even though he put up a brave front, Daddy said he was really scared to death about going in that store. When he reached the counter, Mr. Will asked, "What can I get for you, Charlie?" Daddy replied, "I'm here to pay off my bill; what do I owe you?" Daddy asked the question, knowing that he only owed eight dollars and some change. He even had his last receipt in his pocket to prove it. But Mr. Will pulled out his pad and pencil and began adding up a long column of numbers. Daddy knew this was going to be a trick. The same trick he had played on many a black man before him. "You owe me thirty-one dollars even," said Mr. Will. Daddy knew better than that. He never ran a bill up over twenty dollars. Daddy replied, "There must be a mistake. According to my receipt, I owe you eight dollars and twenty-five cents and I want to pay my account in full." Mr. Will replied, "According to my records you owe me thirty-one dollars."

Daddy was conscious of where he was. He remembered Mr. Will's gun and he remembered his own gun in his pants pocket. He wasn't there to cause trouble, he just wanted to pay his bill and end his trading relationship with Mr. Will. He laid the eight dollars and a quarter on the counter. Mr. Will said, "I want the rest of my money, Charlie." Daddy replied. "All that I owe you is eight dollars and twenty-five cents, Mr. Will." By this time, the white men who had been sitting at the table were all standing. They were carrying on quiet conversations with each other. Daddy realized that he had probably been in the store too long already. Now he figured it was time to get out. He had seen Mr. Will slap a black man across the face for disputing a bill before. He wasn't quite sure why Mr. Will had not hit him yet, but he didn't want to stick around any longer to find out. He began to back slowly toward the door, leaving the money on the counter. No more words were exchanged between him and Mr. Will. Once he was outside the door, he turned and quickly picked up his pace. Before he knew it, he was home. He never once looked behind him.

After he got home, he realized what a crazy thing he had done. No black man ever stood up to Mr. Will and lived to tell about it. He was rumored to have murdered half a dozen blacks. He had beaten men in the street for just looking at him crosswise. To think that he had let a "nigger" stand up to him in his own store was almost unbelievable. Maybe the white folks were right. Maybe Daddy was a biggidy "nigger." Or maybe he just demanded the respect that he deserved, the respect that he had earned as a man.

After that incident, Daddy never did business again with Mr. Will. Although Mr. Will kept sending word that Daddy still owed him thirty-one dollars, that was thirty-one dollars that Mr. Will never got.

Unfortunately, that was not the end of Daddy's dealings with Mr. Will. He had one more run-in with him. A couple of years after Daddy confronted Mr. Will at the store some black men came to our house in an uproar. It was late one evening and they told Daddy he had to come help Mr. Dan. Mr. Dan, an old friend of Daddy's, was one of those poor Negroes who had been trying for years to pay off a small bill at Mr. Will's store. The truth of the matter is that Mr. Dan did not actually owe Mr. Will anything. That was nothing new. Most Negroes did not owe Mr. Will anything, but they continued to pay him week after week. The men explained that he was over at Mr. Will's store and that Mr. Will was beating him with his whip. They had come to Daddy because he was the only black man that they knew who had ever stood up to Mr. Will. There was no one else to turn to. None of those men were brave enough to go alone or with Daddy to help Mr. Dan. Against Mama's wishes, Daddy went to Mr. Will's store to help. When Daddy got there, Mr. Will and Mr. Dan were outside the store. Mr. Dan was dripping with blood. He was lying on the ground and could not get to his feet. He was rolling from side to side and screaming with pain.

Daddy yelled to Mr. Will, "Stop, don't hit him any more," but Mr. Will ignored him. Daddy yelled to him again, "Stop, I said, don't hit him again." Mr. Will looked up and stopped beating Mr. Dan. He seemed stunned to see someone, a black someone at that, telling him what to do on his own property. Daddy loaded Mr. Dan into his car while Mr. Will watched. Daddy carried him to the doctor where it took almost a hundred stitches to close his many cuts. Mr. Dan almost died that night. It is possible that Daddy actually saved his life by showing up when he did. After that night Daddy and Mr. Will never said a word to each other again.

But that did not mean they never came in contact with each other again. Daddy recounted at least three different occasions where he and Mr. Will had met along the highway. On all three occasions Mr. Will had attempted to run Daddy off the road into the ditch. All three attempts were unsuccessful. On one attempt Mr. Will only succeeded in running off the road himself and wrecking his own vehicle. Daddy always enjoyed telling that part of the story and we all enjoyed listening to it.

Mr. Will had failed in his attempt to get Daddy to pay a bill that he did not owe. He had failed in his attempts to run Daddy off the road. And Daddy had humiliated him when he rescued Mr. Dan. He made one final attempt to get back at Daddy. It was the middle of the night and everything was quiet around the house. Daddy was not home. Once again he was off working out of town. Great-grandma Moa was staying at the house with Mama and the children. Everyone was in bed fast asleep except for Moa. All of a sudden, Moa heard something outside, so she went to wake up Mama. There was a full moon. Moa and Mama hid behind a window in the front room and looked out onto the moonlit yard at the night riders, several cars full of them. Everyone knew about night riders. They came around under the cover of darkness to deal with unruly Negroes. Mama and Moa watched as they got out of the cars carrying gas cans.

Moa and Mama were afraid, but not too afraid to take action. Daddy always kept several guns in the house and Mama and Moa went straight for them. They watched as the men approached the house with the cans. Mama recognized several of the men. And there was Mr. Will, right in the middle of the group. They had come to burn the house down with my family still inside. Mama and Moa knew what they had to do. They pointed the guns out of the window and began to shoot. They fired over the heads of the group of men; they did not want to shoot anyone. The punishment for shooting a white man, Klansman, night rider, or not, would be stiff. The gunshots caught the gang off guard. They scrambled and ran to their vehicles, dropping several of the cans as they went. Mama and Moa stood watch for the rest of the night. Mr. Will had failed once again to harm Daddy or my family. The Lord had been with the family that night.

When Daddy returned home from his work out of town, Mama did not tell him about the night riders. She was afraid of what he would do. It was a long time before she told him about the incident. She thought it would be best that he not know for a while. It was probably a good idea, because when she finally told Daddy, he blew his top. It took the entire family to keep him from single-handedly attacking Mr. Will. After that night visit, my family never had another problem with Mr. Will, no problem at all.

While Mr. Will was a horrible, horrible person, his ex-wife, Miz Trudy, was not too bad. Actually, Miz Trudy was a pretty decent person. She and Mama got along well. Miz Trudy and Mr. Will had been divorced for years, and she had become a good neighbor to us. She hated her ex-husband as much as most black folks did. I often overheard her bad-mouthing him to Mama. He had treated her almost as bad as he had treated most of the black folks in the area. She did not need his money, so she left him. Her daddy, John Grant, left her plenty of money; she was wealthy in her own right. Her daddy was the same landowner that Papa,

Mama's daddy, sharecropped for years earlier. He had plenty of money to hand down to his children, one of whom was Miz Trudy.

I went on many pleasant trips with Mama to Miz Trudy's farm house, which had a large wrap-around porch shaded by large oak trees on all four sides. The house was full of doors. There seemed to be at least two doors on each of the four sides of the house. She had several milk cows and she churned and sold butter. Mama bought butter from her during the time our own milk cow was not producing milk.

Miz Trudy also had a green thumb. She could make anything grow. If it was a plant she could make it grow. Her gardens were always full of every kind of vegetable you could name. Her yard was also full of fruit trees of all varieties. There were peach, pear, apple, plum, and fig trees. And she allowed my sisters, brothers, and me to eat our fill. Our trips to visit her in midsummer were the most memorable of all. She and Mama would go inside to have ice cold lemonade. Us kids would sit outside on the porch and swing in the large swings on the porch. It was so cool and comfortable. We also enjoyed the taste of Miz Trudy's sugar cookies. They always tasted so good. She made Mama, me, and my sisters and brothers feel like regular people. When I think back on things now, Miz Trudy was one of the most decent white people I ever knew. It seemed strange, because her ex-husband, Mr. Will, was one of the meanest. Miz Trudy and Mama shared a truly wonderful friendship, the kind so rare for the time. A poor black woman and a well-to-do white woman were friends in southern Alabama in the 1940s, '50s, and '60s. It was an unusual relationship indeed.

V
The Stories

The Sit Up

Papa, Mama's daddy, was born around the turn of the century and in those days things were done a lot different from the way they are done now. People were born, lived, and died all very close to home. Sometimes they lived their entire lives never straying more that twenty miles or so from where they were born. Most families were self-sufficient and took care of things like births and burials all on their own with no assistance from people or agencies outside of their community. Normally each community had a midwife to take care of the births. Some of the midwives were more experienced than others. I suppose that would partly account for the mortality rate for poor people being relatively high. In those days burials were normally handled by relatives and friends, people in the immediate area. Burying a relative was fairly easy for the family to do; there wasn't much embalming going on in those days. Who could afford to pay for it anyway? A deceased loved one never stayed aboveground more than a day or so after death. In the summer months a quick burial was an extremely good idea.

Children were treated differently as well back then. A child was to be seen and not heard. The children were required to work as hard as the adults with few of the benefits. Actually, there weren't many benefits for adults either. Most families were just living from hand to mouth. And speaking of hand to mouth, children also took a backseat to adults when it was time to eat. Typically the adults ate first. After the adults were finished, if there was food left over, the children would get their turn at the table. Normally after the adults were finished, there wouldn't be much left for the children. There would be remnants of bread and vegetables. If meat had been part of the meal very seldom would there be any left over for the younger ones to eat.

There was an occasion around 1908 or so when Papa decided to launch a protest of sorts against being treated as a child. I suppose he wasn't really protesting being treated as a child. His protest had a lot more to do with having to eat after the adults, knowing there would not be much food left over. At the time Papa was about ten years old and his stomach was seemingly a bottomless pit.

It was the fall of the year and a friend and neighbor of Moa, Papa's mama, had passed away. As was the tradition of the time, with the passing of a dear soul, relatives, neighbors, and friends would come from far and near to the home of the deceased to help the family with a "home going" celebration for the deceased. The body would be washed, dressed in his or her finest clothes, and laid out on display in the family "parlor" for all to see, to admire, and to pay their last respects. They called it a parlor, but actually it was just the large room in the front part of the house. The parlor in the house was used for everything, eating, drinking, sleeping, gathering, bathing, living, and as in this case, as a temporary display place for the deceased.

In keeping with tradition, a big meal was planned for the night before the burial at the home of the deceased. Folks in attendance would feast, drink, and "sit up" through the night telling all sorts of stories about the dearly departed. Many of the stories were highly exaggerated, but it was supposed to be bad luck to speak ill of the dead. And it was difficult to do with the person lying there just five feet in front of you. So the sit up was a time to feast, laugh, tell happy stories, and make merry. In essence it was a sending-off party for the soul of the departed. There might have been some crying and a few tears, but most of that type behavior would be saved for the funeral services the next day. The funeral would generally have more people in attendance and would provide a larger audience for those who were inclined to "show off." The sit up was a time for celebration.

It was at this sit up for one of Moa's friends that Papa decided to be rebellious. The evening had started as most such did, with a steady stream of neighbors and friends coming by to give their condolences to the family and to leave food, drink, and homemade spirits. There were cakes and pies of all sorts. There was also pork, beef, chicken, and vegetables of all types being brought to the celebration. People always shared the best of what they had at times like these, even if it meant they would go hungry themselves for a time. So, some of the best food in the community was brought to the sit up. There was also some of the best moonshine brought in for the occasion. In those days wherever there was food and festivities, there was always moonshine, just a little something to get the party going.

Papa watched with excitement along with one of his friends, another boy about Papa's age, as the parade of food lasted all afternoon and into the early evening. People were coming and going in and out of the house, and in and out of the parlor. Moa had warned Papa early in the day to be on his best behavior in front of the neighbors and he did his best to do as Moa had asked. But even Moa knew that expecting him to be a good boy all day and into the night would be a tall order.

Many hours had passed since leaving home and Papa's will to be good was slowly fading away. He and his friend had sat quietly in the parlor watching people stroll by with food on their way to the kitchen. They had also sat quietly while mourners walked through having private conversations with the deceased, wishing the person well after his life of toil and pain. Many held his hand, rubbed his face, and kissed his forehead. After hours and hours of this one of the older women stood in the doorway and announced it was time for everyone to come into the kitchen to eat. The breaking of bread was always the climax of the celebration. All the old women headed into the kitchen first, followed by the men, and then the young adults. When Papa and his friend got to the kitchen door they were stopped by Moa. She didn't have to say anything; she just gave them a stern look and pointed a finger back toward the parlor where the guest of honor was waiting. Children ate after the adults, not with them.

Papa and his buddy slowly walked back into the parlor feeling mistreated. They sat there glaring at the corpse for a few minutes all the time getting angrier and angrier with the folks in the kitchen. After about twenty minutes or so of listening to the good time being had in the other room, Papa could sit still no longer. He wanted to get back at the grown folks. He sprang from his seat and ran across the room to the body that was all laid out and resting peacefully on the table. He looked toward the kitchen and then quietly beckoned for his buddy to come over. Rigor mortis had set in. The man was as stiff as a board. The two of them slowly slid the man off the table. They stood him up and inched him over to the fireplace, which was only a few feet away from his resting place on the table. They did more dragging than carrying but they got him over to the mantle. The man's arms had been folded peacefully across his chest so his elbows were frozen in place and extended out a few inches on each side. That slight extension was all they needed to prop him up against the mantle. There he stood, the guest of honor, leaning against the fire-place as if he was an active participant at his own going-away party. He looked quite natural propped against the fireplace. A closer look would reveal that his eyes were closed eyes, but other than that he could have been anyone at the party.

Papa and his partner in crime slowly walked across the parlor and out the front door, taking care not to make a ruckus or arouse suspicion. Once outside, they made themselves comfortable right in front of the large open window and they watched and waited. After a short period of time, the guests, including Moa, began to return to the parlor. None of them no-ticed that the deceased had left the table and joined the party. Almost everyone had returned from the kitchen before someone noticed that the dearly departed was no longer on his platform. Papa held his breath wait-ing for the reaction when the corpse was spotted. He didn't have to wait long.

Suddenly all hell broke loose when several people noticed the guest of honor leaning against the mantle. Grown men began yelling and scream-ing like little babies. Food, drink, and petticoats were flying all over the place. It was a sight to see. Papa searched the room for Moa and quickly found her running and screaming as well. People who hadn't yet seen the dead man standing at the mantle were yelling and hollering just because everyone else was. Folks started jumping out of windows and doors alike.

There were even a couple of new doors made in that old ragged house that night. Papa said he didn't know grown folks could move so fast. The entire house was emptied in seconds. Everybody ran, jumped, or fell outside; everybody of course except the guest of honor. There he stood all alone in the house, silently leaning against the mantle, the only guest left at his party. And there were Papa and his friend with a front row seat to the best show in town.

It took quite a while before folks calmed down. Then they slowly began to come out of the corn field and from hiding places out behind the barn. A few folks however never made their way back to the house. They had run away screaming on foot all the way back to their homes, leaving their horses, wagons, mules, and their wits behind them. After a little time had passed, people realized that the deceased had not moved at all from his standing position. It was soon determined that he might be in fact still dead and have had a little help getting off the table. It didn't take long to figure out who had helped him. Only two people present were laughing, and those same two people had not made any attempt to run away. Clearly, Papa and his buddy were the guilty ones.

Soon folks began to get angry. Moa was embarrassed and ashamed of the terrible thing that Papa had done. She was considered a pillar of the community, respected by everyone, and her own son had disrupted a sacred celebration. All because he didn't want to wait and eat after the adults. She knew she had brought him up to know better, how could he have done such a thing?

It took most of the rest of the night to get the house back in order and the deceased back in his place on the table. Moa made sure Papa stayed around to help. And Papa didn't get a single morsel of food to eat that night. The food that had been left by the adults for the children to eat had been ruined in the ruckus Papa and his friend had caused. In all the commotion and its aftermath, Moa didn't punish Papa that night. That was a good thing for him; had she been able to get to him that night, the next sit up in the community would probably have been his. But the next day Papa got his punishment for what he had done. He recalled it as one of the worse whippings of his life. After the sit up Papa was not able to sit down for quite a while, and deservedly so.

It has been said that all's well that ends well. I suppose that's true in this case as well. The funeral for the departed went on as scheduled the following day. There were no surprises this time from Papa or the guest of honor. All the mourners, the ones that were brave enough to attend, were on their best behavior. And Moa's friend got an opportunity to participate in his own sit up, a first for the community.

Mornin', Miz Lula

When Papa was growing up childhood only lasted a short time under the best of circumstances. In the worst of circumstances, as in Papa's case when a boy was forced to become a man before his time to help support his family, childhood lasted no time at all. Back when Papa was a boy around the turn of the century, children were raised by the community. Every adult played an active role in the upbringing of a child. If a child was found misbehaving he would be punished on the spot by the adults who witnessed the bad behavior, and then again by his or her parents once the bad news found its way home. This type of discipline made all the adults in the neighborhood natural enemies of ill-behaved children. Papa, by his own admission, was one of those naughty children. He kicked up a ruckus all the time, even knowing that when he was caught he would be punished, twice. He was a very bad boy.

There was one old woman in the community Papa didn't get along with at all. In fact it would be fair to say that he hated her. Her name was Miz Lula and she refused to let Papa or any of the other children get away with anything. If any of the kids did something bad around her, she would exaggerate it, whip them, and then tell their folks so they would get another whipping at home. She seemed to take pleasure in the children's pain. Papa really hated her.

One afternoon Papa and a couple of his friends were walking past Miz Lula's house. They were laughing, playing, and throwing rocks at each other. They were just being kids. Well, as always, once Miz Lula saw them she blew the whole thing out of proportion. She accused them of making fun of her and throwing rocks at her house. Everyone should have known that wasn't the truth. Had the kids hit her ragged house with rocks, the old building would have come tumbling down around her. Or, as Papa would have wished, the house would have fallen on top of her. She was just being the mean old unhappy cuss she always was. She called the children over and gave them each a whipping with the large tree branch she kept propped against her back door. Then she promised to tell their folks about their bad behavior.

A couple of days later Papa found out Miz Lula had made good on her promise. She had indeed told Moa about the rock-throwing incident and about the whipping she had given the kids. Moa was a strict disciplinarian and after hearing about Papa from Miz Lula, she took a strap to him. Moa whipped Papa twice for the same incident. She whipped him once for the part he played in the rock throwing and a second time for not telling her about it. Poor Papa had gotten three whippings for the same incident.

As you can imagine Papa was quite upset with Miz Lula. He desperately wanted to get back at the old witch but he wasn't quite sure how to go about it. An idea came to him a couple of days later when he was walking past her house. He walked slowly past Miz Lula's looking straight ahead. Papa kept his eyes focused in front of him and as he passed directly in front of her, not five feet away, he didn't open his mouth to say a word. In those days as a rule, children had to acknowledge adults when they were in their presence. It was totally disrespectful not to speak to them. Nevertheless, Papa walked right past Miz Lula as if she wasn't even there. He could see her out of the corner of his eye standing there with her hands on her hips and her nostrils wide open glaring at him as he passed. He could see that she was angry but what could she do? What could she tell on him this time? This time he had not done a single thing to her. After he rounded the corner past her house he hid behind a tree and watched her for a while. There she stood, shaking her head, breathing heavy. Papa thought he had really gotten back at her.

Papa was sure surprised later in the day when Moa set in on him again with a strap. Between the hollering and screaming he wanted to know what he had done this time to deserve such a whipping. Moa was happy to let him know what he had done. Miz Lula had come by and told Moa that Papa had been disrespectful to her. Being disrespectful to an adult was about the worst thing a child could do. Papa promised Moa that it would never happen again. He promised to always speak to his elders, especially Miz Lula . . . he promised.

It was several weeks before Papa got the nerve to walk past Miz Lula's house again. He still hated her, but the memory of his last whipping from Moa was still fresh on his mind—and his backside. He knew one thing for sure. He was definitely going to speak to Miz Lula if he saw her. And he was not going to take any chances, he was definitely going to see her.

Papa walked slowly toward Miz Lula's. His eyes were scanning the entire place looking for her. He scanned the house, the yard, and the garden. She was nowhere to be seen. He glanced over by the well to see if she was drawing water but she was not there either. She had to be somewhere. She was always at home, that is when she was not off snitching on some poor kid. As Papa got a little closer to the house, he could see a slight movement over near the old broken fence that ran along one side and across the front of Miz Lula's house. As his eyes focused on the movement, he could clearly see Miz Lula. There she was with her back and her backside to him. She had her skirt pulled up high about her midsection and her underwear pulled down around her knees. There she was oblivious to his presence all propped up against the fence taking care of her business. Papa was afraid to look and afraid not to look. If she saw him watching she would tell Moa. If she saw him go past and not speak again she would tell Moa that also. Papa just knew he was in for another whipping no matter what he did.

Papa quickly decided that the thing to do was to speak to Miz Lula and then keep walking. He silently eased up behind her and said in a loud strong voice, "Mornin', Miz Lula!" Papa never broke his stride. Miz Lula, on the other hand, was quite startled. If she hadn't had her underwear already down about her knees she would have probably had an accident in it. He could hear clothes and petticoats rustling behind him, but he was too afraid to turn around and take a look. Papa walked on but he just knew his life would be over as soon as Miz Lula told Moa about what had happened.

Papa waited and waited for Miz Lula to tell on him for seeing her in such a compromising position, but apparently she never did. In fact, after that incident, he and Miz Lula became good friends. He spoke to her every time he saw her. She would always speak back with a pleasant smile on her face.

Miz Lula never whipped Papa again, nor did she ever tell Moa about anything else he did. Whatever Papa did from that day forward was fine with Miz Lula. Apparently Miz Lula took their secret with her to her grave. As for Papa, he told everybody, everybody except Moa of course.

Chicken Soup

Daddy was a hard and difficult man. He was very hard on us kids especially. But although he was strict and a harsh disciplinarian, he would not allow anyone else to give us a hard time. Daddy had nine daughters, and protecting us from harm was a full-time job. Diane was the youngest, the baby girl. When she came along things were a lot easier for her than they had been for the rest of us. Diane got away with murder. She could pull a stunt on the rest of us and get away with it too. Her only defense would be, "The baby did it." That statement alone in most cases would win her a reprieve. She also enjoyed taunting the animals, at least most of the animals.

It was a hot summer day when Diane finally met her match. We always had all kinds of animals, including chickens, around the house when we were young. Not for fun, but for food. I can't remember ever being without chickens. They were always around, sometimes to eat, sometimes to lay eggs, and sometimes for both. Mama raised between ten and a hundred chickens at any given time. It all depended on the type of year we were having. In lean times we did not have many chickens. If times were hard we had to use them for food, and we definitely could not afford to feed chickens, if we could not afford to feed ourselves. Most of the chickens were mild-mannered, well-behaved birds. But there was always a chicken or two with a bad attitude.

There was one rooster in particular with a temper from hell. This bird was wicked, evil to the core. You could tell by looking at him that he was not a normal rooster. Even the crown on top of his head was unusual. The crown on his head was abnormally large. It was so large in fact that it would not stand straight up. Portions of the crown folded over and hung down the side of his face as if he was wearing some sort of elaborate headpiece. He was a very large chicken as well. His feathers were a dark and shiny brown. His feet had little spurs on them that resembled an additional toe, and boy, were they sharp. He would often use those spurs in fights with the other chickens. Indeed, he was one bad bird.

That rooster was also territorial. His territory was the right side of the house, near the kitchen door. He would attack anyone and anything who trespassed on his property. If you trespassed, he would chase you until he felt that you were no longer in his territory. He first did this with the other chickens. Most of the time Mama kept the chickens in a pen. But occasionally in the summer she would allow them to roam in the yard to find more food. This chicken thought the entire yard belonged to him. As he got bolder, he began to chase us as well. Daddy got more and more annoyed with that old chicken each time he would chase or harass one of us. He would always promise that next time he was going to kill that chicken. But next time never came.

We were all afraid of that old rooster. We would be rounding the corner of the house, innocent and unsuspecting, only to be pounced upon and chased. We tried hard to stay out of his way, but he would often catch us by surprise. It was nerve-racking to say the least.

Even though Diane was just as afraid of this rooster as everyone else, she still tried to taunt him. She would toss things at him and invade his space in an attempt to make him angry, which she did, indeed. That summer day when Diane met her match started out like most days. Diane had decided she was going to taunt that old rooster again. Apparently this was also the day that rooster had decided he was not going to take anymore flak from Diane. There was a showdown in the making.

Diane rounded the corner of the house with three small sticks in hand, prepared to throw them at the rooster in an effort to make him mad. To her surprise he was already mad. In the past, she could usually throw all three sticks at the rooster before he would get angry enough to chase her. Today, she only had to throw one. That rooster shot out at her like a bullet. She had expected to be chased, but she had not expected the chicken to chase her past his normal territory border. Once he chased her to his territory line, he kept going. In fact, he chased her around and around the house. Diane was yelling and screaming all the way. "Help! Help!" It was a sight to behold. That rooster was paying Diane back for the days of torture he had endured at her hand. He must have remembered them all. The faster he chased, the faster she ran. And the faster she ran, the louder she yelled. "Help! Help!" While I didn't want to see the rooster cause Diane any harm, I was kind of glad to see him get back at her.

By this time the pair had gotten Daddy's attention. Daddy ran outside and started yelling at the rooster. He yelled at him as if he were a person and could understand what he was saying. Daddy yelled "Stop! Stop! Stop chasing my baby." But of course the rooster did not have a clue what Daddy was saying. So he continued to chase Diane. And he was gaining ground on her. Daddy ran back into the house. He was inside for only a few seconds and when he came back outside, he had his rifle. Mama was following close behind him. "What are you doing?" she yelled. "I'm going to kill that rooster." When Mama saw that the rooster was chasing Diane, she pleaded with Daddy not to shoot. If he missed the rooster, he could accidentally shoot Diane.

By now, Daddy had loaded the rifle with a single shell. As he raised the gun, he yelled to the rooster one last time, giving him an opportunity to give up the chase. The rooster just kept chasing Diane, Daddy took aim, and with a squeeze of the trigger, it was all over. When the bullet hit the rooster, it went up in the air at least fifteen feet, and then landed with a thud. Daddy was a great shot.

The sound of the gunshot scared Diane. She had been completely unaware that Daddy was going to shoot the rooster or that we were all watching her get chased. She had only been aware of the rooster who was hot on her heels. When she heard the blast from Daddy's rifle, she dropped to the ground. By the time she turned around to see the rooster on the ground about twenty feet behind her, all she could do was cry. She cried for hours. She had been one scared kid. Diane had brought on herself that race with the rooster. She had been taunting him for a long time. That day, even in death, the rooster got even, and we were all glad to see it.

Diane and the rooster were the main topic of conversation for the rest of the day. Like brothers and sisters do, we made fun of her. Even Mama and Daddy laughed over the incident. The rest of the day passed without incident. We went to the fields to hoe and pick vegetables. It was late evening when we all returned to the house to get ready for dinner. As usual, we washed up outside. Dinner that night included a last-minute addition, chicken soup. Everybody enjoyed that soup, except Diane. For some reason, she did not have much appetite.

Full Ain't Nothing but Full

Growing up as poor as my family was meant that there were a lot of days when the dinner that Mama set on the table was not always what I wanted to eat. It was not always what any of us wanted to eat but we were not in any position to be choosy about what was placed on the table before us. We were lucky just to have food on the table. Even so, my family was a lot better off than a number of other families right there in the area. At least we always had something on the table for dinner, even if we didn't always like what it was. Mama was extremely resourceful and good at making meals out of just about anything or just about nothing. Because there were so many of us, she had to make a little go a long way. And even in the roughest of times, she always came through with something. We might eat the same thing for dinner ten days in a row, but we always ate something.

Breakfast in the summertime always included Mama's hot biscuits. That was one thing we never ran out of. I guess flour was one of the few things that were plentiful around the house. I could make a meal out of Mama's hot butter biscuits with syrup. The fresh butter was from the old cow out back, and cane syrup came from our own sugarcane. There were many times when that was the entire meal. But in the summer, when all the vegetables were ripening in the fields, we could count on some of them being on the breakfast table to go along with Mama's biscuits. Fried okra was one of those breakfast vegetables. We had fried okra at least four or five times a week in the summer. Mama had a special way of preparing it. She would get the okra cut fresh from the plant still covered with the early morning dew. After washing the slender parts of the plant, Mama would cut off the tough tip and the hard, furry, fuzzy, sticky head and discard them. She didn't toss out much, but those pieces were too tough to eat. Then she would slice the parts of okra into tiny bite-size pieces. After adding a little salt and pepper she would pour a big mound of okra into a large, hot, grease-filled cast-iron skillet. It only took a couple of minutes for the okra to be cooked clean through and ready to eat. Fried okra and biscuits tasted great.

We didn't eat okra just for breakfast. We had it for dinner also. Mama usually cooked it a little differently for dinner. She would season it and either boil it or she would cut it up in bite-size pieces, bread it with cornmeal, and fry it. Either way it tasted pretty good. We ate okra most of the summer, often two times a day.

Now tomato gravy was another story. I loved tomato gravy, and in the summer there were always lots of tomatoes available. We usually had a pretty good tomato crop. We didn't have much, but it doesn't take much to grow tomatoes. Tomato gravy was a very simple recipe. Mama would put a huge iron skillet on the stove. She would add lard and bacon scraps if we had them. Then she would cut up a large bowl full of ripe juicy tomatoes, add salt and pepper to taste, and add them to the hot grease in the skillet. Once the tomatoes had cooked to a gravylike consistency, it was ready to eat. Of course it too was eaten with Mama's biscuits. Tomato gravy and biscuits would fill a hungry stomach and keep us going for a large part of the day. It wasn't a bad meal either.

Fried green tomatoes were another delicacy. We ate them for breakfast and dinner. Mama would take the large, green, just-beginning-to-ripen tomatoes, slice them thinly, salt and pepper them, bread them with flour or cornmeal, and fry them in a thin layer of hot lard or grease. Honestly there wasn't a taste like them anywhere, north or south. They tasted great. In the summertime it didn't matter. Red and fully ripened or green, tomatoes played an important and tasty part in our diet.

One of my favorite meals was pretty simple. It consisted of warm cracklin cornbread and fresh butter milk. This was a relatively easy meal to make and it didn't cost the family much since all the ingredients were homegrown. We always had a hog or two that Daddy would kill in the fall of the year. Then Mama would make her own cracklins. Cracklins were delicious to eat by themselves or cooked inside fresh hot cornbread. Cracklins were small quarter-size pieces of the outer layer of the skin of the hog. After the hog was slaughtered, Mama would cut up those pieces of fat and cook them all in the big black washpot outside. Since they were mostly made of fat, they served two purposes. Mama used the grease, or lard, that was removed from the cracklins to cook with. We almost never had to buy grease for frying and such. And small cooked pieces of fat were delicious morsels of pork. The cornbread was practically home-grown as well. The cornmeal was ground from dried corn that we had grown ourselves. Mama mixed the cracklins right in with the cornbread batter and baked it all together. The cracklin bread itself was enough for a meal. And if we had fresh buttermilk to go with it, all the better. Mama's old milk cow supplied the fresh milk. Yep, cracklin cornbread and fresh buttermilk definitely went down well.

We always ate a fair amount of bread, whether it was cornbread, with or without cracklins, or Mama's biscuits, bread was on the menu, for breakfast and dinner. I imagine bread was plentiful because flour and cornmeal were always reasonably inexpensive. Mama often made bread by the panful; however, many times she simply made hoecakes, which were fairly simple to make. The batter was always mixed in the same manner, as if Mama was going to make a pan, or waiter, which is a really large pan of bread, with flour or cornmeal. Then she would heat an iron skillet filled with a large amount of lard or grease on top of the stove, drop large spoonfuls of the batter directly into the grease, and fry the bread into small cakelike portions. We ate a lot of hoecakes.

My great-grandmother Moa, on Mama's side of the family, passed down her hoecake recipe to Mama, and she passed it down to my sisters, brothers, and me. Moa, who was a slave as a child, may have learned how to cook hoecakes from her Mama. Moa always said the term "hoe-cake" came from the time when slaves didn't have any cooking utensils so they cooked with whatever they had at hand. Because hoes were always plentiful on plantations, slaves put batter on them to cook bread, hence the name hoecakes. Even though Mama never cooked hoecakes on a real slave hoe, great-grandma Moa did.

We also ate a fair amount of potatoes, sweet potatoes and "ice" potatoes. We raised both kinds. I remember during the summer months after all the ice potatoes were harvested Daddy would bed a large number of them for winter eating and for planting the next spring. To bed the potatoes, Daddy would dig a large hole in the ground and line it with pine straw to store the excess potatoes and keep them from freezing in the winter. During the winter months we would retrieve potatoes from the bed. We had to take care and cover the bed properly after each visit. If not, the cold air would get to the bed and spoil all the potatoes. This would not only ruin the eating potatoes for the rest of the winter but also our potato seedlings for the upcoming spring. Sweet potatoes were bedded in a similar manner. The thing about sweet potatoes was that we never seemed to have enough of them to last for very long. It always seemed as if the good-tasting food was always in short supply. There definitely weren't enough sweet potatoes around to make enough of Mama's sweet potato pies.

During the summer months we were able to eat a fair amount of fish at most meals. Every day either Mama or one of us kids were going fishing, not for fun but for food. Sometimes fish was the only meat we would have for weeks at a time. I guess we were lucky to have meat at all. If we had a good vegetable crop during the summer, we were able to raise a couple of hogs to be killed in the fall. This provided us with meat during the early part of the winter but there was never enough to last all winter. I guess it would be fair to say that we ate better in the summer months than in the winter months; most folks in the area did. In the summer you could fish and grow vegetables, which you could not do in the winter.

There were a lot of times when we didn't have what we wanted to eat, and meat on the table did not automatically come with every meal. But we always had something to eat. Mama made sure of that. Grandpa Allen, Daddy's daddy, used to say when times were hard and he could barely feed his family that when you do get enough to eat, you shouldn't be picky. After all, he would say, "Full ain't nothing but full," and I must say I agree with him.

Stomp and Pack

Religion and churchgoing played a critical part in my upbringing. I always believed, even when I was too young to know just what I believed in. Going to church on Sundays was something that we always did, even if most of the time Mama was literally dragging us kids behind her kicking and screaming all the way. Whether we wanted to go didn't matter. If Mama went, we went, and that was that. We had no choice. I was taught to believe that there was a God up there somewhere looking after, caring for, and loving all of us. I admit there were times when I found believing difficult. I mean, how could you readily believe in a God who seemed to place you, your family, and every other colored family that you knew right smack in the middle of the hardest, cruelest, and most miserable existence there was? We were poor sharecroppers. How could God intentionally put us through that type of life? I never understood the why, but Mama always said that if we trusted in the Lord, He would make a way for us out of no way. The really strange thing about it was that Mama was right. Each time the family faced an insurmountable obstacle, we were able to overcome it—but only after an awful lot of praying. I decided early on that maybe there really was something to the God thing. I figured, if you were going to bet on whether or not God existed, the sure bet would be that He does. I can honestly say that so far, my bet is the winning bet.

Daddy seldom went with us to church. I suppose he never found the need the way Mama did. Since Daddy was the biggest hell-raiser I knew, maybe going to church was too much against his nature.

Going to church with Mama on Sundays was a real eye-opening experience. I guess I could also call it an awakening experience as well. For sure there was absolutely no way you could fall asleep. The preachers made sure of that. Each sermon was packed full of yelling, screaming, gesturing, walking, moving, and pointing. Even if you wanted to fall asleep, you were too afraid to. As a member of the congregation, it seemed that if you let your guard down, even for a second, you could be gathered up by some evil demon, tossed into an abyss, and lost forever. I was always on my guard during church and made sure I stayed awake.

Each sermon had just the right mixture of ingredients. The preacher usually began with about 5 percent Scripture. Each sermon had to start with a little basis in fact, just to keep the preacher honest. Next the preacher added in about 65 percent storytelling. Storytelling was added to keep us interested. Next the preacher would add 5 percent yelling, to keep us awake. Now that we were awake, 5 percent of gesturing and walking was added to make sure everyone was following along. Once the preacher was sure he had everyone's undivided attention, he would tie everything all together with another 20 percent of Scripture. The final 20 percent of Scripture usually got most of the congregation yelling, talking in tongues, and shouting in the aisles. And if the preacher could get folks shouting in the aisles, he had them. You see, the aisles lead right down front to the pulpit and of course to the collection plate. So you see a good sermon went hand in hand with the day's collections. This gave preachers an incentive to do a good job. And on most occasions, they did a very good job indeed.

After some time of being dragged along to church with Mama, I began to enjoy it. I mean the stories were always great, and the preacher was always entertaining. I very seldom heard the same story twice. Each preacher seemed to have a dozen stories to go with each Bible verse. While some of the stories have faded from my memory, I do recall a few favorite stories, or sermons, if you will. One such favorite revolved around a farmer and an old mule.

I am sure that almost everyone has heard the phrase "stubborn as a mule," and we probably all know someone who would fit that description. My father was one of those people. Once he got something in his mind, there was no changing it. Daddy was indeed a stubborn man. A lot of people said that being stubborn was one of the traits I got from Daddy. I never understood why. And as I recall, I never really liked being called stubborn. People made being stubborn sound like a bad thing. I always thought that people called other folks stubborn just because they couldn't convince them to do things their way.

As I remember, one preacher built an entire sermon around the pitfalls of being stubborn. He really had our little church rocking with his renditions of well-known Scripture. He started out with the Scripture about a father who had a stubborn son. This father tried over and over to change his son's habits to no avail. Since the father couldn't get the son to see the error of his ways, he took him out onto the city square to be stoned by the townsfolk. I always thought that was an awful thing for a father to do to a son, even if the son was bad. I thought it was even worse that the preacher could actually find such a story in the Bible, but he did. Those Bible stories were really tough.

To bring the sermon on home, the preacher decided to tell a little story. He said it was for the purpose of clarity. He wanted to make sure that all us poor sinners like me, who didn't quite understand the Scripture of the father and the son, were getting the proper message.

So he told the story of a farmer and his old stubborn mule. In those days everybody I knew had a mule, including Daddy, so that part of the story was believable. The story went a little like this. There was an old farmer who had a stubborn old mule. The farmer had had that old mule for many years, and for all that time the mule had been stubborn. That old mule refused to do anything the farmer asked him to do. If the farmer wanted to plow the fields, the old mule didn't want to plow. If the farmer wanted to ride the mule, the old mule didn't want to give him a ride. If after a long day in the fields, the farmer wanted the mule to drink, the mule wasn't thirsty. If the farmer wanted the mule to gee, the old mule wanted to haw. If the farmer wanted the mule to haw, the old mule wanted to gee. The two of them just could not get along.

One day the farmer decided that if the mule was going to continue to be stubborn and was not going to work with him, he was not going to continue feeding him. After all why waste food on a mule that had a mind of its own? But how was he going to get rid of that stubborn, good-for-nothing mule? He thought about shooting him, and he decided no, that might be too painful for the mule and why waste a bullet. The farmer thought about drowning the old mule, and he decided no, he could never get that stubborn old mule to go near water when he wanted him to, so drowning him probably would not work. The farmer thought long and hard for several days until he finally came up with a way to get rid of his old mule.

The farmer remembered that he had an old well out in back of the house near the barn. That old well had been dry and useless for four or five years. He figured that he could toss the old mule in that dry well and then just cover him over with dirt. He thought that to bury the mule alive would be a relatively painless way to go. He didn't really want to torture the old mule. He just wanted to get rid of him. And he felt that this way would be a lot better than shooting or drowning. The farmer got up early one morning to set his plan in motion. He lured that old mule out back near the old dry well. He began talking to the mule about plowing. He knew that if he began talking about work that old mule would refuse to help and try to get away. The farmer was right. The mule reacted exactly as he expected. The minute he mentioned plowing, the mule wanted no part of the work and started to slowly back up. The mule was backing up directly toward the old dry well. The farmer's plan was working great. When the mule got within a couple feet of the well, the farmer grabbed him by the hind legs and up and in he went. Right to the bottom of the well, about thirty feet down.

The farmer rejoiced, "I did it, I did it. I got rid of that old mule." The mule, standing down at the bottom of the well began to get worried. "I can't believe it, that old farmer, is really trying to get rid of me. He actually threw me into the well. Maybe I should have plowed when he wanted to plow. Maybe I should not have tried to haw, when he wanted me to gee. Now how am I ever going to get out of this fix? Am I ever going to get out of this well?" Before the mule could get his bearings and think straight, a shovelful of dirt hit him square in the middle of his back. The mule couldn't believe it. Not only did the farmer throw him in the well, but he was trying to bury him alive. The mule knew he had to do something if he was going to survive.

The mule went to work. He shrugged his shoulders and dumped the shovelful of dirt off his back to his left side and onto the ground below.

He began thinking, how do I get out of this? As he thought, he stepped to his left and began stomping his feet and packing the fresh dirt into the ground. He was stomping and packing, stomping and packing. The farmer up above was thinking, "I got him now. I got him now." He picked up another shovelful of dirt and threw it into the well. The dirt again landed square on the shoulders of that old stubborn mule. The mule was still trying to figure a way out of his predicament. While deep in thought, the mule shrugged his shoulders again, this time dumping the shovelful of dirt to his right side. Again the mule began stomping and packing, stomping and packing. This ritual continued for some time. Each time the farmer threw dirt in the well on the mule's shoulder, the mule would throw the dirt off his back and stomp and pack the fresh dirt into the ground. All the while the dirt the farmer was tossing into the well was slowly filling it up, and the mule was slowly rising to the top.

By midday, the farmer was getting tired of throwing dirt into the well. He had not heard a single sound from the mule, and all he knew, the mule could be dead and buried already. The mule was getting tired as well. Each time the farmer threw dirt into the well he continued to stomp and pack, stomp and pack.

Around half past noon, the farmer decided to quit. He just knew the mule was long gone. He reached in his back pocket to get a handkerchief. He closed his eyes to wipe the sweat from his brow and turned his back toward the well. Suddenly the farmer felt something warm and moist on this neck. He turned around and found himself face-to-face and eye-to-eye with the mule. He had not gotten rid of that ornery critter after all. Instead, by throwing dirt into the well he had helped the mule build a ramp to get out. That old mule was shocked when he found himself looking at the farmer. While he had been trying to figure out a way to get out of the well, he had been stomping and packing, stomping and packing his way out.

The farmer was disappointed, and the mule was overjoyed. The farmer, being too tired to start all over with a plan to get rid of the mule, decided to give him one more chance. The mule, being too tired to resist, thought it was a miracle that he had survived. He decided that he would try and work a little with the farmer. If the farmer wanted to plow, maybe, just maybe, he could help out a little.

After that the farmer and the mule began to work better together. In fact, they worked well together for many years. The farmer became more tolerant of the mule and his stubborn ways. And the mule became more willing to work and less stubborn.

After hearing this story from the preacher, I never worried much anymore about being called stubborn as a mule like my daddy. The preacher explained that the lesson to be learned was not to be *too* stubborn or you might get stoned or thrown down a well. But that was not the lesson I learned from this sermon. I figured I could be as stubborn as a mule all right. I could even be as stubborn as my daddy. Just as long as I remembered to stomp and pack, stomp and pack.

The Brown Bomber

Daddy often talked about some of the things he had done as a small child and as a young man growing up. Most of the things he talked about were centered on the hard work that he and his family had to do in order to eke out a meager living. Times were hard for Daddy and his family. He very seldom spoke of having any type of enjoyment out of life. With the living conditions as horrid as they were, there weren't many things happening to or for black folks that they could enjoy. On most days just having one meal a day was an enjoyment.

One thing Daddy did enjoy as a young man was listening to the fights on the radio. The weekly fights were a real thrill for him and his friends. The boxing matches came on every Saturday night, and he and his young friends always got together and somehow found a way to listen to them. Saturday afternoons for young blacks in the 1920s and 1930s in the South were always spent in some white man's field finishing up the week's work. There was always a lot of work to do around the large plantations and farms, but by late Saturday afternoon, all the work would be finished for the week. Saturday nights were a time that colored folks, young and old, could settle down and try to live like human beings, at least for a while. Saturdays were also a time to get some much-needed rest. So the young men were on their own from Saturday afternoon until early Monday morning, when the long hard work week would begin again.

In those days there was a professional or semiprofessional fight going on somewhere in the United States almost every Saturday night. All Daddy and his friends had to do was find a place to listen to it, which was easier said than done. The fights were always broadcast over the radio. But in those days not a single colored person had a radio. At least not one that Daddy knew of. It was just as well I suppose. Because in those days not a single colored person had electricity to power a radio either. Though a lot of the white folks in our poor town had both radios and electricity, the poorest white folks, just like the coloreds, had neither.

On fight nights the search was on to find a white person, with a radio, who was willing to allow colored folks to listen. If you worked for a "decent white family" as Daddy called them, he would let his colored folks sit quietly outside his house and listen to the fights through an opened window. And I emphasize "quietly." Most white folks, however, didn't want Negroes around their house after dark. But in those days almost every country store had a radio, and most of those old stores stayed open late on fight night to accommodate their white friends and customers. Some store owners would allow colored folks to sit outside and listen to the fights. The blacks were told, of course, that they had to be extremely quiet, as not to disturb the good white folks inside the store.

Usually the blacks were able to comply with the store owner's demand of silence. However, when the fights got exciting, it was difficult to hold in all the enthusiasm. This was one of the few things they did to enjoy themselves and to ask them to be silent when their favorite boxer was winning was torture. Occasionally they would get too loud and they would all be yelled at like disobedient children. If the noise persisted, they would be run off into the woods and banned from the property, and thus listening to the radio, for several weeks. Being quiet was never easy but it became a real problem when the boxer Joe Louis appeared on the scene. Joe Louis was a black boxer, born in Alabama in 1914. He was just five years older than Daddy, and when he came on the fight scene, he became a hero to my daddy and to colored folks all over the world. Daddy really loved Joe Louis. A lot of folks loved him, and who could blame them. Daddy said that Joe was able to do what millions of colored men wanted to do but couldn't get away with. Joe was able to punch a white man square in the mouth and not get hung for it.

Joe Louis was a great fighter. He began boxing when he was just a young teenager. And by the time he turned professional in 1934 he had a huge following everywhere, including south Alabama. Daddy recalled listening to Joe Louis fights often; he hardly ever missed one. He recalled having to be so careful while listening outside the window of one of the old country stores. He said he had to be especially careful if Joe Louis was fighting a white opponent. It was forbidden for a black man to cheer for Joe Louis to whip a white opponent. Those old farmers would not hear of it. It may have been forbidden, but Daddy and his friends did it anyway. It made those white folks so angry when Joe Louis would beat a white man. It made Daddy and his friends very happy. They would brag about it for weeks. Of course all of their bragging was just among themselves. Bragging was their way of getting back a little at a society that was cruel and unfair.

After Joe Louis went up against Primo Carnera in 1935 and beat him, he was given the nickname "the Brown Bomber." This was difficult for the white people in our small town to take. They were furious and humiliated. So much so, that they banned colored folks from listening to fights outside their windows all over the county for a long time. Black folks were still able to get news of the fights even it they weren't allowed to listen to the fights firsthand. Daddy and his friends were still able to enjoy the career of their hero, the Brown Bomber.

Those times listening to a radio outside white folks' windows were talked about often by Daddy, and it was clear to me that those times troubled him very much. There wasn't anything he could do about it at the time, but he was keenly aware that it was one more injustice inflicted on black people. Daddy often wondered if times would ever get better for black folks. For Daddy's sake and mine, I am glad they did.

Whenever I hear the name Joe Louis, I think about Daddy, the radio, Saturday nights, his young friends, and what the Brown Bomber meant to them and to my small hometown.

The Old Swimming Hole

During the summer months the Alabama heat was often nearly unbearable. It was so hot it was difficult to breathe on a normal summer day. And if breathing was difficult, you can imagine how hard it was to work in the fields day after day, to begin in the relative cool of the morning and work right through the midday heat. Sometimes the days were so hot I can recall actually praying for a heart attack, or sun stroke, or just to be struck down by the mercy of God, anything to ease the pain of the heat. At least death would bring relief from the extreme heat. Of course, death never came, but those long hot summer days returned over and over again. Only the setting of the hot sun in the evenings brought some temporary relief. This relief only lasted until the next sunrise. Then we would begin the long hot work day all over again.

On normal summer days my sisters, brothers, and I would work from sunup to sundown in the fields. There was always plenty of field work to do. I often wondered why field work had to been performed during the hottest part of the year and at the hottest time of the day. It seemed as if field work was some type of evil punishment that colored folks had to endure for some long-ago sin. Even to this day I can't figure it out.

Our only break from the field work came on Sundays. And why not, even God got a chance to rest on Sundays. Though we had to work in the fields on Saturdays, Daddy often allowed us to quit earlier in the day, most times around midday. The little rest time on Saturday afternoon always passed much too quickly. Even so, a little rest was better than no rest at all. When my sisters and I got a break, it was usually spent taking a cool bath, drinking tall glasses of water, and resting comfortably in the shade, that is if we could find any shade to rest in. We took care to make sure that our shady spot was well out of Daddy's line of sight. Even though he had given us a break, he couldn't bear seeing us "lazing around." If we were spotted just relaxing in the shade, Daddy would surely find some other sort of work for us to do. If not field work, yard work. If not yard work, housework. It didn't matter much to Daddy, as long as we were working.

My brothers took a different approach to keeping cool and getting a rest on Saturday afternoons. They liked to cool down by taking a swim in Mr. Buck Henderson's pond. Going swimming in Mr. Buck's pond was not permitted. Mama had warned us kids over and over not to do it. Mama didn't usually have to repeat warnings to us. In most cases she only had to make her wishes known once. As a rule, we were quick to comply, considering the fact that we knew the consequences. Mama usually had a good reason for her warnings anyway. Not that she had to have a good reason. Simply telling us not to do something was usually enough. In the case of Mr. Buck's pond, one reason she warned us against it was that not all of us could swim. Every summer we would hear of some poor colored child who had drowned in some lonely creek or pond while trying to learn how to swim. We had lost several friends that way and Mama was afraid that one of us would accidentally drown. She didn't have to worry about that. All of my brothers were great swimmers. To hear them tell it, they were experts. They were great teachers too. So while Mama worried about us drowning, we never worried about it at all.

A second reason Mama warned us to stay away from Mr. Buck's pond was that Mr. Buck had told us to stay off of his property. This was a man with hundreds of acres of land, yet he refused to allow my family or any other colored family to set foot on any of it except to chop and pick his cotton, and to plant and harvest his vegetables, to cook his food, wash his clothes, and clean his house. He just didn't allow us on his property unless we were actually working for him. Mama thought that Mr. Buck's warning was a good enough reason to make us stay off his property and away from his pond. We thought he was just pure selfish. And the way we figured it, he had more property than he could keep an eye on anyway. My brothers didn't worry about Mr. Buck's warning any more than we worried about drowning.

Another reason Mama warned us to stay away from Mr. Buck's pond was snakes. That old pond was infested with snakes. The pond was located way back up in the woods in a low-lying area completely surrounded by trees, thickets, and kudzu. It was the perfect habitat for all sorts of critters, especially snakes. The area around the pond was crawling with all sorts of snakes. There were black snakes, chicken snakes, and rattlesnakes. And the pond itself was inhabited by dozens and dozens of water moccasins. They were everywhere. The old folks used to call them cottonmouth moccasins because of the white cottonlike insides of their mouths. As for me, I just called them snakes. In my opinion, the snakes were the only really good reason for us to stay away from the pond. I thought you had to have a death wish to want to go swimming with snakes. My brothers disagreed. They went swimming in that ol' pond in spite of the snakes. Mama had tried everything to convince them that hanging around that old pond could be dangerous, but they never listened. Whenever we got a break from work, they simply waited for Mama to turn her back and then off they went to sneak a quick swim in Mr. Buck's old snake-infested pond. Of course they knew better, but that didn't matter. Like the old folks used to say, knowing better and doing better are two different things.

Each time Mama turned her head, my brothers were off and running. She needed help keeping watch over them. And with nine sisters multiplied by two eyes each, Mama had quite a bit of help. After all, spying on and telling on brothers is what sisters are for. At least that is what I thought we were for.

One Saturday afternoon, when we had an early end to a long hot day in the fields, three of my brothers thought it would be the perfect time for them to sneak away for a quick swim to cool off. They thought they would be back in plenty of time before Mama missed them. And Mama didn't miss them, but my sister Ediffie saw them sneak out of the house and decided to follow them.

She knew right away where they were going. And sure enough they headed out in the direction of Mr. Buck's pond. They were careful, looking back to see if Mama had spotted them. But they weren't careful enough. Ediffie followed them closely, taking care not to be seen, as they crossed over one fence after another onto Mr. Buck's property. When they made a step, she made a step. When they paused, she paused; closer and closer they crept toward the pond.

When they reached the pond, they were home free. They got undressed, taking off every single stitch of clothing. If they came home with any wet clothes, Mama would know right away what they had been up to, so, naked as jaybirds they started to swim. Ediffie watched and waited. They were having so much fun they didn't notice her at all. She sat there in the woods watching them have a good time and trying to figure out how to tell on them. She only took her eyes off of them now and then to watch for the occasional snake or critter that wandered across her path. Ediffie was known for telling on folks all the time. She wanted proof this time so it would not just be her word against theirs. She came up with a brilliant idea: She would take their clothes back to Mama. They would be hard pressed to get out of trouble this time.

Ediffie began to put her excellent plan to work. She slowly worked her way around the pond to where the boys had gone into the water. Piece by piece she removed their clothes from the stumps and branches where they had left them. She was good. They never saw a thing. After she retrieved every stitch of their clothing, she headed straight for the house and Mama as fast as she could go.

After a while Mama spotted several figures in the distance. They weren't walking normal at all. They were kind of hunched over and were hiding behind trees, bushes, and such. And they were headed home by way of the pigpen, which was not on the way to house. To the contrary, they had to go at least fifty yards out of their way to stop by the pigpen. What on earth were they doing?

As the figures got closer to the house, you could see why they made a side trip to the pigpen. You see Daddy always kept a few burlap sacks thrown across an old post near the pigpen. They were there to carry corn, grasses, and other foods to the pigs. The boys had stopped by to pick up three of the sacks. Mama and the rest of us were waiting for them as they got to the house. When they saw Mama they lowered their heads and their eyes. They had been caught red-handed, or rather butt-naked. Surprisingly, they made no attempt to explain. Mama had not spent all her time just sitting and waiting for them. Once Ediffie reported in, she had spent part of her time collecting some of the largest switches you could imagine. There was definitely a big whipping coming on.

Without saying a word Mama pointed downward and all three of my brothers lay face down on the ground. Mama commenced to giving the three of them a good old-fashioned butt whipping. She hit one bottom and then the next, hit one bottom and then the next, making sure they all got it good. They were all yelling and screaming so loud that Mr. Buck could probably have heard them. By the time she was done, there was not much left of the old burlap sacks that they had used to cover themselves with, not much at all. It is amazing what punishment a body will endure just to go for a cool swim on a hot summer afternoon.

This whipping stuck in Floyd, Sonny, and Calvin's minds for many years. But it was not enough to stop them from sneaking off and going swimming in that old swimming hole, not at all. They did however learn to be a lot more careful. No longer could they simply watch out for Mr. Buck and cottonmouth moccasins. No, now they had to also watch out for Ediffie, and from that time on, they did just that.

Baptism Day

From the time I was born, religion was an important part of my family life. Sometimes it seemed to me that the poorer you were, the more religious you were. If that was so, then my family would have been one of the most religious families in the community.

Everyone in my family grew up and joined the church. And when the time came for me to join the church, I had very few questions regarding the matter. I was not going to question God. And the thought of questioning my mother never entered my mind. So when the time came for me to become a full member of Mount Ida Baptist Church, I was excited about it. This was something I had waited for all my life, all eight years of it.

The events of that Sunday had been carefully planned well in advance. A lot of important things had to be attended to before committing my life to Christ. One of those important things was to prepare my dress for the baptism. It would have been nice to have had a rare store-bought dress for the occasion, but there surely wasn't enough money in the household for that. Buying food was considerably more important. So as Mama had done on other special occasions, she made a dress for me for the occasion. It was beautiful. No store could have done better. It was a floor-length white gown that had a tiny collar with a little ruffle around the edges. The dress had short sleeves, which was a good thing since I had decided to join the church in the middle of the summer. I am not sure what material the dress was made of. It had a glow about it and it felt heavy and slick. Mama had the dress finished weeks in advance of the event. She was looking forward to my being baptized almost as much as I was.

Another important matter that had to be taken care of was my hair, which was long, thick, and hard to manage. I hated getting it washed and combed because it was such a painful experience. Mama did not have much patience with us younger girls when she was fixing our hair. I figured she had simply gotten tired of doing hair over the years. After having nine girls with long thick hair to do who could blame her? Anyway, I didn't mind much when Mama decided not to do my hair but to let Miz Jenny do it instead.

Miz Jenny was a nice older woman with long beautiful black hair of her own with lovely gray streaks. Her hair was always tidy. In fact, even on hot summer days, her hair, her person, and her house were all well kept. She lived on a dirt road that wound through the woods between our house and town, near Grover Adkins and the old Simpson Chapel School. Like most colored folks, Miz Jenny did a number of things to earn money. One of those things was doing hair. And she was very good at it. For a dollar, if you brought your own hair grease, Miz Jenny would press your hair, no matter how long and thick it was, even mine. In those days the best hair grease for pressing was that stuff in a red and blue can. It was called royal something or another. It was thick and heavy on the hair. It was used to keep the hair from burning while you were running a hot comb through it. I hated all that grease. The longer the hair, the more grease had to be used to keep it from burning. Since Mama had decided to let Miz Jenny do my hair for the baptism off I went on the Saturday before I joined the church. Off to Miz Jenny's house, me, my can of hair grease, and my one dollar bill.

When I arrived at Miz Jenny's, she and her straightening comb were already waiting for me. As always she had prepared a place in one of the bedrooms in the front of the house. I handed Ms. Jenny the can of grease and she sat me down in a straight-back chair, right beside the bed and close to a window. Because I was short, she had already piled three pillows in the chair for me to sit on. It took Miz Jenny a little over an hour to finish her work. She would patiently separate my hair into small sections, pile on a double fingerful of hair grease, and then slowly run that hot comb through my hair pressing it as straight and as flat as possible.

Section by section, she worked her way around my head, greasing and pressing. Even though Miz Jenny had placed a towel around my shoulders to protect me from the hot metal comb and grease, an occasional errant drop of hot liquid grease would reach my neck. After she was finished she handed me a mirror so I could take a look at my new hairdo. I looked pretty good, burned neck and all. I left Miz Jenny's house with long silky hair. Not at all like when I had first arrived. I had my new dress and my new hairdo. I was ready for baptism day.

After I got home the only thing left to do was to wait for tomorrow. I was so excited it seemed as if tomorrow would never arrive. I woke up early the next morning. I didn't even have to wait for Mama to call me over and over like she normally had to do, especially on a Sunday morning. I was already up and waiting when Mama came into the kitchen to start breakfast, which was a sure sign that the day was actually beginning. After breakfast, we all began getting ready for church. I was surprised when Mama told me that I was not going to be wearing my new white baptism dress to church. Isn't that what she had made it for? I was told that I had to wear a regular dress to the Sunday service and would change into my new dress at the actual baptism. Even though I was a little disappointed, I quickly got into another dress and was ready to go in minutes.

The whole family arrived at church like we had a thousand times before. Reverend Gandy gave a regular sermon, not much different from many I had heard him give in the past. It was so regular in fact, that I can't remember a single thing about it. Toward the end of the sermon, like he always did on the first Sunday of the month, Reverend Gandy announced that "the doors of the church are open" and asked for all people who wanted to become new members of the church to step forward. This was the prompt that I had been waiting for. Without hesitation, I stood up and went toward Reverend Gandy. I was followed by my younger sister, Diane, who had also decided that today would be her baptism day as well. We were followed by several other young people about our ages.

After Reverend Gandy read from the Scripture and said a few words of wisdom, he made the announcement that we, all the new members, would meet after church at a pond down the road. That is where we would actually be baptized and have all our sins washed completely away. After the church services were finally over, my baby sister and I were able to change into our lovely white dresses that Mama had made special for the occasion.

We all assembled at the appointed time under a large oak tree right at the edge of the pond. The tree was so close to the pond in fact, that several of its large roots stood naked out of the water. The tree was huge, spreading its large full limbs in all directions and providing shade to all who were assembled. The shade was very comforting as we waited for Reverend Gandy in the hot summer sun. There was not a breeze to be felt. The air was hot, dry, and still. Diane and I waited patiently for what was to come. I must confess, however, that I was puzzled about a couple of things. For one, the pond water was filthy. It was muddy, cloudy, and full of bugs and floating objects. I had been told that to be baptized was to be cleansed of all my sins. How could I be cleansed of anything in dirty water? Even though I was young, I was sure that it was not a good idea to allow my new white dress to be dipped in that filthy water. It would be ruined for sure.

Another thing that struck me as odd was that the pond was completely surrounded by cows. They were everywhere, dozens of them. They were pooping and peeing all over the place, in and out of the pond. I looked down to find that the mounds and mounds of cow poop were even under the oak tree where we were standing. Seeing those piles made me realize where that horrible odor was coming from. By the time Reverend Gandy showed up I was totally disgusted with the whole situation. There was no way I was going to go into that nasty pond with those nasty cows in my new dress and new hairdo, no way. This couldn't be what I had been looking forward to for so long. As I started to back up, I bumped right into Mama, who stopped me dead in my tracks.

Reverend Gandy approached the pond with a deliberate stride, which he broke only momentarily to remove his shoes. I couldn't tell for sure what he was wearing because his regular clothing was covered by a long white robe, not much different from the dress I was wearing. He walked into the pond until the water was about knee deep, reached out his hands and called for the first victim who had so willingly agreed to take part in this ritual. The poor soul was led helplessly into the water by the Reverend, who ordered her to cross her hands over her heart and to close her eyes. The reverend said a few words and swiftly lowered her into the dirty pond, then pulled her right out and said "Amen." This amen was loudly repeated by everyone lining the banks of the pond including Mama.

Soon it was my turn. Reverend Gandy called my name and slowly walked toward the bank to meet me, probably because I was making no effort to start in his direction. By the time his hands touched mine Mama had already removed my shoes and started pushing me in his direction. As I walked slowly toward him I could feel what was probably mud, but could have been cow poop, squishing between my toes. For a moment that was all I could think of. What on earth was I stepping in? My thoughts of cow poop vanished when the water was about waist high. I was ordered by the reverend to cross my arms at my chest, close my eyes, and hold my breath. Those were a lot of orders for a young person to try and follow all at once but I did. Within the space of a couple of seconds I was thrown backward in the pond, totally submerged in the dirty water, and retrieved almost as quickly.

Just like that it was over. I could feel the cool, dirty water running down my face. As I opened my eyes I could see Mama on the bank of the pond looking at me with a huge smile on her face. I was a new person. I had been born again. I was saved, absolved of all the sins that I had committed at my young age. As I walked slowly toward Mama, I began to cry. I'm not sure why I started crying, but I did. Maybe it was because the long-anticipated event was finally over. Maybe it was because I was convinced that cow poop was between my toes. I can't say.

I don't remember much more about the events of that day. Everything else is just a blur. Oh, there was one other thing. Miz Jenny had done such a good job on my hair, slathering on all that grease, that after Reverend Gandy pulled me out from under the water, the water simply rolled right off my hair. So, not only was my soul saved on baptism day, my hair was saved as well.

Simpson Chapel

When I was growing up Simpson Chapel was the name of a little white-washed church and the name of a school for colored children. In the days before desegregation, each black community had its own neighborhood school for the proper matriculation of little colored minds. Almost every colored church had a one-room outbuilding that was used as a school-house for the neighborhood children. Our community was no different.

In most cases, colored children didn't go to school at all. There simply wasn't time for it. Those who were fortunate only attended school during the agricultural off seasons when the white landowners and farmers did not need workers for planting or harvesting. It seemed like there was always some field work to be done most of the year and this left very little time for learning. At least my sisters, brothers, and I had it better than Mama and Daddy. When they were children going to school was low on the list of priorities. Having a roof over their heads, leaking or not, and getting something to eat, preferably at least once a day, were what they strove for each day. Survival was the name of the game, which is why very few people in Mama's and Daddy's time learned to read or write. There just wasn't enough time for it. Staying alive was far more important. I suppose that is pretty easy to understand. What good was learning to read and write if you were going to starve to death. Folks had to make a choice, tend the fields or go to school. But as times began to change in the South, it became more important for colored folks to get an education.

Simpson Chapel was a tiny one-room building located not far off

Highway 185 on a narrow winding unpaved one-lane road. There were two ways to reach the school. One was to travel for a couple of miles off Highway 185 on a paved blacktop road and then for several miles on gravel and then red clay. The second way was the route my sisters and brothers took, winding through the woods on a narrow dirt road on foot. Going through the woods would take miles off the trip. They would go past Grover Adkins's house where he still lived with his elderly mother. They were colored folks who had a small homestead by the side of the road. It wasn't large enough to do anything more than raise a few animals and have a small vegetable garden, just enough to feed Mr. Grover and his mama.

After they passed Mr. Grover's house, in about another mile or so they would go past Miz Jenny Boling's house. Miz Jenny lived in a neat little house very close to the road. She was an attractive older black woman with long, flowing well-kept hair. No matter when you saw her or what you saw her doing, she always looked very well groomed. She was the woman who pressed our hair for special occasions when we had the money to pay her. The little dirt road was so narrow that if two wagons met, one would have to pull off to let the other pass. It was narrow for riding but not too narrow for walking. And in those days there was a lot more walking than riding.

Each school day began very early in the morning. We all had to get up at the crack of dawn to get started on the many chores we had to do before we could even think about heading out to school. Just like in Mama and Daddy's time, chores had to come before school. The old cow had to be fed and milked each day. That old cow provided milk and butter, much-needed commodities for the entire family, and no matter what, she had to be taken care of. The chickens that roamed around and found food on their own during the summer months were kept in pens in the fall and winter. This meant we had to make sure they all had food and water each morning. There was almost always a hog or two that also had to be attended to before any book learning could take place. Slopping the hogs was one of the nastiest jobs and my brothers usually took care of that task.

While the older children were busy taking care of the animals before school, the younger kids were catching another minute or two of sleep before getting up to get dressed and start their own chores. According to Daddy, you were never too young to do some type of work around the house. While chores were attended to outside, Mama was in the kitchen preparing breakfast Almost every morning started with the smell of hot biscuits and fatback wafting from the kitchen. I recall being awakened on many occasions by the satisfying odor of pork cooking, which is not a bad way to be awakened. During lean times, the smell of anything cooking was a good thing.

By the time the animals were fed and watered, it was time for all us kids to come in and get a bit of breakfast before actually starting our day. It took no time at all for my sisters, brothers, and me to eat breakfast. In about five minutes or so we were all done and ready to head out for school.

Mama would have our lunches for the day already packed and ready to go. Lunch usually consisted of more of what we had just eaten for break-fast. Hot or cold, biscuits always tasted pretty good. Small bits and pieces of fatback or other scraps of pork went well with the biscuits. It didn't matter much what we had to take along for lunch, as long as we had some-thing to eat. We were much better off than a lot of the kids who went to school with us. Most of them could not afford to bring anything to school for lunch. There were a lot of hungry kids and hungry days at Simpson Chapel.

With lunch in hand, we were off to start our day before the sun was up. We were all in line, one behind the other, like baby chicks follow-ing the mama chick as we headed off to school. Though school was sev-eral miles away, the walk didn't seem to take very long. There was always something to see or some practical joke to play on each other or some scary story to tell. As we walked we would meet up with other colored children in the community also heading for Simpson Chapel, the one place that for a few short hours we could just be young people. We could forget about the animals back home that had to be fed; we could forget about the dinner tables that would have no food at dinner time. And we could forget about the injustices and indignities meted out daily to col-ored people throughout our little community and the South as a whole.

After reaching the school we were separated by grade levels. There were never more than three or four students in each grade. There was no such thing as overcrowding. There were enough children in the community to overcrowd the school, but there weren't enough children able to go to school to make it happen. Classroom participation was a big part of the learning process. This was a good thing because there were never enough books and learning materials to go around. The single-room school was supplied with two chalk boards up front for the teacher to explain assignments and work through mathematical problems. There always seemed to be plenty of chalk and erasers, just not a lot of books.

There was also a pot-bellied stove up near the front of the room. Of course the stove was not used during the warmer months but it was an absolute necessity during the winter. It was the duty of all the larger boys in the school to make sure there was plenty of wood to burn in the winter. They had to chop the wood and keep a fire going throughout the school day. Out in back of the school there were two outhouses, one for the boys and a separate one for the girls. For water, there was a well with cool drinking water not thirty feet from the school. Simpson Chapel had all the comforts of home and it provided a welcome escape for a short time each day.

It was very difficult for the majority of the children at Simpson Chapel to actually concentrate on the three Rs. It was hard to imagine how learning to read and write and do sums would be helpful to us. None of the older colored folks we knew who could read and write appeared to be much better off than the ones who could not read and write. But for my sisters, brothers, and me, going to school was not an option. Mama said it would pay off some day, so regardless of whether we could imagine the payoff, we went to school.

While Simpson Chapel was our community school, it only served elementary through middle school. Many colored kids would stop their education at that level. But there were always a few who continued. There was a larger school in town called Greenville Training School, which was there for the older colored children who were lucky enough to be able to attend. This high school was attended by all the colored children in the county who had made it past the lower level of training in the many small country schools in the surrounding area.

My sisters, brothers, and I were very fortunate. We all made it through the lower level grades and were able to attend the high school in town.

This was not an easy task by any means, and many less fortunate children never got beyond middle school. Simpson Chapel was not the best place to start one's education, but for some colored children in our community, including my siblings and me, it was enough. It laid the groundwork for our future. Of course when we were attending school there, we had no idea what a significant part it would play in all of our lives and our memories. But it turns out Mama was right. Education did pay off one day.

The Boogeyman

Most colored folks, young and old, were afraid of the boogeyman, even though they didn't know very much about this mysterious creature or even whether or not he really existed. The more intelligent colored folks figured out early on that the boogeyman was just a character made up by white folks who wanted to keep the Negroes tucked in tight at night instead of wandering around and "making trouble" as they put it. The boogeyman's sole purpose was to scare poor colored folks back into to their place when they got out of line, or out of hand, or out of sight. And in most cases just the mention of his name did the trick. Colored folks had endured such hard times for so long, they were susceptible to just about any tale or threat no matter how far-fetched it was.

There were many stories told around town about how the boogeyman had manhandled, whipped, or beaten some poor wayward soul half to death in an attempt to get him back on the right track. Papa, my grand-daddy, used to tell us stories all the time about his encounters with "the man." And Papa had had many encounters in which he almost got caught by "the man."

Even though I was young it seemed odd to me that all of Papa's boogey-man stories apparently occurred right after he had consumed large quantities of moonshine. Somehow he never encountered a boogeyman when he was sober. Now Papa was a strong, hardworking man, and he was brave when it came to standing up to folks for what he believed in and taking care of his family. But he wasn't too brave when it came to the boogeyman. Most of Papa's income came from the sharecropping for Mr. John, but he also found time to make a run or two of moonshine now and again to supplement his income. The tradition of making moonshine had been handed down from generation to generation in my family since before the Civil War, back during the time when cotton was still king. So most of the family had learned to make it, and Papa was very good at it.

After making a large run of moonshine, Papa would hitch up his old mule and wagon and head out around dusk to make his deliveries. The darkness was a cloak used to avoid being caught by the sheriff, who was always on the lookout for such activity. The delivery roads were dark and lonely. And Papa's only companions were his trusty mule and a half gallon or so of his own shine. Papa said it was comforting to have a little moonshine along to ease his weary bones as he made his rounds, moving from house to house, door to door, leaving a quart here and a gallon there for six bits to a dollar. It was a hard way to scratch out a living.

One night in late spring, around 1935 or so, Papa set out on one of his moonshine delivery trips. This one started as they always did, slow and lonely. As the evening grew late he had made all but a couple of deliveries. The sun had long since set and after a long, hard day Papa was tired and ready to get some rest. To that end he had decided to skip the last deliveries and take a shortcut home that would save him at least an hour in time. The downside was that the route would take him past an old church and cemetery. It was a creepy place that he didn't even like traveling through in the daytime, let alone at night. Papa had grown up hearing tales of the boogeyman and ghosts and goblins, and they were definitely on his mind as he thought about traveling through a cemetery.

Papa said he knew something was wrong as soon as he approached the cemetery. An eerie calm lay over the night and everything was in slow motion as he entered the cemetery. *Clop, clop, clop,* the mule plodded along. He began to hear and to see strange things right away. The night was dark and only the glow of the moon lit his way. The first thing he saw was a possum. Possums were a common sight in those parts but this one was different. This possum walked slowly across several graves until he picked up his pace, began to run, and then poof. He disappeared into thin air. Papa had seen hundreds of possums in his life, in daylight and at night, but he had never before seen one disappear into thin air. He was scared out of his mind. Had he really seen what he thought he had? There he was, all alone going through a cemetery and watching possums vanish. He knew that if by some chance he survived this ordeal, no one would believe his story.

Before Papa could shake off the thoughts of that disappearing possum, he felt a presence creep onto the wagon seat beside him. He felt the seat move as if someone had actually sat down next to him. He was sure something was there; he could feel it. He was afraid to look and afraid not to look. He rode on for a little while without saying a word, but finally decided he had to see what was sitting beside him. When at last he gathered enough courage to look, he immediately wished he hadn't.

There was a small white figure sitting all close and tight next to him. It was neither man nor beast, and certainly not possum. Papa wasn't quite sure what it was. But what Papa found out right away was that it didn't care much to be looked at. As soon as Papa turned his head toward it, the small figure began to attack Papa, hitting him about the head and face. Papa fought back with all his might. He was punching, yelling, and screaming, and tugging on the reins leading the old mule. It takes a lot for a mule to quicken its pace, that ol' mule began to run for dear life, which, for a mule, is little more than a fast trot.

There they all were, Papa and the boogeyman yelling and fighting and the ol' mule running for his life. Papa said he struggled with the boogeyman for more than a mile when suddenly, as quickly as it had appeared, the figure disappeared. Just like that it was gone. Papa caught his breath and thanked his lucky stars. He knew he could not have lasted five more minutes in that fight.

He slowly continued on his journey home, taking special care to look only straight ahead for fear of seeing something else beside him. By the time Papa arrived home it was very late. Most of the children had already gone to bed, but like always Mama, his oldest child, had waited up for him. He sat on the wagon for a spell before going inside. He told himself he was a very lucky man to have survived the ordeal he had just been through. When he entered the house Mama was horrified at the sight of him. He had indeed been in a fight with someone or something. He had a bloody nose, a swollen left eye, and bumps and bruises all about his head and face. Right away Mama began giving Papa the third degree. Each time Mama asked what had happened to him, he patiently explained that a "haint" in the cemetery got him. The haint had started out as a possum that had disappeared and then had climbed up on the wagon beside him. And that haint had a great right hook.

For the rest of his life Papa never changed his story. Whenever he was asked about the incident he always said that the "haint," or the boogeyman as the white folks called it, had attacked him in the cemetery. There was just one thing that Papa never could explain no matter how hard he tried. He never could explain just what the boogeyman did with the two gallons of moonshine that Papa had with him in the wagon when he went into the cemetery.

Uncle Snow's Hole

I loved to go fishing when I was young. I took after Mama; she loved to fish as well. Mama would go fishing anytime of the year anywhere she could. She would fish in any river, lake, creek, or pond. Anywhere she could wet her hook, she would. Mama did not fish for fun. Fresh fish was an important part of our family's diet. It broke the monotony of pork, that is, when there was any meat at all. Fish was always a welcome addition. I can recall many times when fish was the only meat we had to eat for weeks at a time.

There was one fishing trip Mama made to an old creek that was particularly memorable. The creek was somewhere around the old Halso Mill just east of town. The weather was cool, not really good fishing weather at all, but Mama didn't care about that. She had an opportunity to go fishing and she wanted to take it. She didn't get a chance to go fishing very often because most of her time was spent working in the fields or doing housework for white folks. With thirteen kids to feed, work was always the main activity of her day. So on the rare occasion when Mama got an opportunity to go fishing, she took it, cool weather or not. At the very least she would a few moments away from most of us kids. And with luck she might even catch a fish or two.

One of my older sisters, Sadie, was the baby at the time and she went along with Mama on the trip. Mama had Sadie all bundled up to keep her warm in the cool air. Sadie was a toddler and barely able to walk; even so, she was able to move about enough to get into trouble. Mama had been fishing for about an hour and had gotten only a nibble or two on her hook. She had not caught a single fish, and this fishing trip looked like it would be a wasted one.

All of a sudden Mama got a bite. The fish must have been big because it nearly pulled the fishing pole right out of her hand. Hook, line, and sinker all went under the water. Mama began struggling with the fish and completely lost track of where Sadie was. Almost simultaneously, the fishing pole, Mama, and Sadie all fell into the creek at the same time. Mama couldn't swim a lick and Sadie was too young to even try. Mama went straight to the bottom of the creek. The water was several feet over her head. Sadie floated on top of the water. And the pole, being dragged by the monster fish on the hook, headed straight for the next county.

History tells us that only Jesus could walk on water. That may very well be true. I do know for a fact however, that Mama could surely walk on the creek bottom, and that is exactly what she did. After she went under, her feet hit bottom right away. She was scared to death and didn't know what to do. She began to walk toward the bank on the other side of the creek. After she had taken about a dozen steps or so her head surfaced. Sadie had drifted across the creek and was directly in front of Mama, who grabbed hold of her as she floated by. With Sadie in tow, Mama continued to walk, step by step, until she had walked right out of the creek and was safely on the other side. It was little short of a miracle that neither Mama nor Sadie drowned that day. But what really upset Mama was that this was one of the few times she returned home without any fish. The only thing she caught that time was a cold.

That incident didn't deter Mama in the least from wanting to go fishing. She still went every chance she got. My brother Floyd and I were her constant companions because we enjoyed fishing just as much as she did. My daddy, on the other hand, didn't care much about fishing and would seldom go with Mama. Mama, Floyd, and I fished all over the place in our small community. One of our favorite fishing spots was a place called Uncle Snow's Hole.

Uncle Snow's Hole was off a dirt road that went through the woods in the Wald community. That old road went on for miles, from our house all the way to town. The pond was way back up in the woods; it was in sort of a scary spot. No more than fifty feet away from the pond ran a set of railroad tracks. The pond was surrounded by large pines and oak trees that towered toward the sky. The trees were so tall and full that in the summer when their branches were full, they would partially block out the sun, which added to the eerie feeling when we were near the pond. Uncle Snow's Hole was located at the bottom of a ravine. The slope of the sides of the ravine leading up from the pond was very steep, so steep that we could not actually walk down to the pond. In order to get there, we had to slide down feet first, with our hands and butts dragging along the ground behind us. We had to do all this carrying an assortment of fishing gear. Of course the fishing gear really consisted of just a cane pole for each of us, a tin can filled with worms for bait, an old bucket for our catch, and a hoe in case we ran into a snake or some other animal that we might have to fight off. Considering how difficult it was to get to Uncle Snow's Hole, I don't know why it was one of our favorite fishing spots, but it was. It could have been a favorite spot because we never left empty-handed. We always caught fish at Uncle Snow's Hole. Without fail. Some days would be good catfish catching days. And there were some days when we would catch a full five-gallon bucket of brim, just right for frying. We always caught something.

Floyd would lead the way to the pond carrying all the gear, followed by me and Mama always brought up the rear. When we left the edge of the old dirt road, we would begin winding our way through the woods toward the old pond. The distance from the road to the pond was about a quarter of a mile, but it seemed much further than that. After making our way past the trees, stumps, and briars, we would soon arrive at the ravine. Next would come the long, slow crawl down the steep slope of the ravine to the pond below. Once there, the fishing would begin. There were all kinds of fish in that old pond, from hand-size brim, to trout, catfish, and jacks. Fishing at Uncle Snow's Hole was always successful.

During the middle of the summer, Floyd, Mama, and I fished at Uncle Snow's Hole about two or three times a month. We alternated a trip there, with a trip to another creek or pond that was much easier to get to. But we never stayed away from Uncle Snow's Hole too long. Until one terrifying trip.

It was a typical summer day when Floyd, Mama, and I headed out to Uncle Snow's Hole. We left the edge of the road and made the trip through most of the woods. We had almost reached the clearing on the other side, when Floyd, who was in the lead as usual, encountered a huge rattlesnake. He had almost stepped right on top of it. Floyd threw all the fishing gear to the ground except the hoe. Then he proceeded to chop that rattlesnake all up into pieces. Floyd was lucky that he had not been bitten by the snake. The snake had given me a scare and at this point I was perfectly willing to end the fishing trip early and go back home empty-handed. But we had already traveled so far, and Mama and Floyd wanted to go on. I was outnumbered, but I had a bad feeling about the trip. Floyd picked up the fishing gear and we continued on our trip to the fishing hole.

In a few minutes we arrived at the ravine and began our climb down the steep slope to the pond. We soon forgot about the snake we had encountered along the way and settled down to fishing. We were having a good day. Every time my hook touched the water a fish seemed to hop on it. I was catching fish so fast that I begrudged the time to take them off my hook. Mama and Floyd were having the same good luck. The fish were biting like crazy. The bucket we had brought to put our catch in was overflowing with fish in no time. We were enjoying ourselves so much, in fact, that we failed to notice the dark clouds gathering overhead.

Before we knew it the skies opened up and we were caught in the middle of an old-fashioned gully washer, also known as a frog strangler. It was raining so hard we could not see our hands in front of our faces. The drops of rain were huge. They were beating down on us so hard they actually hurt as they hit my bare skin. Instantly we were trapped. On a dry day it was difficult enough to climb out of that ravine. With rain-slicked sides, it would be nearly impossible. Each time we scrambled a foot or so up the slick slope, we would lose our footing and fall right back to the bottom of the ravine, right to the edge of the pond. I didn't want to die there at Uncle Snow's Hole, but it began to look as if I would. It began to look as if we all would.

The rain was falling harder than ever. Each time we made it partially up the slope, we would lose our footing and slide back down. We were all completely covered with mud. Floyd was faring a little better than Mama so I grabbed Floyd around the waist and hung on. Together we would climb and slide, climb and slide. We would climb up five feet and slide back four. Climb up five and slide back four. We were making a little headway, not much but a little. After what seemed like an eternity, Floyd and I reached the top of the ravine. I was exhausted and covered from head to toe with mud. I even had mud in my eyes. Floyd's work was not done. While I lay there trying to wash the mud from my eyes with water from the hard-falling rain, Floyd had returned to the ravine to get Mama. Mama was much heavier than I was, but Floyd jumped back into the ravine and Mama grabbed hold of him. They began the slow climb to the top, climbing and sliding, climbing and sliding. They would climb up three feet and slide back two. Climb up three feet and slide back two. Floyd grabbed hold of roots, branches, and limbs as he slowly climbed upward.

Finally Floyd and Mama reached the top of the ravine. The three of us were a sight to behold, all covered with mud, lying at the top of the ravine to Uncle Snow's Hole, the rain beating down on us. After a while we were rested enough to start our journey back though the woods to the old dirt road. Floyd had done a great job of saving Mama and me, but we had lost all our gear: three fishing poles, the bait can, the hoe, and of course our bucket filled with fish.

By the time we returned home, muddy and empty-handed, the rain had stopped. The family didn't believe that we had caught a single fish. Everyone thought that we were just telling one big fish tale. I knew meeting up with that old rattlesnake at the beginning of our trip was a bad omen. And sure enough it was.

Mama, Floyd, and I continued to fish for years all over the area. We went just about anywhere we could wet a hook. But it was a long, long time before we returned to Uncle Snow's Hole.

Turtle Soup

Daddy never really liked to go fishing with the rest of the family. That may have had something to do with the fact that he was always called upon to do the worst jobs: bait hooks, kill snakes and other critters, and remove fish from the lines of everyone else who was fishing. Or then again it may have been because Daddy had very little patience. He did not want to wait for anything. Placing a baited hook in the water and simply waiting for a fish to happen along and bite it was torture for him. He simply could not sit still for a long period of time.

While he may not have enjoyed going fishing with the family, he surely enjoyed going fishing by himself, which he did quite often. On lazy summer evenings, Daddy would often go to his favorite fishing holes, alone, and set out hooks. He would place bait on several hooks, attach those hooks to lines, and then tie those lines off to a sturdy tree branch near the water. But he would not sit around and wait for a bite. He would leave this contraption set up overnight and then return early the next morning to see what fruit his labors had produced.

Daddy always caught something. But not always fish. He caught everything. I remember one fishing trip when Daddy set out hooks at an old creek east of town. As usual he had gone the night before and left bait on about a dozen or so hooks. When he returned the next day to see what he had caught even he was amazed. He hadn't caught any fish, not a single one. Instead, he had caught about seven or eight of the largest eels I had ever seen. Daddy brought them home all right, but I don't know why he even bothered. They were huge, and to me they looked like very large snakes. Why on earth would he catch snakes? Mama refused to mess with them. She thought they looked like snakes as well. She told Daddy that for all she cared, he could take those eels back to the creek where he had caught them. There was no way she was going to touch them let alone cook them. Daddy was forced to take all of his catch to town to try and sell them.

When it came to getting rid of one of his strange catches, Daddy always had a place to go: the Seawright family, a really weird group of folks. The huge family consisted of mostly women and children. Occasionally you would catch a glimpse of a man around the house but not often. The average woman in the house stood well over six feet tall. Even the children were large, and they would buy and eat anything, literally. Maybe that is how they got so large. So whenever Daddy caught something that even Mama wouldn't touch, he could always take it to the Seawrights. There was almost nothing they would not eat. Daddy headed in to town with his passel of eels. He returned home a short time later empty-handed. He had found a taker for those eels. After trying a couple of places, he had ended up at the Seawrights' house, as suspected. And yes, they were happy to take the eels off his hands. Daddy charged a few cents for his catch. He tried never to give anything away.

Sometimes Daddy would return from one of his fishing trips totally empty-handed. Not because he hadn't caught anything, but because he was afraid to show anyone what he had caught. There were other times when he would come home with enough fish to feed our entire family for days. He would even have enough to take some to town and sell. On most of his fishing trips he would return with at least two turtles as a part of his catch. They averaged between twelve and eighteen inches across. While turtles were by no means a favorite meal of the family, they were food nonetheless and all food was considered a blessing. They were a supplement to our sometimes-poor diet and they were better than nothing. Mama said the turtles Daddy usually brought home were just the right size to bake. They were also the right size to have for a little turtle soup. The Seawright family hardly ever got any of Daddy's turtles. There was one turtle, however, that Mama did not even consider making a part of our diet.

I remember the incident well. It was in the middle of the summer. I could not have been more than seven or eight years old but it's still fresh in my memory. I remember Daddy going out the night before as he often did to set out hooks, not knowing what to expect the next day. By the time I got up the next morning, Daddy had already left the house to retrieve his hooks and what everyone hoped would be a huge mess of fish. Mama had not made breakfast yet and we were all hoping that fresh fish would be on the menu; fresh fish for breakfast was a delicacy. We waited and waited, but there was no Daddy. It was getting late. Daddy usually returned home from a fishing trip quite early in the morning, I mean how long does it take to remove a few fish from hooks? Mama was getting worried that something had happened to him. At a creek alone, he could have easily fallen and gotten hurt. If he had fallen into the water, he could have even drowned. A dozen things could have happened to Daddy, none of them good.

By the time Mama decided she had better go and look for Daddy, there he was slowly driving up to the house. When he got out of his truck he was hardly recognizable. He was covered from head to toe with mud. He looked as if he had taken a bath in the stuff. He looked as if he had been in a fight with the devil, and lost. To hear Daddy tell the story, he had. Daddy beckoned for us all to come outside. Mama, my sisters and brothers, and I walked slowly, single file behind Daddy toward his old beat-up truck, all wondering what was waiting for us in the truck. It must be something terrifying to have gotten the best of Daddy. Mama was the first to reach the truck. She looked in the truck bed and let out a gasp and stepped away from the truck. My brothers Floyd and Sonny were next. They too peered into the back of the truck, gasped, and moved away from the truck. I was afraid to get any closer, but I had to see what was in that truck. When I reached the truck I still couldn't see anything. I was too short to see into the truck bed. I tugged on Floyd's pants until he lifted me up and put me on his shoulders. I leaned forward to look inside the truck. I grabbed hold of Floyd tightly and let out a scream.

There, in the back of Daddy's truck, was the largest turtle ever seen by human eyes in the state of Alabama. It was possibly the largest turtle ever caught in the southern United States. That turtle was huge. I had never seen anything like it. It was as wide across as the bed of Daddy's truck, at least five feet or more. It stood at least two feet tall, and it had a head the size of a grapefruit or larger. His jaws were snapping and cracking, clearly wanting something or someone to bite down on. I am sure that turtle weighed more than two hundred pounds. It was rocking from side to side trying to get off the back of the truck. The truck itself was swaying under its weight. We all stood there, mouths agape, staring at that monster turtle. After a time, Mama said, "Charlie, how in God's name did you catch this thing?" Daddy began to tell us the story of his ordeal.

When he got to the creek where he had left his hooks the night before, there were fish on the first couple of hooks he checked and nothing on the next two or three. A couple of the other hooks had caught fish on them, but the fish had been eaten, up to their heads, by something during the night. Usually when Daddy set his hooks out, he would use standard hook and line on most of the hooks, but on at least one or two of the lines he would use a heavy-duty cord and a large nonstandard hook, just in case he caught a really big fish. When Daddy checked the last hook, which was one of the heavy-duty ones, the line was still tied to the tree and very taunt. There was something on the other end of the line, something very big. He grabbed hold of the line up near the tree and began to pull. He couldn't see what was on the other end of the line because it was still underwater. As Daddy pulled the line a few feet out of the water, something on the other end was pulling back toward the water. There was a real tug of war going on and Daddy was losing.

At one point Daddy was able to pull about six or seven feet of the line out of the water, and for the first time he was able to get a glimpse of his prey. He saw a portion of its head. It was a turtle. But Daddy said it was hard to tell that at first. There had been stories told by old colored folks for many years about large creatures being found in creeks and rivers in the area. Daddy thought he had run across one of those creatures. Many people had seen alligators in the creeks and lowlands in the area. Daddy said he was praying he hadn't gotten hold of one of those. When Daddy saw what he thought was the tip of the creature's head he decided it was not an alligator but one monster turtle. Then that thing flipped his head once and pulled Daddy and all the line into the creek right alongside him. Daddy began struggling to get out of the creek, all the while being scared the turtle might turn and take a bite out of him.

By the time Daddy managed to get out of the creek he was exhausted. He thought about just leaving the darn thing on the line and going home with the few fish he had. But he was sure no one would believe his fish story, rather turtle story, without proof, so he decided to give catching the monster turtle one more try. Again he began pulling the line out of the water, inch by inch. This time, as he got slack in the line, he wrapped it around a nearby tree stump. Slowly, slowly he dragged the turtle out of the water. Inch by inch, he pulled up the line and wrapped it around the stump. The outline of the monster turtle began to emerge from the water. He was much bigger than Daddy had thought. There was no way he was going to be able to lift him alone. Then Daddy had an idea.

Daddy kept all kinds of rope, chains, and tools in his old truck. Daddy went to his toolbox and began gathering objects. He found a chain, rope, and a small tackle, rigged a rope and tackle contraption, and placed it over the strong branch of a nearby tree. He attached one end of the tackle to his truck. He then tied the other end of the contraption to the huge turtle. Daddy had to be careful because the turtle was snapping and biting at him.

Once Daddy got the turtle attached to the tackle, he was able to hoist the critter up to the truck and lower him into the truck bed. It took Daddy more than two hours to maneuver his monster turtle into the truck and bring him home. Now that he had him, what was he going to do with him? We all stood around the bed of the truck staring at Daddy's monster turtle. None of us had ever seen such a critter. What could be done with him? Mama often made turtle soup from the turtles Daddy brought home, but there was no way she could make turtle soup from this one. If she did, there would be enough turtle soup for the entire county. The thought of even just plain cooking the animal seemed far-fetched. Cook him, my God, how could you clean him? In fact, how could you kill him? He was just too big. After a time, Mama decided we could not keep the turtle. She knew Daddy had struggled and worked so hard to catch it, but there was nothing she could do with it. There was no way to turn it into food. It was probably seventy or eighty years old and wouldn't be very good to eat anyway.

Deciding that we couldn't keep the turtle was one thing. Figuring out what to do with it was another. That was a decision we put off for tomorrow. For the rest of that day we all sat around laughing, talking, and asking Daddy over and over about how he caught the biggest turtle in the whole state of Alabama. Daddy had told a lot of fish stories in his time and we surely would not have believed this one if he had not brought him home to show us. Before we all went to bed that night, Daddy made sure he secured his prize catch for the night. One end of a rope was still tied to the turtle. Daddy took the other end of the rope and tied it to the bumper of his old truck. Securing that monster was a good idea because by the time we all got up the next morning, that big old turtle had some- how gotten off the back of Daddy's truck and tried to make his getaway. Daddy and my brothers put him back on the truck. Daddy had a much easier time since he had plenty of help.

After breakfast, Daddy decided it was time to try to sell his catch in town. *Try* turned out to be the operative word. He tried everywhere. He went to all his usual spots but no one wanted to take a chance on his huge turtle. People were afraid of it, just like Mama was. No one had ever seen such a large turtle and nobody had any idea how to cook it. A couple of folks called it a demon turtle, saying that nothing normal could grow so large. Daddy couldn't even give his catch away in town. Finally Daddy went to the Seawrights' house, the family who would buy and eat al- most anything. Even the Seawrights were afraid of Daddy's turtle; they wanted no part of it. Daddy tried for most of the day to get rid of his prize catch, but no one would take him. Many people thought there had to be something wrong with a turtle so large, and no one wanted to take a chance with it. By late afternoon, Daddy returned home with his mon- ster turtle in tow. Yesterday, he had been proud to make such a catch. To- day he just wanted to get rid of it.

Finally Daddy did what he had known for a while he would have to do. He did not have much of a choice. Late that evening Daddy and his turtle returned to the creek. He watched as his prize catch climbed slowly off the back of his truck and plodded toward the water. He stared into the water long after his monster had disappeared under the surface. In the end the turtle had won; he had survived. All Daddy had left was the story of the capture of the largest turtle in the state. If turtles could talk, Daddy's big monster had a story of his own to tell. Who knows, he may still be out there telling his tale right now.

Civil Rights

I don't recall the first time I heard the term "civil rights." But although I may not have been aware of the term, I have always been aware of the condition, or the lack thereof. Growing up black in the South in the 1950s and 1960s was a challenge to say the least. Things were bad for black folks for a long, long time. In my earliest memories I was keenly aware of who I was and of my role in society. I was aware of the different roles that blacks and whites played. And I was always aware of "my place." While I was aware of my place that did not mean that I accepted it. I know that Daddy most certainly did not. As if living on white folks' land, working in white folks' fields, washing white folks' clothes, and cooking white folks' food was not enough, there were other reminders that there were a lot of civil wrongs taking place.

Cottonreader

While Atlanta, Birmingham, and Montgomery had Dr. Martin Luther King and Rosa Parks, Greenville had Cottonreader. At the time, I didn't know if that was his real name. I did know, however, that Cottonreader wasn't from around Greenville. When Cottonreader came to town, he evoked fear in the hearts of many white men.

Cottonreader was a freedom fighter, a civil rights advocate, and a northerner. They called him a northerner, but in reality I only know that he was from farther north than Butler County. Now the white folks around Greenville had another name for him. They called him a "nigger" agitator. Agitator or not my family saw Cottonreader as a vision of hope in a time when there wasn't much of it around. He opened the eyes of a lot of black people in the area. When he showed up, in the early sixties, black folks in Greenville were blind to a lot of things. Perhaps blind is not the right word. Let's just say that we were not fully aware of the civil rights movements going on throughout the country. Oh, we had heard about Dr. Martin Luther King, but what could King do to help us? Cottonreader turned that question on its head and asked what could we do to help ourselves. Cottonreader was one of Dr. King's foot solders and an active member of the Southern Christian Leadership Conference, an organization sworn to fight for the equality of all men.

Cottonreader started out bringing news of the movement to the churches. That was always a good place to start because you knew a lot of black people would be there. He began organizing protests, marches, and sit-ins. Nothing on the scale of Atlanta or even Montgomery, but to even talk of such things in Greenville was unheard of until he arrived. While the civil rights movement would have brought respect and equality for blacks to Greenville eventually, I think Cottonreader gave it momentum and direction. There was a lot of opposition from the white folks in the area. White people in Greenville were just like white people all over the South. They wanted to hold on to the status quo, to keep things the way they were. They wanted to keep segregated schools segregated. When white folks heard that civil rights workers were in town, they began to warn their Negros not to talk to, associate with, or be seen with the "outside agitators." All the black families had been warned, even mine, not to associate with Cottonreader and his kind. It was warnings like that that made Daddy more adamant than ever to see things change for black folks. He had a vision. He saw a light at the end of the tunnel. Until the beginning of the civil rights movement, the only future Mama and Daddy saw for us kids was the same future they had. And that was no future at all.

Some things worth having are worth fighting for. And as so many black folks learned, freedom is not free. There was a price to be paid. Daddy decided to host a gathering at our house for Cottonreader to speak. Participating in a meeting was bad enough; hosting a meeting could be detrimental to one's health. But that did not scare Daddy. It scared Mama, but not Daddy. So my family hosted a meeting. We also provided Cottonreader with a home-cooked meal and a place to spend the night. In those days it was not as if he could stay in the Holiday Inn or have a sit-down dinner at a local restaurant. Cottonreader had no sooner left our house than the news that he had stayed there spread all over town, to black areas of town and white areas alike. Black folks were very good at telling on other black folks.

A couple of days after Cottonreader had been in our home Daddy started getting harassed by the white folks in the community. The first bit of harassment came when he went to one of the local country stores to trade. Daddy was stopped at the front door. "Charlie," said the white store owner, "what is this I hear about you feeding that old 'nigger' agitator at your house?"

"I feed who I want to feed at my house," said Daddy, "just like you feed who you want to feed at your house."

"Not with food bought from my store," the white man said.

"Then I will trade with someone else," Daddy replied. Needless to say, that was the end of us being able to buy goods and supplies at local stores for a while. We often had to cross the county line to shop at stores where no one knew us. That was a small price to pay in the fight for civil rights.

Not until many years after Cottonreader's visit to Greenville did I find out the truth about how Daddy ended up hosting a meeting at our house. Cottonreader had been scheduled to speak to the community at Old Elam Church, near our house. But the church deacons and elders, along with everyone else in the community, had been warned by the white folks to turn him away. The small sliver of land that the church sat on had been donated to the black community almost a hundred years earlier by white landowners. The church fathers were told that the church and the land it sat on would be taken away if Cottonreader spoke there. That type of threat was typical for the time and most black folks had little choice but to comply. The church deacons stood in the door to keep Cottonreader from entering.

But the white community did not own my Daddy's land just fifty yards away. So that meeting went on as planned. Cottonreader delivered his message to the community. And the rest, as they say, is history.

A New Pair of Shoes

Most people probably don't give much thought to buying a new pair of shoes. When I was a child the biggest hurdle was having the money for shoes. With so many sisters and brothers, one pair of shoes a year for each of us was rare. We wore a lot of hand-me-down clothes, but we did not wear a lot of hand-me-down shoes because there was no such thing. We didn't wear shoes until they got too small; we wore shoes until they fell apart. Our shoes never got too small for us anyway. As I recall, Mama used to buy them several sizes too large. We had to stuff paper into the toes of the shoes until we grew into them. In my family, shoes were worn until they wore out.

When money was available to buy one of us a pair of shoes, we would get all excited about it. The lucky person would be called into the kitchen. Mama would be standing there with a pencil and a piece of cardboard. We would place a bare foot onto the cardboard and watch while Mama traced the outline of our foot. If more than one of us were to get shoes, our name would be written inside the outline. I never really understood why Mama bothered tracing our foot size anyway if the shoes were always going to be too large. But I guess she had her reasons. Mama would then take the pieces of cardboard with her on an all-day trip to town. After a few hours, she would return with a plain ol' black pair of shoes that was at least a couple of sizes too large. It didn't really matter that the shoe was plain. It was a new shoe. I always asked if I could go to town with Mama when it was time to buy my new shoes but I was never allowed to go. I thought that if I were able to go with Mama, I could try on the shoes for myself and get a better fit. Mama always gave me reasons why she wouldn't let me go with her, but I never understood them. I suppose I was too young. Well, childhood does not last very long, I was eventually told the bitter truth. I was not allowed to go to town to try on shoes because colored folks weren't allowed to do such a thing. Coloreds were not allowed to put their feet inside new shoes in the stores. The merchants said that no white person would buy a pair of shoes that had been tried on by a Negro. The cut-up pieces of cardboard that Mama traced around our feet were what the white merchants used to fit shoes for colored people. Cardboard was allowed in shoes, but not colored feet.

Now that I think back on it, I appreciate Mama shielding us from the humiliation of merely buying a pair of shoes. I don't know how she survived it. Each time one of us needed a new pair of shoes, we looked forward to the shoes. Mama looked forward to once again going through the pain and humiliation of having been born black.

The Picture Show

My first trip to the picture show was another lesson in race relations. When I was very young, I heard about this place where there was a very large screen, sort of like a television screen, and dozens of people got together to watch a picture. My older sisters and brothers had been to this place, and I enjoyed listening to their stories about it. You had to pay money to get inside. And you could have popcorn, sodas, and other goodies while you watched the picture. My brothers and sisters told me that when I got older, they would take me to the picture show with them. I couldn't wait to get older. I was dying to see what all the fuss was about.

My day finally came. My sister Ediffie had told me early in the week that she and her boyfriend Johnny were going to go to see a picture on Saturday night. They had decided that for the first time I could go with them. I was so excited. It was the only thing I thought about all week. I couldn't wait for Saturday. That was one of the longest weeks of my life. By the time Saturday morning rolled around I could barely contain my enthusiasm. And by the time Johnny showed up on Saturday night, I was more excited to see him than Ediffie was.

The seven-mile drive to town seemed long, but I didn't mind. I didn't mind because I knew I was finally going to get to see a movie. No longer would I have to wait up to listen to the stories my sisters and brothers told about the picture show. I would be able to tell a story myself. Now my younger sister, Diane, would have to listen to me talk about a place she had never been. It was going to be great.

Finally, we reached town. The Front Street was all lit up with lights and awnings. The street's actual name was Commerce, but everybody called it "the Front Street." It was not very long, and you could almost see from one end of it to the other. By the time we passed under the big railroad bridge by the depot, I could see the theater. I had seen it before in the daytime, but it looked very different at night with its bright lights and glittering marquee. As we approached I could see people going in the front door and there was a line forming at the entrance. To my dismay Johnny drove right past the front door. I asked him where we were going. He told me not to worry, that he had to park the car. There were parking spaces right out front; I couldn't imagine why we drove past all of them. We drove to the corner of Commerce and Church Street. Johnny parked the car in an alleyway behind a row of buildings, one of which was the movie theater.

From that vantage point I could see several other cars loaded with black folks parking back there. Johnny, Ediffie, and I got out of the car and made the short trip around to the front of the theater. Ediffie and I stood on the sidewalk while Johnny went up to the line in front of a large glass window. When he got up to the front of the line he bought tickets for the three of us. Then he headed back out to the sidewalk where Ediffie and I were waiting. I was confused. I saw people, white people, buy their tickets and then go inside the door to the right of the large window. I didn't understand why we were headed back toward the parking lot in the alley behind the building. I wanted to know what was going on but I was afraid to ask. I did not want to be a bother to Ediffie and Johnny. I figured if I was too much trouble, they would not take me with them to the movies again. So I went along quietly, very puzzled, but not saying a word.

We didn't make it all the way back to the parking lot. Instead, we stopped at the side of the theater building. The building was two stories tall, and there was a narrow, rickety set of stairs attached to the outside of the building. There was a metal landing at the top of the stairs, just large enough for two or three people and a single door at the landing. It was very dark out there away from the bright lights in the front of the building. The only light around was from a single bulb at the top of the stairs. I didn't know what to expect and I was getting a little scared as we climbed the stairs. By the time we had climbed the first flight of stairs, I was also tired. Sensing that, Johnny carried me up the second flight of stairs. We reached the landing at the top and opened the door. There was a tall skinny black man standing just inside the door. He held out his hand. Without exchanging any words, Johnny placed the tickets in his hand, and still carrying me, stepped inside.

It was so dark inside I could not see a thing. I was scared to death. I could hear people talking, and I could see shadows moving, but I could not distinguish any figures. Inside there was another set of stairs. After climbing a few steps, Johnny stopped and began to walk sideways; Ediffie followed him past a row of people and chairs. When Johnny reached three empty seats together, we sat down. By the time my eyes had adjusted to the low light, I could see that there were only black people around us. What had happened to the white folks who had bought tickets in front of Johnny? Where had they gone? The white people had not gone any-where at all. They were all downstairs. All of the stair climbing was fi-nally making sense to me. We were in the balcony. All the black people were in the balcony. You could look over the edge of the railing and see the tops of the white heads down below.

I don't remember what movie was playing that night. I do remember however, the separation. I remember the balcony and the colored-only seating arrangement. I remember the stairs and the colored-only door. I remember the colored-only parking in the alley in the back of the build-ing. No, I don't remember anything about the plot or characters in my first movie. But I remember the important things about that night.

When we got home, I didn't boast to my sister Diane at all. I did not like what I had seen. Racism and disappointment were not lessons I wanted to have to teach her.

Separate but Equal

"Separate but equal" was the term whites used when talking about segregated facilities. One thing that all blacks knew was that separate was never equal.

I recall riding the school bus to school as an elementary school student. There was a white family with children my age that lived about a half mile down the road; their children rode a bus to school just as we did. The bus I rode in was old. It was almost worn out. The school bus my white neighbors rode in was shiny and new. And it wasn't just my bus; there wasn't a single bus going to the black school that was anything close to new. They were all old hand-me-downs that were worn out before we got them.

The same was true of school books. I remember the year I went into the fourth grade. The teachers were so excited because our school was supposed to get new textbooks. The colored school hadn't had new books for years. I was being taught from the same books my sister who was ten years older than me had been taught from. I don't mean the same edition of a book. I mean the exact same tattered and torn books. The books were so old pages and covers were missing; they were literally falling apart. But my fourth grade year would be different. We were going to get new books.

We were well into the semester when the new books arrived. The teachers had worked late the night before, cataloging and sorting the books so they could distribute them to us the next day. I was in English class when the teacher told us to come up front one by one and place our old spelling books in a neat stack by the door. We were all happy to comply. When all the books were neatly stacked she went over to some boxes that were piled in the far corner of the room. She began removing books from the boxes, three and four at a time. She went up and down the rows of chairs and placed a new speller on each desk, one by one. She continued until each and every one of us had a new book on our desk.

By the time she finished handing out the new books, we were all examining our books, turning pages, flipping through the indexes, even smelling the books to enjoy that new book smell. We were giving those books a good going over.

After a careful examination, I could tell that something was amiss. My book was not new at all. It was not even close to new. I admit I did not see any missing pages or covers but my book was not new. It didn't look new and it didn't smell new either. It even had writing in it, as if some kid had been practicing his or her spelling words and later erasing them. No, my new book was not new at all.

I was heartbroken. I began to question the teacher. I wanted to know what went wrong. What could have possibly happened to our new books, the ones that we were expecting? Where could they be? I began to cry. The teacher put her arm around me and explained what had happened. There had not been a mix-up in the delivery of the new books. The new books had arrived just as planned. The book in front of me was indeed the book that I had been waiting for. Black schools, she told me, never really got "new" books. "New" to black schools meant that the students at the white schools were done using the books and the board of education was passing those books down to us black kids. They were only called new because they were new to us and were in better condition than the books we had been using for the past decade.

I cried a lot about those books. My fourth grade speller was one of the many lessons I learned about the doctrine of "separate but equal." Separate and unequal is what it should have been called.

Sadie vs. the United States

The year 1968 was a memorable one. It started out in much the same fashion as 1965, 1966, and 1967 had started out. These were still poor and desperate times for black folks in the South. I remember those times very well. The civil rights movement had been going on in earnest for many years, but in Greenville, Alabama, black folks were still waiting to reap the benefits the movement had supposedly brought. My family was among those still waiting for equal rights. Even though the Voting Rights Act of 1965 had been passed, I did not know a single black person who was allowed to cast a vote in my hometown. Just because the right to vote was the law did not mean that law would be enforced.

There was no way the white folks around Greenville were going to let a little ol' law convince them to break the age-old tradition of discrimination and segregation, no way at all. The Voting Rights Act of 1965 was supposed to prohibit discrimination in voting practices and procedures because of race or color. Of course colored folks thought many of the laws already on the books, some for a hundred years or more, were going to protect the rights of colored folks.

In 1863 when President Lincoln issued the Emancipation Proclamation black folks assumed that equal rights would soon flow like water to them. They assumed wrong. In 1865, when the Thirteenth Amendment to the Constitution abolished slavery everywhere in the United States, colored people assumed they would soon be given equal rights under the law. Again they assumed wrong. Then, in 1868, the Fourteenth Amendment made former slaves citizens and guaranteed equal protection under the law to all U.S. citizens. And two years later the Fifteenth Amendment made it against the law to deny any citizen the right to vote because of his race or color, or because he was formerly a slave. Surely this time colored folks would be able to take their rightful place as free and productive members of the United States of America. But no. Despite the promises of all those laws, the former slaves and their descendants did not receive equal treatment under the law nor were they allowed to vote.

Then, in 1896, the U.S. Supreme Court ruled in *Plessy v. Ferguson* that state governments could separate people of different races as long as the separate facilities were equal. What on earth was the Court thinking? This was a step backward for equal rights. This separate but equal doctrine remained the law until 1954 when in *Brown v. Board of Education* the Supreme Court overruled its previous decision. Voting rights laws were enacted in 1957 and 1960. Those laws, like the ones that came before them, failed to deliver on their promise of equality.

So by 1968 it really was no surprise that Mama and Daddy and most of the colored folks in our community were still not registered to vote. But it wasn't because they hadn't tried. While the poll tax had been outlawed by the Twenty-Fourth Amendment, there were a number of communities, mine included, that still subjected poor colored folks to literacy tests. The tests were not tests of literacy at all. They were a tool to dissuade blacks from even attempting to vote. The tests were daunting and humiliating. How many soap bubbles does one bar of soap make? That was one of the questions my Daddy was asked when he tried to register to vote. There is, of course, no right answer to such a question. There was always some reason why colored folks should be denied the right to register. We were also denied the right to an equal education. Separate but equal was the doctrine; separate and unequal was the reality. In 1968 I was only in the second grade, but I knew even at that young age that something was wrong.

My entire family—from Daddy down through all thirteen of us kids—was involved in the civil rights movement. We all knew the horrors of discrimination and we desperately wanted things to get better. When I thought about it, the only thing my Daddy wanted for us is what daddies all over the world have wanted since the beginning of time. He wanted a better life for his children. My family was not the only family in Greenville trying to make things better for colored folks; there were others. But as a small child, sometimes it seemed as if my family had the entire weight of the world on its shoulders. My father was a stern and hard man. Mama always said that his rough childhood made him that way. Nevertheless, many folks in the community, black and white looked up to him. Many didn't like him, but they all respected him, and his children.

While all my sisters and brothers participated to some degree in the civil rights movement, my sister Sadie stood out from the rest. She was a lot like Daddy. She had a strong opinion about everything, and equal rights for colored folks was at the top of her list of concerns. Sadie was an active participant in civil rights activities at school and in the community. For her teachers at Greenville Training School and Southside High School, she was a little bit too active. She was a smart girl, an honor student, in fact. And she believed in speaking her mind, which landed her in trouble with her teachers more often than not. Each time there was a demonstration, she demonstrated. Each time she demonstrated, she got in trouble at school. Sometimes we wondered which side of equal rights those teachers were on.

Most of Sadie's teachers were simply products of their times. They had grown up in segregated communities, had attended segregated colleges, and had managed to get jobs in segregated schools. They had achieved the colored person's American dream. But that was not my Daddy's dream and it was not Sadie's dream either. She wanted much more for herself and for her little sisters and brothers coming along behind her. She wanted an opportunity to compete with her white counterparts for the American dream, not the colored American dream. During the 1960s there was always some demonstration going on or a picket line somewhere. And that was where you would find Sadie. She threw herself wholeheartedly into protesting the separate but equal doctrine. In 1968 while black and white schools were still being maintained in Greenville, families were allowed to send their children to the other race's school. Not a single white family chose to send their children to the all-black school across town. And why would they? They knew the black children learned under inferior conditions; they would have been crazy to send their kids there. At that time, black kids couldn't even get a hot lunch at school. But several brave colored families did send their kids to the white school. My family was one of those.

Daddy did not send his younger children to the white school, but he was perfectly willing to allow his older children to take their chances across town. Except for Sadie. Daddy thought she was old enough to attend the white high school across town; he did not think she was tolerant enough. She was just like him and could not be trusted to hold her tongue, especially if she felt that an injustice was being done. Nope, Daddy was smart; he did not allow Sadie to attend the white school, and she didn't actually mind. She believed there should only be one high school in the community; Greenville was not large enough for two high schools. Sadie thought if there were only one high school, then the white folks would simply have to make it a good school, with good teachers and good books and a good education. She was fervently opposed to busing black kids to the white school across town. She was also against busing the black kids to the inferior black school. Sadie wanted an equal opportunity for everyone.

One brisk autumn morning Sadie decided to help lead a special protest. The issue that day was that black children were being bused to inferior black schools, to attend inferior classes taught by inferior teachers, use inferior books, eat cold lunches, and receive inferior educations. So that day the protesters decided to make a stand. Sadie was not alone of course. There were other brave students, such as her close friend Dorothy Wilson. R. B. Cottonreader was also on hand. Whether the kids were going to be bused across town or across the street was not what mattered. What mattered was the inferior conditions black students were subjected to day after day, week after week, year after year. The plan to shut down busing for a day was a way for the protestors to express their outrage at this continued injustice.

As the children boarded the bus in preparation for their journey across town, Sadie and her fellow protesters put her plan into action. They leaped in front of the buses and lay down crossways in the street completely blocking the road. The busing system in Greenville did not run that day. The news spread quickly across town. Soon everyone knew what Sadie and the others had done. And the people who knew Sadie knew she was a leader in the protest.

Of course every action has its consequences. Sadie, along with the rest of my family, suffered the consequences of her actions that day. Sadie and the other protestors were suspended from school. And for months everywhere Mama and Daddy went to do business they had to endure white people complaining about the behavior of their insolent, disrespectful, undisciplined daughter. Daddy nearly came to blows with one white merchant. Daddy could hold his tongue when the man was making negative comments about the civil rights movement. But when he referred to Sadie as "that 'nigger' bitch daughter of yours," Daddy lost his temper. In fact, he threatened to kill the man if he repeated himself. Yes, there are always consequences to your actions, but I am sure that Mama and Daddy were proud of what Sadie had done.

By 1968 the civil rights movement had spread across the country, even to places as remote as Greenville, Alabama. The U.S. Commission on Civil Rights had been established by the Civil Rights Act of 1957, however it took the commission, which traveled all over the country holding hearings, almost a decade to want to know what was happening in our area. The commission interviewed hundreds of colored folks, seeking their opinions on the state of civil rights in the United States. The commission came to Montgomery barely three weeks after the assassination of Dr. Martin Luther King. In April and May 1968, the commission held hearings in Montgomery, Alabama. And lo and behold, one Sadie Mae Allen, the daughter of Charlie and Willie Joe Allen and the big sister of Peggy Allen, was called before the commission to testify about the conditions of colored folks in our community, more specifically, the colored folks in Greenville, Alabama.

The hearings convened on April 27, 1968, at nine o'clock in the morning. Black folks came to testify from all over central Alabama: from places like Selma, Sardis, Prattville, Camden, Tuskegee, Ozark, and Boykin. And Greenville. The testimony of folks who came before and after Sadie reads like a script. Everyone spoke of discrimination in the schools, businesses, and workplaces throughout the state of Alabama. Their testimony revealed a sad state of affairs, a sad state of affairs indeed. Sadie, like those before her, told a tale of racial discrimination. All the students told of being above-average students turned down by colleges and trade schools because of the color of their skin. They told of working in the fields most of the school year in order for their families to have a place to live, a place on some white family's land. Sadie's story was the same as the others. At one point during the hearing Sadie was asked, "Do you think there is a difference between your generation and the older generation?" Sadie replied, "Oh, yes. I do. Because the things I get up and say my mother wouldn't have attempted to say twenty years ago. My mother believes in waiting on the Lord. And I believe in waiting on the Lord true enough. But I also feel that you have to help yourself. Because I mean the Lord isn't going to come down here and tell this white man who is beating your head to stop. I think He gave you enough common sense to stop him from beating your head by hitting him back." That said it all. All those kids were doing by protesting was using their common sense and trying to help themselves. I turned out like Mama in a lot of ways because I believe in waiting on the Lord. But I guess I'm a little like Sadie too; I also believe in helping myself.

One of the things that came out of those hearings was validation of what a lot of people already knew: Black people were being discriminated against and treated like second-class citizens. Sadie was ostracized at school, by teachers and even by some students, for fighting for equal rights, but she never gave up and she never gave in. I am still very proud of my big sister who helped pave the way for me and for others. As I said, 1968 was a memorable year. And though it started out like many other years, things were different when it ended.

To Be Continued

Well, through everything somehow we survived. Mr. Will, those cotton fields, pecan orchards, segregated schools, the sheriff, even slavery could not get the best of the Allen family. We are a strong family. There were times when our future was not so certain, but we managed to get by somehow. And if I do say so myself, as a family we did all right. We worked hard together and saved money for many years. We eventually moved out of that sharecropper's shack in the middle of Ol' Man Standoff's pecan orchard. Mama and Daddy bought a few acres of bottomland less than a mile away, over behind Old Elam Baptist Church.

My oldest brother, Thomas, grew up quickly. Not because he wanted to but because he had to. Like most young black men he had to find work even before he graduated from high school. He was luckier than most and landed a job at the W. T. Smith Lumber Company in Chapman, the same sawmill where Daddy began his long hard life of supporting his family. Thomas worked at the sawmill for years. He eventually fell in love and married Wrilla, one of Mr. Time Harris's daughters. Her family lived out west of town. The two of them started a family and eventually moved north to Michigan, where Thomas found a really good job in the automobile manufacturing industry. They raised four fine children, three sons and a daughter.

My oldest sister, Mae Nell, did all right as well. She was one of the smartest of the children and one of the prettiest girls. Mae Nell graduated from high school at sixteen; because she was so smart, she was allowed to skip ahead a grade or two. They did that a lot back then because there was no mechanism in the black schools to accommodate bright and gifted students. She graduated from high school with honors and continued her schooling at Alabama State University where she received her bachelor's degree. By the time I was born in 1959, Mae Nell had left home. She was brilliant and beautiful. She won a beauty contest in Florida then continued her education, getting her master's and then her PhD. Not bad for someone who started life in a poor, black sharecropper's shack in the middle of a pecan orchard.

Mae Nell married Ted Chenier who was a pilot in the U.S. Air Force. Ted was a looker, tall, not so dark, and very handsome. Ted and Mae Nell loved each other but they just couldn't manage to stay together. They eventually divorced but remained good friends.

Divorce did not stop Dr. Mae Nell Allen Chenier in the least. She became a tenured professor at Pensacola Junior College in Florida. When she was about fifty Mae Nell developed a lung ailment. My dear older sister eventually succumbed to the disease, but not before she had made her mark in the world. Pensacola Junior College named an African American memorial scholarship fund in her honor. The entire family is still very proud of her.

Betty graduated from high school and married a handsome chap by the name of Leo Crenshaw. Together they brought up three children, two daughters and one son. Betty struggled to get all three of her children off to college. Once her youngest child entered college, Betty did the near impossible. She went to college and put herself through nursing school. Betty still works as a nurse.

Ediffie grew up and married Johnny Bogan, a very attractive fellow from down the road. Johnny was a good, hard-working man with even more sisters and brothers than I have. Johnny, who was part American Indian, learned the art of basket weaving from his mama, Miz Ollie, who had learned it from her mother. Ediffie and Johnny brought up two children, a son and a daughter. Ediffie was always good with her hands and she and Johnny started a basket-weaving business and even opened a shop on the Front Street. They were the first black people in Greenville to have a business of any kind on the Front Street. They make baskets of all kinds and sizes, from key chains to clothes hampers. They also make woven furniture from oak they harvest themselves. They continue to ship beautiful handmade baskets all over the country. President Ronald Reagan once owned one of their baskets.

Gracie was a quiet child but I think secretly she was a rebel. After Gracie graduated from high school she wanted to go to nursing school. She and her best friend, Betty Sue Brown, went to New York City, which was a far cry from Greenville, Alabama. Gracie worked as a live-in nanny to earn money for school. Gracie saved every dime she made for a year. By the time she returned to Alabama, she had earned enough money to put herself through nursing school. She fell in love and married a tall, dark, and handsome man by the name of Walter Womack, who spent a tour of duty in Vietnam. They raised three children, two daughters and a son. Gracie enjoyed a long, successful nursing career.

Floyd was a kind and gentle soul. He was Mama's and my best fishing buddy and a good brother to me. I depended on him for many things and he always came through. After high school Floyd moved off to New York where he met and married a northerner, Evelyn. She too was a kind and gentle soul; they were a perfect match. Together they raised three children, two daughters and one son.

Sadie, our rebel, was an active participant in the civil rights movement while she was in high school. Wherever there was a protest against injustice, Sadie was there. She graduated from high school soon after she testified before the U.S. Commission on Civil Rights. Sadie worked her way through nursing school and became a well-respected member of the medical community. The old white man who had called her "a 'nigger' bitch" in front of Daddy was once a patient of hers. Like the true professional she was, she gave him the same tender loving care she gave all her patients. Sadie fell in love with a local boy, Jeffery Shepherd. They married, moved to Michigan, and raised a son and a daughter.

Charlie Allen Jr. (Sonny) looked just like Daddy when he grew up. Sonny graduated from high school and went on to run track, his favorite sport, at Alabama's Troy State University (now Troy University). He was as smart as a whip. After college, he joined the marines and served several tours of duty overseas. Sonny married Cherry and together they raised a son.

Calvin was the most mischievous of us all. He was constantly getting into trouble. He was also very good with his hands. He could make any kind of toy imaginable, everything from miniature horses, to merry-go-rounds, to race cars that actually worked. As a teenager Calvin rebuilt the engine of a 1947 Plymouth. I learned a lot from Calvin. I helped Calvin rebuild that car; we were a good team. Thanks to him I can fix a flat and give my car a tune-up. He also taught me how to shoot a gun. The only person in the family who was a better shot than Calvin was Daddy. Calvin was a good-looking fellow. He got married right out of high school but that only lasted a short time. Calvin was a free spirit and never stayed put. He had one son and a daughter. His talent for building and repairing things stayed with him and he became an electronics whiz.

Brenda was always a quiet one and never caused much of a ruckus. Actually we all worked so hard none of us had enough energy to cause much of a fuss. We thought Brenda would turn out all right. When she was in high school she was first runner-up in Greenville's very first racially integrated beauty contest. Of course we all thought she should have won the whole thing outright. Before she graduated from high school she became the first black person to get a job at Elmore's Five and Dime on the Front Street. Brenda received her undergraduate degree from Alabama A&M University. She married Eddie Harrison and has one daughter. Quiet Brenda now works for a Fortune 500 company in the Chicago area. I would say she definitely turned out all right.

I always thought Janice was Daddy's favorite. If you asked her, she thought Daddy singled her out and picked on her. She looked a lot like his mother, Betsy, and he would sometimes refer to Janice and his mama as if they were the same person. When Jan grew up she joined the Greenville Police Department. She really looked cute in her uniform; it fit her small, trim figure quite well. Unfortunately, as a policewoman she was required to carry a gun, and she was by no means proficient with a firearm. Jan eventually decided law enforcement was not for her—but not before she accidentally shot a hole through Mama's living room floor.

Jan married Joseph Freeman, her high school sweetheart. Together they raised a son and a daughter. Jan and Joseph later divorced and she married Tim Stamps, a really nice fellow from the Georgiana area just south of Greenville.

Jan went on to single-handedly develop the enhanced 911 system for Butler County, Alabama. She did a great job and became the director of that system. She also started her own business and is the owner and operator of a liquor store. She is the first Allen to sell liquor legitimately, paying taxes to the state and all.

Diane was the youngest child. Though she did not experience all the hardships the rest of the family did, she lived through her share. While in high school Diane joined the army reserves. By the time she realized the military was not for her, it was too late to change her mind. Eventually Diane received her honorable discharge from the army. She attended the University of Alabama School of Nursing. At one point she received the Florence Nightingale award for having the highest grade point average of the class. She became a dedicated member of the nursing profession. She met Clifton Mosley in Michigan. They fell in love, got married, and had two sons.

As for me, I guess I turned out all right too. I am the deputy director of an engineering department for a large company in the Metro Atlanta area. I survived all the hard lessons of my childhood and even learned from them. I know the value of a dollar because of the many hours my family and I had to work in the pecan orchards and cotton fields just to earn one. I know the pain caused by prejudice because I lived in the segregated South with its separate schools, separate restrooms, separate water fountains, back doors, and balconies. I also learned tolerance. There were many occasions during my childhood when hatred of others would certainly have been justified. But hatred was not one of the things taught by Mama and Daddy. Daddy did teach us that we were just as good as anyone else, black or white, and we all grew up believing that. He taught us never to ask for a handout, but rather an opportunity. I learned the love of family because I shared that love with a great one. We had our rough moments like all families do, but when the chips were down, and they most often were, we stuck together. And there is no power stronger in this world than God and family.

I have learned to love and admire my great-grandmother Moa more with each passing year. What a strong, admirable woman she was. She started life as a slave, was separated from her family as a young child, raised her own family, then stepped in to rescue her granddaughters when their daddy was in jail. She was a rock to my family and, oh, what a treasure.

Other people besides my family have contributed in one way or another to the person I have become. Miz Rosie taught me the value of strength. Mr. Steve, who despite having a wooden leg supported his family in any way he could, taught me perseverance. Miz Rachel, who gave a helping hand to everyone, even those who could not pay for her services, helped teach me compassion. I like to think that I carry a little of her with me each day. From Mr. Gary I learned both the joy of giving and the grace of accepting gifts. Miz Lady Bug was always one of my favorite people growing up. To me she was not a jealous wife who had abused her husband and murdered her tormentor. To me she was a kind and gentle soul who watched over me and my younger sister. From Miz Trudy I learned that kindness and grace can come in all shapes, sizes, and colors. She was truly a good woman.

The surgeries and medical treatments brought on as a result of my childhood rickets were just another painful chapter in my life. Although I still bear the mental and physical scars, I wear them proudly as a badge of courage. Over the years I have grown accustomed to the chronic pain and it hardly bothers me at all. It seems too trivial to mention compared to other things my family and I went through.

I graduated from high school in the top of my class. I was even voted most popular and most likely to succeed by my classmates. I attended the University of Alabama. Those were very good years for me. I worked hard in school and graduated on the dean's list with a degree in civil engineering. I guess all those days of being stuck inside reading books paid off for me. I also received a black belt in karate. This was no small accomplishment for a person who couldn't walk for the first three years of her life. I even had an opportunity to do my duty in the fight for racial equality. In 1987 I participated in a march in Forsyth County, Georgia. I marched alongside Hosea Williams, a famous civil rights activist who once marched with Dr. Martin Luther King. Even as late as 1987, Forsyth County was still segregated. Thanks to me and tens of thousands of my closest friends, that is no longer the case. I even found R. B. Cotton-reader. He lives in the Metro Atlanta area. I told him he owes me dinner for the one he took from me so many years ago. Actually it is I who owe him.

I learned at an early age from Daddy that there is no such thing as a good excuse. So I never make excuses. I also learned it's not always important that you finish first. But it is important that you finish. I still have part of the little custom-made hoe that Daddy fashioned for me so many years ago. The wooden handle has long since rotted away but a portion of the metal blade has survived. I will cherish it always. It reminds me of my childhood and the people who were such an important part of my growing up. It reminds me of where I've been, and of my history and my heritage. I am only three generations removed from slavery and my little hoe helps me remember that.

Mama and Daddy did the best they could rearing thirteen children in the rural, segregated South. And their best seems to have been good enough. There were more hard times than good. But through it all we persevered. I am thankful for the good times and the bad. All of my experiences together have made me the person I am today.

But my story is not done. There are many places I have not yet seen and many things I have not yet done. This is only the beginning. I look forward to tomorrow's sunrise.

I was born the daughter of a poor black sharecropper on November 29, 1959, in Greenville, Alabama, and this is my story.

To be continued . . .